Joseph H. McCarty

Fact and Fiction in Holy Writ

Book and World wonders

FACT AND FICTION IN HOLY WRIT

OR

BOOK AND WORLD WONDERS

BY

REV. J. HENDRICKSON M'CARTY, M.D., D. D.

AUTHOR OF

Two Thousand Miles Through the Heart of Mexico, Inside the G.., The Black Horse and Carryall, etc.

" Inspired theology, the haven and sabbath of all our contemplations?"—*Bacon.*
" *Lucerna Dei spiraculum hominis.*"

NEW YORK: HUNT & EATON
CINCINNATI: CRANSTON & STOWE
1891

TO

THE YOUNG MEN AND WOMEN

WHOM

I HAVE SERVED IN MANY PLACES AS A PASTOR

THIS VOLUME

IS

𝕷𝖔𝖇𝖎𝖓𝖌𝖑𝖞 𝕴𝖓𝖘𝖈𝖗𝖎𝖇𝖊𝖉.

INTRODUCTORY.

THIS book has had its birth in a desire to show that most of the objections, if not all of them, made by people of a skeptical turn of mind against the Bible are not well founded.

We know there are some things in the Scriptures which do not accord with the observations and experiences of mankind in these modern times, and hence by some have been relegated to the domain of myths and legends, and classed with the vagaries and superstitions of unlettered tribes and ages. We also have endeavored to make plain the fact that in the natural world and in history as well there also have been some strange, yes, very wonderful things, which, had they been written in the Bible, would have been declared impossible, unbelievable.

Throughout we have endeavored to be as true to the teachings of science as to Scripture, for both lead the mind to God. But is it not a fact that very many people think more about the mysteries in this book than they do about the simple statements of belief and the duties which are inculcated?

More time is spent by some persons over the unessentials than over the essentials. This grows, in part, at least, out of the natural desire of the mind to seek out hidden things.

The reader, doubtless, is aware that for over three hundred years the governments of the civilized world have been fitting out expeditions at great cost of life and treasure to solve the problems of the polar regions. We presume the search will be continued even if it takes a thousand years, or at least until some brave-hearted adventurer reaches the pole. We hope this will come to pass, for until then we shall not have come into the full possession of our earthly kingdom. It was written in the great charter in the beginning: "Thou shalt have dominion . . . over the earth."

In the study of the Bible much valuable time is spent in endeavoring to unravel the minor mysteries—to find answers to questions which have no practical value. For instance, Whom did Cain marry? Was the beast which personated Satan in the garden of Eden a veritable snake, or was it an ape? What sort of animals did Samson employ in setting fire to the grain-fields of the Philistines? What was Paul's "thorn in the flesh?" Many other questions of a similar character have been asked again and again, as if the soul's highest good depended on their correct answer.

Many a minister has dwelt so much upon the disputable and doubtful things in the Scriptures that all positive teachings have been passed by, and hungry-hearted people have gone out from the Church unhelped and unfed. Many a Christian has passed by with comparative indifference the "weightier matters of the law" and dwelt on the trivial things, "seeking rest, and finding none." They are like one who cavils over the chemistry of water while dying of thirst.

Others seem eager to sound the hidden depths and to unveil what God has purposely concealed. No wonder they are dazed and bewildered. Still others must find the Bible, because professedly written by men under divine guidance, in absolute accord with the "latest developments of science." We believe in science and we believe also in Scripture, and have no fear that the former will ever overthrow the latter.

There are some things very clear, some not so clear. There is here and there a doubtful passage in the Bible. A few errors have crept in during the last few thousand years, mainly through the blunders of transcribers and printers, but none that harm its sublime teachings. There are numerous figures of speech and poetic representations which, if taken in a literal sense, would rob the Bible of its meaning.

The Scriptures have been given to help us *live*, not to interest the mind merely. That they do the latter is not to be denied; but the Bible is a heart-book. It teaches us that the best way to live is to follow its teachings; that vice is secession from God; that holiness is essential to true happiness.

How far must a soul fly to escape the dominions of the Eternal? The largest telescope in the world cannot answer the question. A Christian on his knees can see farther into the universe than the astronomer through his glass. To a prayerful soul the heavens are always open. We are lifted out of self and sin by a power outside of and above ourselves. If it be true that the sun in the heavens colors the rose, it is equally true that in human life conformity to the law of God is the way to grow spiritually pure and beautiful. Two cannot walk together unless they be agreed. We should walk with God, for we are in his keeping, and are upheld by his power every moment; but to walk with him aright we must love what he loves and hate what he hates.

Refuse to do this, and there is only one alternative, and that is to fight the universe. What would any of us think of the commander of a ship who should stand on the quarter-deck and curse the wind and the waves? Let the winds roar and the waves beat, his business is to guide the ship.

The Bible exists to banish sin from the heart and the life of man. So let us steer clear of sin. There is no use of singing lullabies over human depravity. Sleep will not change the blood-thirstiness of a tiger or neutralize the venom of a serpent; asleep or awake they are the same. Sin asleep, if it can be, is sin still. Some say the world is very wicked. Alas! we know it; but what would it be if all these hundreds of agencies for good were withdrawn, or if these ten thousand voices calling us to the right were silenced?

The world needs science, commerce, art, and it has them. But what is better than the gospel of love? "Ye must be born again" rings down over the ages. A man may confess his sins and sin on. He may resolve on reformation and yet not reform. What he needs is help—the Bible is a helper. It is an old book, a much-loved book, a much-hated book; but somehow it manages to stay in the world.

There are some things in it which some of us imagine we could improve. Most of us think we could improve the weather and the seasons were they left to us. The Bible is the only key that can turn this human lock—the heart of man; and that shows that He who constructed the lock furnished also the key. If every thing on the pages of this book which offends the taste of the fastidious reader were eliminated, there would yet be left more simple and beautiful truth than the average believer puts in practice— enough surely to save the guiltiest. Any thing can be criticised, even a landscape or an anthem; the Bible has not escaped it.

We submit these pages to a generous public hoping that they who read them may turn to the old book and find in it not only food for thought, but abundant spiritual consolation. THE AUTHOR.

SYRACUSE, N. Y., *April* 7, 1891.

CONTENTS.

CHAPTER I.
	PAGE
The Old Book	13

CHAPTER II.
The Old Book in its Relation to Science 24

CHAPTER III.
The Old Book and its Themes 37

CHAPTER IV.
The Stone Book 46

CHAPTER V.
Fact and Fiction in Human Life 61

CHAPTER VI.
Fact and Fiction in Holy Writ 77

CHAPTER VII.
Fact and Fiction Among the Heathen 92

CHAPTER VIII.
Man the Monarch 100

CHAPTER IX.
What is Life? 122

CHAPTER X.
Life in Larger Forms 134

CHAPTER XI.
Life—A Study 141

CHAPTER XII.
Death 148

CONTENTS.

CHAPTER XIII.
Longevity—The Patriarchs............................ 162

CHAPTER XIV.
Noah and the Flood.................................. 174

CHAPTER XV.
Book Wonders—Samson the Mighty................... 190

CHAPTER XVI.
A Group of Samsons................................. 204

CHAPTER XVII.
World Wonders—Chord and Canvas................... 215

CHAPTER XVIII.
World Wonders—Trees............................... 232

CHAPTER XIX.
World Wonders—Animals............................. 247

CHAPTER XX.
Struggles with Unbelief.............................. 259

CHAPTER XXI.
What is Truth?..................................... 271

CHAPTER XXII.
The Age of Science.................................. 285

CHAPTER XXIII.
Responsibility for Our Belief........................ 308

CHAPTER XXIV.
The Logic of Experience 318

CHAPTER XXV.
The Goal... 332

FACT AND FICTION IN HOLY WRIT;

OR,

BOOK AND WORLD WONDERS.

CHAPTER I.

THE OLD BOOK.

THIS old book which lies open before me, a copy of which may be found in nearly all the homes of the civilized world, whatever may have been its origin, whether absolutely and in every part a revelation from God to man, inspired in every paragraph, line, or expression, and consequently a divine book in the fullest sense of the word; or part divine and part human, as most people believe; or entirely human—a sentiment with which we do not accord—the fact remains indisputable, the Bible is a wonderful creation.

It is more than mere rhetoric to compare it to the ocean on whose broad expanse the navies of the world are launched, whose hidden depths lie almost beyond the reach of the mariner's plummet, and yet into whose plashing surf a child may wade. This old book is an ocean; it too has depths which cannot be measured by the fathom-line of human science and philosophy, and yet is so simple that the merest rustic, the child in either years or intelligence, may read it, find comfort and direction in its wholesome revelations, and be made strong by its spiritual truths. It requires a good deal of faith to believe all the Bible; but that is no impeachment of the book any more than it is an impeachment of Nature that she has things too deep for our comprehension.

Faith, or belief in things above and beyond our sight, is the secret of all spiritual growth as well as of all true progress. No man grows strong in any direction in whose heart the faith-principle is not supreme. There is no conflict between faith and reason. In the development of a human life there is first the exercise of the senses, then reason, and next faith. We touch, taste, hear, and see things before we reason about them. It is through our faith-faculty that we come into relationship with the invisible world. By faith we are enabled to reach the loftiest summits of human excellence; it is faith that supports us when we descend into the deepest recesses of life; on the wings of faith we may sweep out into the spaces and mount up to the very throne of God. God has spoken to us in nature, through star and flower and worm, but who understands all his speech? To the eye of Him who watches over a sparrow's fall there is nothing great, nothing insignificant. The man of science trains his eye to a similar impartiality in the study of nature. A little patch of moss to the common eye seems destitute of interest—to the eye of the accomplished botanist it is a little world in itself. Some one complained to the great Swedish naturalist, Linnæus, that Sweden did not afford scope enough for the study of nature. The naturalist, pointing to a clump of moss, replied: "No man will live long enough to master the mosses on the rocks of Sweden."

One day, when lost in an African desert, Mungo Park came across a tuft of moss. This bit of green growing in an arid waste was a messenger from God to the desponding explorer. "If God cares for the moss," he said to himself, "surely he cares for me." And he went on his way, cheered by the sight of a bit of moss. Do we not remember the beautiful lines of Wordsworth?

> "To me the meanest flower that blows can give
> Thoughts that do often lie too deep for tears."

There are some people who seem to think, judging from their speech, that the Bible should be reduced to the simplicity of an ordinary human volume. If such were the case, then who would believe it to be a divine book? The natural world about us is made up of a few simple elements—sixty-four or five in number, so far as we know at present. Not only is the whole earth constituted of these, it is supposed, but possibly the entire material universe—their combinations are infinite. No man can ever hope to understand this great volume of nature. It has come from the mind of God, and to know all would be to know God. So the Bible is made up of simple moral truths, variously combined and presented to us in scraps of history, biography, poetry, metaphor, incident, parable, hyperbole, and allegory, etc. And coming from God, like the earth, must it not necessarily partake of his thoughts? And are not his thoughts too deep often for human thought?

The facts of Scripture are at least as well attested

as those of any history; and though it may contain many figures of speech they are to be understood as such, for through them some of the sublimest truths are set forth. Hence we think it is not irreverent to speak of "Fact and Fiction in Holy Writ." But of this we shall have more to say farther along.

All that is asked now is that the reader will follow us patiently and impartially. This is not a vindication—the Bible has reached beyond the need of any man's defense or apology. It is buttressed in the affections of millions of our race, and only Omnipotence himself could banish it from human society. It treats more of the supernatural than of the natural, for the supernatural is the natural of the universe. Many things are recorded upon its pages which all do not believe. These remarkable statements and occurrences belong either in the realm of fact or fiction. We know that some of the grandest truths are taught in fiction.

In both the Old Testament and the New there are accounts of miracles wrought through human agencies as incontestably proven as any of the ordinary events of secular history. Shall they be accepted or rejected? At this point many people are divided in their opinions. One thing, however, has not been, to any great extent, a matter of dispute—the Bible is a book of morals such as is not possessed by any people on earth, except Jews and Christians. How are we to account for this fact? Only by admitting its divinity. One thing is certain: to abide by its precepts, to revere its mysteries, and to drink in its spirit is the sure pathway of ascent to the highest personal, social, and national development in both intelligence and virtue. There are those who read the Bible to find fault with little things—the minor portions—as if one should repudiate the Declaration of Independence because its author neglected to dot an i or cross a t. No scholar denies the fact that there are obscure passages in the Bible, as well as a few spurious ones; but they are easily pointed out and do not mar the teachings of the book. How they came there is not very clear, nor is it very important, but they are there. There are spots on the sun, but who thinks less of the sun on that account? He who searches for these and for the seeming discrepancies, and who reads every strain of poetry as if it were prose, and deals with every metaphor as if it were a mathematical equation, who applies to Scripture language the exactness of law or science, who sees in every expression born out of a luxurious Oriental imagination a plain matter of fact, is not only doing injustice to the book but to himself. He may fitly be compared to a traveler belated at nightfall miles from his destination who stops to read the inscription on the guide-board by the road-side, and instead of pushing on to where the index-finger points, thus escaping the darkness and the impending storm, falls to criticising the lettering of the board.

But let us consider this book as a production—a book merely. It divides itself into sixty-six sub-books, which are attributed to about forty different writers, and who lived through a stretch of nearly or quite two thousand years. As a whole it is a unit. The New Testament quotes the Old frequently, while the Old Testament is the foundation of the New. Not far from one half of the New Testament was written by St. Paul. The next most extensive writer was the gentle and loving John. Of all the New Testament writers Paul was the only one who could claim any eminence in point of scholarship. The writers are mostly men of good native ability; but if any, except St. Paul and possibly the "beloved physician," Luke, ever enjoyed the benefit of academic training both history and tradition have failed to make note of it. And yet how ably did they write! What lofty themes inspired them, and what eminent characters have they chronicled! These writers present different types of character. They were as unlike as musical instruments or trees. There was Jeremiah the sorrowful, Daniel the sagacious, Isaiah the sublime, David the poet, and Solomon the philosopher. The same varied talents appear among the writers of the New Testament. All seemed to have exercised their natural gifts, whatever may have been the degree of their inspiration. Moses and Solomon were the most learned of any of the writers of the Old Testament. The former, with his vast knowledge and proud intelligence—the legislator, reformer, and deliverer, brought up in the learning of Egypt—began the work of writing the Bible. John, with his tender depths of feeling and spiritual insight, completed it.

But how little we know of the inner lives of these men, even the last two mentioned. There was certainly nothing in them calculated to foster or exalt human vanity. Moses was a foundling rescued from the oozy rushes of the Nile; and John a lonely exile at last amid the rocks of Patmos, an island in the Ægean Sea, whither he had been banished by a decree of one of the Roman emperors "for the word of God and the testimony of Jesus Christ."

The Bible, humanly speaking, emanated from the pens

of a class of men whom the world never would have selected as authors capable of writing for all time. Is it not a proof of their inspiration that what was written in that age is so fresh—so interesting and applicable in this and all the ages?

It is a peculiarity of the holy writings that they hide no man's faults and cover up no man's sins. The greatest characters of the Scriptures were imperfect, and some of them at times were notoriously immoral. Even Abraham did not tell the truth—the whole truth, at least—on one or two occasions, when his own highest good would have been subserved by the strictest integrity of speech, which he afterward learned. Noah, David, Solomon, Peter, and some others were not always guiltless. There is no attempt at the concealment of their moral imperfections. Sin is always called by its right name. The entire frankness of this book in dealing with its chief characters is strong proof of its divinity. Is the Bible charged with being unchaste in its language, in some instances? It should be remembered that it is a reflection of the age in which it was written. Its authors were honest enough to make record of the evils in human life and society, calling them by their true names. If it had described only the virtues of its chief men, sinking out of sight their errors and sins, we might then indeed have had reason to suspect it of being untrue to what we know has ever been characteristic of human life.

It does tell of events quite impossible of belief to some minds. For instance, the story of the creation of the first woman from a rib of the first man; the first human transgression and "fall," provoked and precipitated by a "serpent" gifted with the power of speech; the Noachian deluge; the prodigious strength of Samson; the account of Jonah in the whale's belly, and some other equally remarkable statements. Let us be frank. To many these records savor of the mythical, the legendary, and consequently are disbelieved. The fact is, some people judge of the Scriptures by the standards of their own local and temporary experience, and hence injustice is done to the sacred writings.

This book is owned by millions and read in hundreds of languages all over the earth. Six hundred years ago the wages of a laboring man in England were only about two pence (four cents) a day, while the price of a Bible at the same period was, in our money, about one hundred and eighty dollars. A common laborer in those times must toil on industriously for thirteen long years devoting his entire income if he would possess a copy of the word of God. Now it can be owned by the poorest of people; for the earnings of half a day by a farm-hand will pay the cost of an entire copy of the sacred book; and besides, if any are too poor to purchase it, the Bible societies will furnish it freely and gladly. What a contrast! What an illustration of the power of the press!

You may eliminate from these pages every seeming contradiction of statement between the writers, every crude story, of which there are many, all the long chapters, with their almost unpronounceable names, and yet there is left a mine of truth—a magazine of spiritual force. If it be asked why it is that so many millions of our race accept this book as inspired of God, relying implicitly on its teachings and its promises, notwithstanding the many strange and mysterious things it records, the answer is that in reading it and in following its precepts the heart is comforted and the life is made strong.

At a recent Bible anniversary Mr. W. E. Gladstone gave utterance to these words:

"If we are in any measure to grasp the office, dignity, and authority of the Scriptures, we must not suppose we are dealing adequately with that lofty subject by exhausting thought and time in examining whether Moses edited or wrote the Pentateuch as it stands, or what was the book of the law found in the temple in the time of Josiah, or whether it is possible or likely that changes of addition or omission may have crept into the text. If the most greedily destructive among all the theories of the modern critics (so seriously at variance with one another) were established as true, it would not avail to impair the great facts of the history of man with respect to the Jews and to the nations of the world, nor to disguise the light which those facts throw upon the pages of the sacred volume; nor to abate the commanding force with which, bathed, so to speak, in the flood of that light, the Bible invites, attracts, and commands the adhesion of mankind. Even the moral problems which may be raised as to particular portions of the volume, and which may not have found any absolute and certain solution, are lost in the comprehensive contemplation of its general strain, its immeasurable loftiness of aim, and the vastness of the results which it and its immediate accompaniments in institution and event have wrought for our predecessors in the journey of life, for ourselves, and for the most forward, dominant, and responsible portions of our race."

It may seem almost like a waste of time and energy at this late day to write upon this subject. We do it because old truths are often lost sight of in the whirl and excitement incident to the discovery of new ones. Moreover, the sons and daughters do not always walk in the footsteps of their fathers and mothers. We boast of our science and our civilization, but forget that they are the outgrowth of Bible teachings in a great degree.

The claims of the Bible are based on its antiquity, its history, and its contents. That which is old, and consequently has survived the wear of long periods of time, has some claim upon the respect of thoughtful people. We gaze upon the Egyptian obelisk, the ivy-mantled castle peering out upon us from the Middle Ages, or upon some ancient tomb that possibly once held the dust of a king, with peculiar feelings of veneration. No matter how we criticise these objects, they command us by their very age. Whatever men may say of the Bible, its pages bear the impress of the buried centuries. It is a message from the past to the present, from generations dead to generations living. Its utterances are the echoes of voices which were hushed in silence ages ago. Astronomers tell us of stars which are so remote in the fields of space that were they stricken out of existence by the power of God at this hour their light would continue to flow toward us for hundreds, if not thousands, of years to come. So of the men who wrote the books which in the aggregate constitute the Bible; they, being dead, yet speak the words of truth to us. We do not mean to say that age alone sanctifies any thing, for even time cannot convert falsehood into truth. There are some old books that might well be burned, and some old customs that need to be forgotten in order that the world may make progress. But this cannot be said of the Bible. Let us be respectful as we enter this temple, over whose archway is cut deeply the inscription, "Thus saith the Lord." Come to this book then, dear reader, as you would go to a well of pure and sparkling water gushing from the rocks below, not to find fault with its depths, but to draw thereof and drink to the quenching of thy thirst, remembering the words of the great Teacher: "Whosoever drinketh of the water that I shall give him shall never thirst; but the water that I shall give him shall be in him a well of water springing up into everlasting life."

CHAPTER II.

THE OLD BOOK IN ITS RELATION TO SCIENCE.

THE Bible has a mission, and that mission is not to teach every thing we ought to know. This thought we shall try to develop as we proceed. It is not the purpose of the Scriptures to teach the world science. The Bible occupies a plane above the natural world. To open it at random, with a view to being directed in the ordinary affairs of life by the first passage upon which the eye happens to rest is not only an unwarranted use of Scripture, but a veritable superstition. It brings the Bible down to the level of a dice-board.. And furthermore, when we speak of the holy writings we mean the original writings, the languages in which they first appeared. When we speak of inspiration it is not claimed that the translations are inspired, though the work has been done well enough for all practical purposes. But every question of absolute verbal accuracy must be referred to the originals. Then, in reply to the objection that the Bible is not always true to science, I remark it does not claim to be, for it never was intended to be a text-book on geology, astronomy, or natural history. Neither the prophets nor the apostles ever made any pretensions as teachers of science. They did not profess even to adhere closely to the exact order in nature. At the time they wrote science, in the modern sense of the word, was unborn.

Mere glimpses, it is true, appear in the writings of Moses, Job, and some others, as they studied the phenomena of the heavens and of inanimate creation. David, moved especially by these phenomena, gives frequent utterance to his feelings in sublime poetic strains. Solomon was a naturalist of high order, but he was an exception to the generality of mankind in his own times.

The ancients had very vague ideas of the natural world. In their conceptions the earth was a plane, and not a sphere; the sun was a great ball of fire which sank into the ocean at night, and, of course, must have arisen out of it in the morning. It was currently reported, too, that they who lived far to the westward could hear the hissing noise made by the sun as he plunged his fiery mass beneath the billows of the great sea in the evening.

Bible writers believed these same things, and their inspiration did not correct their science, for wrong science, then as now, might exist with a right heart.

The Bible speaks of the earth as "stretched out," and also of the "ends of the earth," expressions at variance with the idea of the earth's rotundity. The thought of a great globe floating through ethereal space, "hung upon nothing," would have seemed an impossibility to them; and any one inculcating such dogmas would have been regarded as insane.

The earlier Greek astronomers introduced a system of crystalline transparent spheres, revolving, one within the other, and carrying the planets with them around the earth as a center. Far beyond these spheres was the *primum mobile*—the starry sphere revolving from east to west every twenty-four hours.

This system was incorporated in the philosophy of Aristotle, and seems to have commanded the assent of mankind for ages. Its truth was hardly drawn into doubt till the revival of letters, the commencement of the true astronomical science of the seventeenth century, and even then the clearest and strongest intellects were slow in extricating themselves from the Aristotelian philosophy. It was not until the time of Kepler that any real progress was made in discovering the true laws of planetary motion.

These old Hebrews, in common with the classical writers, understood the sky or firmament to be a solid vault as it appeared to an ordinary observer. Moses had said, "God made the firmament, and divided the waters which were under the firmament from the waters which were above the firmament." Again, the same writer, in describing the rain-fall at the time of the deluge, said, "The windows of heaven were opened." Even if it was a figurative expression, to the unscientific mind it seemed descriptive of something material.

In like manner, Job speaks of the "pillars of heaven." Samuel said, "The foundations of the heaven moved and shook." David sang, "He commanded the clouds above, and opened the door of heaven."

There are many other similar expressions, such as the "rending of the heavens," the "skipping of Lebanon," the floods and trees "clapping their hands." To these same people the earth was a stationary body, around which the sun revolved. Let us not visit any undue reflections upon them on account of their ignorance of the physical world, for at a much later period the same condition prevailed until Copernicus, Tycho Brahe, Galileo, and Newton broke forth in a darkened firmament as stars of the first magnitude.

A great commotion was raised when these scientists began to teach that the sun was the central point in our system, around which the earth revolved. They could not deny the evidence of their senses. Galileo constructed a telescope which revealed to him the true motion of the heavenly bodies, so that the plain teachings of astronomical science could not be successfully denied. For this overturning of old-time notions he was twice imprisoned by the irate monks, and each time recanted, so that the young astronomer lost the honor of martyrdom. As he came out of prison, however, he stamped the earth with his foot and said, "Yet it does move!" But why this opposition on the part of the monks? Because they preferred to interpret nature by Scripture rather than the Scriptures by nature.

"Is it not written in the Bible," they said, "'The world is established that it cannot be moved?' And do not the Scriptures say again of the sun that it is as a 'bridegroom coming out of his chamber, and rejoiceth as a strong man to run a race. His going forth is from the end of the heaven, and his circuit unto the ends of it: and there is nothing hid from the heat thereof?'" The Roman Inquisition took the matter in hand and decreed as follows: "First, The proposition that the sun is the center of the world and immovable from its place is absurd, philosophically false, and formally heretical, because it is expressly contrary to Holy Scripture. Second, The proposition that the earth is not the center of the world nor immovable, but that it moves, and also with diurnal motion, is absurd, philosophically false, and, theologically considered, at least erroneous in faith." It is due to the infallible Church to say that in A. D. 1818 the papal edict was formally repealed, and the Copernican theory is now taught alike in Jesuit colleges and Protestant divinity schools. Until comparatively recent times science and natural history had no very conspicuous place in the religious training of men, and, as a consequence, many were ignorant of the important bearings which a right understanding of nature has upon the written word. Indeed, Christian teachers were afraid of science, especially that of geology. The author of this book, when a student, was urged by an old and conscientious divine to "let geology alone," for its teachings, he said, "tended to atheism." Times have changed; it is now understood that both books are God's faithful records; and if it be so, then it follows that either without the other cannot be fully understood. Cowper said, "An undevout astronomer is mad." So an undevout geologist or chemist or botanist is mad. The Rev. Richard Watson, afterward Bishop of Llandaff, England, who wrote a book entitled *An Apology for the Bible*, in reply to Paine's *Age of Reason*, was elected professor of chemistry in the University of Cambridge in 1769, and at the time, he informs us, he knew nothing at all of chemistry, had never read a syllable on the subject, nor seen a single experiment in it. The remarkable part of this is that at so late a date the physical sciences should have been held in such low esteem that a student could receive his degree without knowing any thing of chemistry. In his honor, however, it may be recorded that he studied it fourteen months and then began to teach it.

In the Bible all these questions relating to the natural world were merely incidental to the main subject, and hence the writers might use the language of common life or the more exact language of implied, if not real, science without in either case doing violence to the word of God. "It frequently," says Professor Maury, "makes allusions to the laws of nature, their operation and effects; but such allusions are often so wrapped in the folds of the peculiar drapery with which its language is occasionally clothed that the meaning, though peering out from its thin covering all the while, yet lies in some sense concealed until the lights and revelations of science are thrown upon it; then it breaks out and strikes us with exquisite force and beauty."

The Bible contains repeated instances where not only the ordinary speech is employed, but makes reference to things that were purely fictitious or legendary. There is one instance which has been a stumbling-block to many.* The questions have been asked myriads of times, "Did the sun and moon really stand still at the command of Joshua?" "Must we believe that the law of gravitation was suspended and the machinery of the whole heavens interfered with while a couple of small armies were fighting a battle on the plains of Beth-horon?" There is not an intelligent youth in Christendom who will not find himself tempted to doubt this when he reads it. He may believe that

* Josh. x, 12-14.

the Almighty had power to arrest the planets in their orbits; but, somehow, he instinctively calls this in question. He cannot help it, for he cannot see that the issue at Beth-horon was of sufficient importance to warrant so stupendous a miracle. We all reason in about the same way. That would have been indeed a wonderful miracle, but then all miracles are wonderful *per se*, and yet a Christian accepts the miracles, believes in them. Take these away, and you have not much left but the two lids of the Bible. Admit the existence of God, then certainly all miracles are possible. The rationalistic dismemberment of the Bible history begins with the negation of miracles, which is a denial of the supernatural. With the belief or disbelief of miracles the entire system stands or falls, for all religion rests on the supernatural. But in asking too much we may get nothing.

This account of the standing still of the sun and moon has generally been held to commit believers in the Bible to its literal truthfulness, when in fact, as any one can see by a careful reading, it is a quotation introduced into the sacred writings from the lost book of "Jasher." To receive this as literal Scripture, therefore, is not required. Let us cling to the Bible, but not at the expense of a correct rendering; if we do, we shall only drive some intelligent and honest people away from it. The standing still of the sun and moon, though entirely possible, is no more to be understood literally than the statement that Mount Lebanon "skipped like a calf." David says it did, but then David was a poet. If we are to take these statements in a literal sense we are simply converting poetry into prose. The above quotation from the lost book of Jasher, "Book of the Upright," describing the standing still of the sun and moon, is a poetic rhapsody, invoked as a sort of "grand march" in a triumphal procession after a great victory. In another place in the Scripture we are told that "the stars in their courses fought against Sisera." Are we to believe that the planets were transformed into warriors and came into Palestine and fought battles with men? when it is only meant that the heavenly powers were on the side of the Lord's hosts, or rather that Barak, the commander of the Israelitish army, assaulted his enemies under the cover of darkness, or in the dim light of the stars, and thus it was that the "stars in their courses fought against Sisera."

The Bible contains frequent instances where not only the ordinary speech is employed, but where allusions are made to things that were purely legendary. We are told in one place that "Saul and Jonathan were lovely and pleasant in their lives; and in their deaths they were not divided; they were swifter than eagles; they were stronger than lions." This, too, is a poetic rhapsody from the lost book of Jasher, and has been accepted by all critics as a very pretty piece of elegiac poetry, very much like some modern funeral sermons where the real is lost in the ideal. Saul was not a very "pleasant" sort of character, judging from what we know of his history. Again, current notions and opinions of the people were often alluded to, as, for example, the belief that the color of the clouds indicated an approaching change of weather. Jesus himself made use of this: "When it is evening, ye say, It will be fair weather: for the sky is red. And in the morning, It will be foul weather to-day:

for the sky is red and lowering." He was not delivering a lecture on meteorology; if he had been he most likely would have told them that neither the color of clouds nor the quarter of the moon had any influence whatever on the weather, and that all the so-called weather-prophets are mere guessers, who may sometimes happen to guess correctly; that all these popular signs are very uncertain.

An old saying has come down to us from a remote past which may or may not be true:

> " Red at night is the sailor's delight,
> Red in the morning, the sailor takes warning."

It is most likely that Jesus attached a symbolical meaning to what he said about the signs of the weather. The "red at even" of the Old Testament betokened fair weather at hand. The red sky of the morning signified the storms of persecution which should descend upon the early Christian Church. At all events, these people were better prophets of the weather than interpreters of those prophecies which it was their duty to expound; or possibly he meant that the signs of the sky are uncertain, and may deceive us, but moral signs, if properly understood, never mislead. Who has not read that beautiful passage in one of the psalms of David: "Thy youth is renewed like the eagle's?"* Now, the fact is, the eagle does not renew his youth; he lives sometimes for thirty or forty years and dies. But there was a belief in ancient times that when this kingly bird found himself growing old he spread his wings and with one mighty effort soared aloft into the sun,

* Psa. ciii, 5.

where his youth was renewed. The figure is most beautiful and expressive, but judged of from the stand-point of natural history is not true. David does not say it is true; he only makes use of the myth to show how man, as "age creeps on apace," may look away into the heavens, where his powers shall be renewed and eternal youth be gained.

Scripture terms are true representations of natural phenomena. Had the Bible been written in the language of the exact sciences it would have been to the great anxious world seeking for spiritual truth and comfort a sealed volume. The psalmist said in one place, "The sun knoweth his going down." Suppose he had uttered this in scientific form; then it must have read something like this: "There is a law by which is determined for any particular day the precise time at which a line drawn from the sun to a given point on the earth will be tangential, and in what azimuth that line will fall," etc. Alas for that psalm! To have used the language of science would have left the world without a Bible for thousands of years. If written in the language of the exact sciences every one would have needed a university education in order to understand it, and even then many might have failed, for the language of science is sometimes very hazy.

Moses came the nearest of any of the sacred writers to teaching science in the necessarily brief account he gives of the beginnings of things; but it was only to show the world that God is the Creator of all things, and thus to banish from the mind of mankind any possible thought of the eternity of matter.

Indeed, whether it be Moses, Job, David, or Peter,

all allusions to natural history, philosophy, and science are made simply to illustrate moral and religious truths. Even modern astronomers talk of "sunsets," and of the "ascension" and "declination" of the heavenly bodies, as though the Ptolemaic system were yet believed, and no one protests against it.

When we come to the gospels we find them to be somewhat diverse in their general features. They agree, and yet do not agree. The writers were intent simply on giving to the world great spiritual facts and truths. Jesus was the great Teacher, "sent from God," and yet he did not instruct the world upon all the questions which were of interest to men. He could have revealed the possibilities of steam-power, railroads, telegraphs, electro-motors, phonographs, and all other modern inventions and discoveries, for they were just as possible in that age as in this; all the forces and all the materials existed then as well as now, but he said nothing about them. Nor did he assume to settle disputes among men about their philosophies or their politics. He did not tell the world which school was the true one in philosophy, nor did he settle the thousand social questions which have agitated the world through all its ages. The earth was a globe and revolved on its axis, carrying both teacher and disciple around the whole circle of the heavens every twenty-four hours, and yet these same disciples thought it was an extended plane resting on they did not know what. Why did not this great Teacher inform the world of its erroneous opinions? Because it was not his mission to teach science, politics, and philosophy.

All mere intellectual questions have been left to

the natural powers of the mind, and mankind must learn by observation and experience in every thing. We are placed here to study the stars, the flowers, insects, birds, animals, the earth, and man, and in these studies to grow wise and strong. How little these innocent people of the olden times knew about the universe! What were the stars above to them? Mere points of light in the dome of the heavens. They knew far less than we with our telescopes and spectroscopes, and yet even we are only beginning to know something of God's great temple. The only large body of water of which they had knowledge was the Mediterranean, which they spoke of always as the "Great Sea." Of the Atlantic and Pacific Oceans they were profoundly ignorant. The little strip of country on the east of the Mediterranean Sea—Palestine and its adjacent neighborhood—comprised in their thoughts the "whole earth," and such it was to them. Of the average man of those times Alexander Pope's lines would have been true:

> "He thought the visual line that girt him round,
> The world's extreme; and thought the silver moon
> That nightly o'er him led 'her virgin host
> No broader than his father's shield."

Injustice is done the Bible when it is demanded that it shall acquaint us with the things we ought to learn by our own efforts.

Shall it be rejected with all its wisdom, because, forsooth, a few small discrepancies or verbal inaccuracies have crept into it during the last four thousand years? A few minor errors have found place there mostly through human mistakes or neglect. In the British Museum there is a collection of the different

Bibles printed in England a couple of centuries or less ago, among which there is one edition that contains six thousand verbal errors of one kind or another! But, thanks to modern scholarship, the Bible of to-day is about as free from human mistakes as would be possible.

But what if in Matthew's gospel the word "whale" is used in reference to Jonah, when in the original the term signifying *sea-monster* is employed, which may have been some other species of fish; what if one writer does say that the robe put upon Christ at the crucifixion was "scarlet," another that it was "purple," and still another that it was a "gorgeous robe;" no one's salvation is affected by the variation. Any good commentary will explain the seeming discrepancies. We must remember that in translating from one language to another a word is often made to do service in several relations, and sometimes there are seeming contradictions when in reality there are none. Shall we discard the Bible because of these? No.

CHAPTER III.

THE OLD BOOK AND ITS THEMES.

THERE are two main topics of which this old book treats, namely, creation and redemption. All other subjects are subordinate to these. The Mosaic account of the creation of the heavens and the earth lies at the foundation of this record. There is a loftiness of style about it which contrasts strongly with all mere human attempts to account for the origin of the present system. The history of all nations, Rome, Greece, China, Mexico, goes back to an age of myths. All have their legends and their divinities, weird and fanciful. The old Hebrew nation is the solitary exception. Here, in the sacred books of the Hebrews, it is simply and sublimely declared, "In the beginning God created the heaven and the earth." If all other nations have had their myths and traditions alike confused and conflicting it is not just to assume that the Hebrews followed the same delusions.

Reasoning from analogy is never safe, for analogy proves nothing, though it may illustrate and fortify an argument. The traditions concerning the beginnings of other nations are characterized by an air of extravagance from which that of the Hebrews is exempt. Let us take the account given by Berosus, an educated priest of Babylon, who lived about two hundred and sixty years B. C. He wrote in the Greek language, and was a man of large information on many subjects. Fragments of his writings have been preserved by Josephus, Eusebius, and others. Even these fragments are said to be of great value, as they relate to the most obscure portions of Asiatic history.

This eminent author has given an account of the creation which we present here for the sake of contrast. "In the beginning," wrote Berosus, "all was darkness and water, and therein were generated monstrous animals of strange and peculiar forms. There were men with two wings, and others even with four, and with two faces; and others with two heads, a man's and woman's on one body; and there were men with the heads and horns of goats, and men with hoofs, like horses, and some with the upper part of a man joined to the lower parts of a horse, like centaurs; and there were bulls with human heads, dogs with four bodies and with fishes' tails, men and horses with dogs' heads, etc. A woman ruled them all, by name Omorka, which is the same as 'the sea.'

"And Belus appeared and split the woman in twain; and of the one half of her he made the heaven, and of the other half the earth; and the beasts that were in her he caused to perish. And he split the darkness and divided the heaven and the earth asunder, and put the world in order; and the animals that could not bear the light perished.

"Belus upon this, seeing that the earth was desolate, yet teeming with productive power, commanded one of the gods to cut off his head, and to mix the blood, which flowed forth, with earth, and form men therewith and beasts that could bear the light. So man was made, and was intelligent, being a partaker of the divine wisdom."

We are almost led to believe that the Darwinians found their theory of development in this heathen account of the creation of man. There is about as much reason in one as in the other. But turn now to the Mosaic record, and what a difference is seen! What childishness in the one, what manliness in the other! How misty the one, how clear the other! How foolish the one, how grandly reasonable the other!

" In the beginning God created the heaven and the earth.

" And the earth was without form, and void ; and darkness was upon the face of the deep. And the Spirit of God moved upon the face of the waters.

"And God said, Let there be light: and there was light.

" And God saw the light, that it was good : and God divided the light from the darkness.

" And God called the light Day, and the darkness he called Night. And the evening and the morning were the first day.

" And God said, Let there be a firmament in the midst of the waters, and let it divide the waters from the waters.

" And God made the firmament, and divided the waters which were under the firmament from the waters which were above the firmament: and it was so.

" And God called the firmament Heaven. And the evening and the morning were the second day.

" And God said, Let the waters under the heaven be

gathered together unto one place, and let the dry land appear: and it was so.

"And God called the dry land Earth; and the gathering together of the waters called he Seas: and God saw that it was good.

"And God said, Let the earth bring forth grass, the herb yielding seed, and the fruit-tree yielding fruit after his kind, whose seed is in itself, upon the earth: and it was so.

"And the earth brought forth grass, and herb yielding seed after his kind, and the tree yielding fruit, whose seed was in itself, after his kind. . . .

"And God said, Let us make man in our image, after our likeness: and let them have dominion over the fish of the sea, and over the fowl of the air, and over the cattle, and over all the earth, and over every creeping thing that creepeth upon the earth.

"So God created man in his own image, in the image of God created he him; male and female created he them.

"And God blessed them, and God said unto them, Be fruitful, and multiply, and replenish the earth, and subdue it; and have dominion over the fish of the sea, and over the fowl of the air, and over every living thing that moveth upon the earth. . . .

"And the Lord God formed man of the dust of the ground, and breathed into his nostrils the breath of life; and man became a living soul."

The cosmogony of Moses is the only one in the world which has in it sufficient merit to warrant serious consideration. It is the most complete of all documents bearing on the origin of things. Hugh Miller called it "science poetically expressed."

But the Bible deals with another subject, namely, redemption, in which more particularly it touches the heart-life of the world. The trend of all its teachings is toward the spiritual welfare of mankind. Almost the first chapter in Genesis points to a coming Deliverer. All the histories, prophecies, songs, and parables cluster about the idea of a mysterious man, a messenger who should come to earth in a miraculous way and upon a lofty mission, and prove his authority by laying down his life for that of all other men.

The Bible influences in a very high degree the literature of the world. Its phrases are woven into the tissues of human speech wherever the book is known. In the conversations, not alone of the common people, but of the educated classes, it is constantly quoted; its expressions are so sharp, its sentences so plethoric of meaning, its proverbs so like pearls and diamonds, that their use is an embellishment of human speech. When we cannot say a thing to suit our idea, for want of proper language, what do we do but draw on the Bible, and often irreverently? Indeed, people sometimes do this in jest, alas! and thus "steal the livery of heaven to serve the devil in." There are but few books, whether of science, history, art, or life, in which there will not be found some Scripture quotation, or reference, or expression used to illustrate a thought or make more forceful the ideas of the author. So in novels, in newspapers, in great senatorial debates, in almost every sort of literary production, written or spoken, we find more or less of Bible, and often in a form which shows most plainly that the authors had not "searched the Scriptures" very carefully. The Bible is a repository of gems of thought which have stood the critical test of the ages, crystallizations in speech as much above the ordinary as diamonds are above crude charcoal; and often when a speaker wishes to give point to a remark, or finish up a sentence nicely, and thus say something well, and beautiful, what does he do but go to the Scriptures, not to "obtain eternal life" for himself, but to give life to his speech or sentence, which might be dead without it.

Nothing interests people so much as the doctrines of redemption. How to escape an offended Deity and placate his wrath has absorbed the thought of both the heathen and Christian world in all ages. It is only in the Gospel of love, the Gospel of the mysterious Man on whom the world's thought is being centered more and more, that we find answer to the longings of the soul. It is not strange, therefore, that the literature of the world has been tinged, if not permeated, with Bible language and influence. So widely has it been scattered, and so universally has it been read and quoted by writers of all classes, in all departments of letters, that should every printed copy in existence suddenly become by some magic process blank paper the entire Bible could be reproduced from other books. Thousands of commentaries have been written upon it, in whole or in part. Then, besides, there have been dictionaries, encyclopedias, reference-books, works on archæology, philosophy, sacred geography, natural history, narratives of travel and exploration, monographs on special themes, works on Christian theology, Christian experience, and biography, tracts, and hymns—the latter to the number of one hundred and fifty thousand! Blot these all out, and more than half the literature of the world would be destroyed.

Could the suffrages of scholars be given on the question, as to which are the three greatest names in the literature of modern times it is quite certain that most would agree in naming Dante, Milton, and Shakespeare. The name of Dante, most likely, would never have been so universally known and immortalized in the *Divina Comedia* if its author had not possessed an accurate knowledge of the Scriptures. Milton's great poem, "Paradise Lost," was the outgrowth of distinctly Christian culture. His figures may be too strong, his coloring too severe, yet had there not been a Bible there could not have been a "Paradise Lost." How is it with Shakespeare? Some one has said that if all he borrowed from the Bible were eliminated nothing characteristic would be taken away. No judgment could be more radically wrong. English literature names no secular writer who gives clearer indications of a genuine Christian culture, so far as the understanding is concerned, than the author of "Hamlet." The passages in his writings in proof of this are quite numerous. The reader can search them out at his leisure. But as an example take the oft-quoted speech of Portia to Shylock:

> "The quality of mercy is not strained;
> It droppeth as the gentle rain from heaven
> Upon the place beneath: it is twice blest;
> It blesseth him that gives and him that takes."

Or this:

> "It is an attribute of God himself;
> And earthly power doth then show likest God's,

> When mercy seasons justice. Therefore, Jew,
> Though justice be thy plea, consider this,
> That, in the course of justice, none of us
> Should see salvation: we do pray for mercy;
> And that same prayer doth teach us all to render
> The deeds of mercy."

Had not a far greater than Shakespeare long before said, "Blessed are the merciful, for they shall obtain mercy?" We cannot speak of Shakespeare as a devout believer and as a pure-hearted Christian man; but that he understood the Bible is as certain as that Bunyan understood it, in a certain sense, and out of it wrote the immortal fiction, *Pilgrim's Progress.*

Such is the Bible, a hated book by some, a much-loved and prized book by others; one that touches the springs of human life as no other ever did or can. He who starts out on the perilous voyage of life without this chart incurs the risk of being dashed on the rocks of sin and error.

Let it be known to the young reader especially that the world's greatest and best men, through all the ages, have been students of this book. It is the one volume which stands out alone among all the myriad volumes that have been printed as the sun shines out of the heavens paling all the stars of night. It not only pictures life but reflects it and elevates it. It is a mirror in which we see ourselves, a dispenser of remedies which heal our soul-maladies, a key which unlocks hidden and mysterious things, a magazine of power to move onward the society of the world toward millennial glory. When Sir Walter Scott was nearing death, sitting by an open window one morning, looking out upon the beautiful Tweed in silent contemplation, he suddenly aroused and said to his attendant, "Read to me." "What shall I read?" questioned the attendant. "There is only one book in the world," answered the great novelist, "the Bible." The volume was brought and opened at the fourteenth chapter of St. John, which was read to him throughout. "There," replied Sir Walter, "that is beautiful, that is comforting." Soon after he fell peacefully to sleep, to wake no more.

"If I err," wrote one who declared his belief in the Bible, "it is in a heavenly region; it is in fields of light. I am content to cheat myself in fields of light with visions of eternity. If I err it is with the disciples of philosophy and virtue, with men who have drunk deep at the fountain of human knowledge, but who dissolved not the pearl of their salvation in the draught: I err with Bacon, the great confidant of Nature, fraught with all the learning of the past and almost prescient of the future, yet too wise not to know his weakness and too philosophic not to feel his ignorance; I err with Milton, rising on an angel's wing to heaven, and, like the bird of morn, soaring out of sight amid the music of his grateful piety; I err with Locke, whose pure philosophy only taught him to adore its Source, whose warm love of genuine liberty was never chilled into rebellion with its Author; I err with Newton, whose star-like spirit shot athwart the darkness of the spheres too soon to re-ascend to the home of its nativity. With men like these I shall remain in error. Nor shall I desert those errors for the drunken death-bed of a Paine or the delirious war-whoop of those men who would erect their altar on the ruins of society."

CHAPTER IV.

THE STONE BOOK.

BY whatever process the earth came into existence, whether created by the fiat of the Almighty in six literal days of twenty-four hours each, or six minutes, or six indefinite periods of time measured by thousands or even millions of years each, one thing is certain, it does exist; in this we have a great and undisputed fact.

There is a small sect of philosophers who live in the misty mazes of speculation, holding to the belief that there is no outside objective world of material entities. With them all is ideal—all is within us—ideas and their relations, that is all! But when one burns his fingers with a piece of red-hot iron, or gets a cinder in his eye on a railway-train, or stumbles over something in the dark to his injury, somehow the impression becomes very strong that there is something besides ideas in the world. We can scarcely read some things which have been written, with even seeming sincerity, without wondering why the insane asylums are not more populous.

Not very long ago the writer stumbled upon a definition of plant life in a learned book,* the author of which says: "These forces are developed by the retrograde metamorphosis of the organic compound generated by the instrumentality of the plant, whereby

---

* *Correlation and Conservation of Force.*

they ultimately return to the simple primary forms, water, carbonic acid, and ammonia, which serve as the essential food of vegetables." The same author, alluding to animal life, says: "Of these organic compounds one portion (*a*) is converted into substance of the living body by a constructive force which (in so far as it is not supplied by the agency of external heat) is developed by the retrograde metamorphosis of another portion (*b*) of food. And while the ultimate descent of the first-named portion (*a*) to the simple condition from which it was originally drawn becomes one source of the peculiarly animal powers— the *psychical* and *motor* exerted by the organism— another source of these may be found in a like metamorphosis of a further portion (*c*) of the food which has never been converted into living tissue." We do not know but the author perfectly understood what he was writing about; but suppose the Bible had been written in language like this, what would have been its fate?

There is a universe of matter, and it is under the control of Almighty God in every part, with whom "all things are possible." He works to-day by means of agencies which were ordained in the beginning. The universe is a vast mechanism, and it is not irreverent to speak of God as a great world-builder. This mechanism, with its majestic movement of suns and planets, light and heat, oceans and tides, seasons and men, is shaped, moved, and guided by infinite power and wisdom, and is animated by infinite love. The power which alone could create the universe could also endow it with all its beauty and capacity. This universe was born out of the marriage of elementary atoms by the joining of lesser unities to form the greater, in accordance with a principle of absolute order and harmony. Thus, Nature took her perfect form. With this type of creation ever before us—the manifestation of God in his works—let not the word mechanism, if it affects only the humblest organism, appear low or unworthy.

It may be proper at this time to give a brief *résumé* of the nebular hypothesis originated by La Place, a French mathematician and astronomer who lived in the sixteenth century. This theory teaches that "the matter of this earth, as well as that of all other planetary bodies of our solar system, originally constituted an immense nebula, extending out into illimitable space; that this nebular mass had an exceedingly high temperature, which gradually cooled off during the long periods of time, and as it cooled and contracted its velocity of rotation increased. From a motion which was very slow at the first it continued to increase until the centrifugal force arising from the rotation became equal to the attraction of the central mass, when this zone necessarily became detached from the central mass. In this way a number of zones of nebulous matter were successively detached until by gradual condensation the central mass became of comparatively small dimensions and great density. These zones thus successively detached would form concentric rings of vapor, all revolving in the same direction around the sun. If the particles of each ring continued to condense without separating from each other they would ultimately form a liquid or solid ring. But generally each ring of vapor would break up into masses, revolving about the sun with velocities slightly different from each other. These masses would become spheroidal in form—that is, they would form planets in a state of vapor. If one of them were large enough to attract each of the others in succession to itself the ring of vapor would be converted into a single spheroidal mass of vapor, and we should have a single planet of great bulk for each zone of vapor detached. But if one of these masses had a preponderating size they would all continue to revolve about the sun in independent orbits, and would form a zone of little planets such as we have actually discovered between the orbits of Mars and Jupiter, known as asteriods."*

Such, in brief, is the nebular hypothesis of La Place. The oneness of the solar system is seen in the light of recent discoveries. Nor does this view interfere with the Mosaic account. Science has shown that the earth at one time formed a part of the sun. The investigations of scientists with the spectroscope have revealed in the sun no fewer than twenty-five distinct elements which are known among things terrestrial, and there is every reason to believe that the remaining elements either existed formerly or exist now in the body of the solar orb. Among the metals discovered in the sun's atmosphere is iron, which along with the other metals is in a state of vapor. Not only is the presence of iron unmistakably made out, but its position among other metals is found to be just where it might be expected, having respect to gravity and the atomic weights which these metals are known to possess.

Whether this be a true or false theory we shall not

* *Exposition du Système du Monde*, 6me édition, note vii, p. 465.

4

discuss it here, only to say that God is the Creator of the earth by whatever process it came into being. His power is unlimited. Let us view things as we see them.

In nature at the present time forces are busily at work which have been in operation through all the ages in the past, though we think not to the same extent, nor with the same degree of energy. Changes are constantly going forward under the silent and persistent influence of natural law. We know that the Gulf of Mexico is being filled up gradually by the millions of tons of sediment borne into it by the Mississippi River and its tributaries. The day will come when the great gulf will not exist, and when what is now its bottom will be dry land, and cities will rise where now the waves beat. Forests are falling before the ax of the settlers; rivers once broad and deep are dwindling to shallow creeks. The ocean is continually encroaching upon the land in many portions of the world, and the old coast-lines are melting away before the beating surf, while the habitations of mankind are being driven inland farther and farther. A coal-bed is most likely being formed at the present time in the heart of the Atlantic Ocean in that triangular space between the Azores, Canaries, and Cape de Verd Islands. When Columbus was crossing the Atlantic Ocean on his voyage of discovery he was astonished when, on the 19th of September, 1492, he found himself in the midst of that great bank of sea-weed, the "Sea-weed meadow of Oviedo," as it has been called by sailors, or the Saragossa Sea, which has a varying breadth of not far from three hundred miles, and stretches through twenty-five degrees of latitude, embracing an area of two hundred and sixty thousand square miles, equal to the whole of the Mississippi valley in extent, a huge floating garden in which countless myriads of animals find food and shelter. It is so thickly matted over with these weeds that vessels are retarded in their speed in passing through it. When the companions of Columbus saw it they thought it marked the limits of navigation, and were alarmed. To the eye at a little distance it seems substantial enough to walk on. What becomes of the dead remains of that vast marine growth? May it not even now be accumulating into deposits of a certain kind of coal, which the generations to come, in the far-off ages, may use when the bed of the Atlantic Ocean shall have become habitable by man?

If this does not turn into coal it at least shows us how the ancient coal-beds may have been formed. Great changes are going forward in this age, but there were greater and doubtless more violent ones some tens of thousands of years ago, when the almighty Father was fitting up the earth for the home of his children.

The earth every-where reveals the fact that there have been great convulsions in nature. The scientists tell us that when our planet was cooling off and taking on its present form the nucleus, or core, shrank, and the crust which had formed on its outer surface, as the heat was radiated off into space, followed the shrinking mass within, and was consequently broken and contorted. When we examine it we behold every-where what seems to be confusion; but that which often appears to be disorder is the most perfect order. We are taught that God is in history, and who doubts it? Equally is the earth replete with evidences of an overruling Providence.

God has as certainly put his signature on the very rocks in their deep beds as anywhere. The ripened grain-fields of our western prairies are the banners which wave over the dominion of the Eternal. How could this grain grow in our fields if it were not for the soil? During the lapse of uncounted ages in the history of the earth rocks have been ground into soil, and soil has been recemented into rock, and to-day the same transformations are slowly and silently going on.

"When the earth first cooled down from its primal heat it had no soil, but must have been a mass of crystalline granite rocks and volcanic scoriæ, incapable of supporting animal or vegetable life. When the vapors condensed upon the surface, then began the strife between fire and water which, under the mild forms we call weather, has never since ceased. Rains began to fall upon the mountains—the mere wrinkles produced by the contraction of the cooling crust; streams flowed downward into the valleys, cracking the still hot rocks, whirling fragments along in their courses until they settled as gravel, sand, or fine powder to the bottom of quiet seas or were dissolved in boiling wells. Then vegetation began to flourish, and after slow centuries had passed animal life appeared; each department of organized existence in its own way adding to the list of terrestrial changes. From the very beginning atmospheric oxygen was omnipresent; carbonic acid gas, too, began to act upon the rocks, and as the result of these solvents decomposing, breaking up, and commingling, the course of operations thus carried on through long periods of continual action has given us the soil in its present character and aspects."* Thus was the earth fitted up for man, to whom almost every thing in nature points.

In no one thing is the providence of God more clearly shown than in the creation of the soil. Some speculative philosophers have predicted that the time will come when the soil of the world will be exhausted and the human race become extinct—"starved out." Such a prediction has no foundation in fact. God has made ample provision for his children. One foot in depth of a fairly good agricultural soil contains per acre 4,000 pounds of phosphoric acid; 8,000 pounds of potash; 16,000 pounds of nitrogen; and lime, magnesia, soda, chlorine, sulphur, and silica to afford food for all the crops which these three elements can feed. After farmers, by careful and skillful cultivation, have exhausted all this great store of plant food in the uppermost foot of this soil, which will require several centuries, will the soil be exhausted? Not at all. As the land is gradually changed into vegetable growth, and the surface is removed as farm crops, it gradually deepens, and the subsoil, which contains the very same elements, becomes fitted for plant food. And thus the imperishable nature of matter applies to the soil, which can never be exhausted during all the ages which are to come. All that mankind has to do is to use its arts under the instruction of science to develop this latent fertility, and to go on feeding the human race until the end, if an end ever shall come when the earth will no longer exist as a fit habitation for mankind.

We have another illustration of this superintending providence in the formation of coal, which means

* Professor Samuel Johnson, Smithsonian Institution Lectures, 1859.

more than a black carbonaceous matter in the earth. It was formed for man's use, and to-day constitutes not only an important article of commerce, but furnishes employment to thousands of men besides adding to the world's wealth and comfort. Coal is of vegetable origin, but was formed from a vegetation differing in character, in abundance, and in rankness very widely from any thing we see upon the earth at the present day. Mr. Lyell, whose writings have usually been quoted with authority on such subjects, is of the opinion that, time sufficient being given, the forces now in operation are adequate to the production of all the changes which have taken place in the earth's crust. But it seems to the writer that one cannot look upon the geological formations presenting their immense strata, marked and scored with traces of the most terrible convulsions, without at once concluding that the forces which operated in past ages were vastly more violent than those of the present. Coal was formed when an atmosphere composed largely of carbonic acid surrounded the earth. That was the wonderful carboniferous period, for then it was that God was preparing, not only the air for our lungs, by extracting the poisonous carbonic acid, but as well the fuel to warm our dwellings and a force to propel our machinery. The great Father has not been parsimonious in bestowing his gifts upon his children. Long ago the elder Professor Hitchcock* estimated that in the United States there were 225,000 square miles of coal area, which, averaging all the beds at a thickness of fifteen feet, would give us 1,061 cubic miles of coal. One cubic mile would

* *Geology of the Globe.*

furnish 7,000,000 tons annually for one thousand years. Since then new fields have been discovered in the West and South-west of great extent. This estimate of the learned professor may be a little fanciful, but one thing is certain—even though a hundred million tons were mined each year the supply would last for ages.

Much has been said about the possible dearth of coal in England. It has been estimated that in the South Staffordshire and Shropshire districts there are 10,000,000,000 tons of coal existing at workable depths beyond the present limits. Then there are 2,494,000,000 tons in the present Warwickshire coal-fields, and 1,760,000,000 tons in the Leicester fields; surely the dearth is not imminent. As a source of wealth the coal-mines of the world greatly exceed the gold-mines. In them the children of men have abundant evidence of the goodness of God, who cared for us even before the foundations of the world were laid.

The earth may have at one time floated in space as a vast cloud of fire-mist, which through uncounted ages slowly condensed into a fluid mass, with a temperature far beyond our conception; or it may have been a fragment of cosmic matter hurled by some vast sun-cataclysm into space, adjusting itself to orbital movements under the law which God ordained to govern the spheres; or it may have been evolved in some mysterious manner out of God himself, the Author of all things, who "in the beginning created the heavens and the earth;" but one thing we know, it does exist as a planet in space. it is our home, and was fitted up for the habitation of mankind. We can hardly expect ever to know just how this world-house was prepared; we must be willing not to know some things at present. It is a source of consolation, however, to know that eternity is before us, in which we may learn what is now hidden beneath a veil of mystery. Nevertheless, it is lawful for us to attempt to uncover even these sublime mysteries. Man is not a mere barnacle, clinging to the rocks that form the sea-wall which hems in his life, but an intelligent student persistently bending over the leafy tablets of Nature, and deciphering her strange hieroglyphics; he is a patient sculptor, chiseling out of these same rocks forms of imperishable beauty. It is more than poetry, then, to say that the earth's crust is a book written by the finger of God. Rock has been piled on rock, and ledge upon ledge, not in confusion, but in the most perfect order, an order that implies man; for though this earth-crust is composed of numerous formations, from garden soil to granite, and is fifty or sixty miles in thickness, yet every layer or stratum comes to the surface somewhere. The granites, and some other rocks needed in the construction of our great buildings which are intended to stand for ages, have been formed under heat and pressure, and are consequently the more durable. What use would they be to us if they were lying miles below us in the earth's deep bed? The coal of which we have spoken when *in place* is about ten thousand feet beneath the surface of the earth. If God had not made provision for it man never could have seen it. But he has placed all these minerals within reach of his children by means of fire and flood and quaking earth. These great convulsions of nature

are indeed terrible visitations, but they show us the benevolence as well as the power of the Infinite One. It is the mission of the human mind to search out the secrets of nature; but to all things there is a limit, and because we are unable to comprehend all that is written in this stony volume it illy becomes us to say with the "fool," "There is no God." Professor M. F. Maury has eloquently said: *
"To one who has never studied the mechanism of a watch, its mainspring, or the balance-wheel, is a mere piece of metal. He may have looked at the face of the watch, and while he admires the motion of its hands, and the time it keeps, he may have wondered in idle amazement as to the character of the machinery which is concealed within. Take it to pieces and show him each part separately, he will recognize neither design nor adaptation, nor relation between them; but put them together, set them to work, point to the offices of each wheel, spring, and cog, explain their movements, and then show him the result; now he perceives that it is all one design; that notwithstanding the number of parts, their diverse forms, and various offices, and the agents concerned the whole piece is of one thought—the expression of one idea. He now rightly concludes that when the mainspring was fashioned and tempered its relation to all the other parts must have been considered; that the cogs on this wheel are cut and adapted to the ratchet on that, and his final conclusion will be that such a piece of mechanism could not have been produced by chance, for the adaptation of the parts is such as to show it to be according to design and

* *Physical Geography of the Sea.*

obedient to the will of one intelligence. So, too, when he looks out upon the face of this beautiful world, he admires its lovely scenery, but his admiration can never grow into adoration, unless he will take the trouble to look behind and study in some of its details at least the exquisite system of machinery by which such beautiful results are brought about."

It is not irreverent to speak of God as a great mechanic. The artisan goes to his shop to push the plane or strike the heated metal, and sometimes is tempted to murmur at his toilsome lot and humble life. But let him cast his eye upward toward the stars and know that God is a great mechanic—we speak reverently—and by his wisdom and power has set the whole universe into motion. Planets and systems alike are traveling through their orbits in the deep spaces of the universe.

Look up into the face of thy Father, put thy hand into his hand, and he will surely lead thee aright. The great Teacher said, "My Father worketh hitherto, and I work." Labor is man's great function. The earth and the atmosphere are his laboratory. With spade and plow, with mining shaft and furnace and forge; with fire and steam, amidst the noise of swift and bright machinery, and abroad in the silent fields beneath the roofing sky, man was made to be ever a worker, ever experimenting. He is nothing, he can be nothing, fulfill nothing, without work.

The word science is not a term which needs to give any one alarm; it is only the window through which we look at objects of nature. We study the laws of mind, and call our studies metaphysics; we study the elements about us, and call our studies chemistry;

we study the stars, and we have astronomy; we study the earth, and call it geology. But alas! how little we know to-day, after all these years of observation, reflection, and investigation, compared with what there is to learn! Nature is only partially understood by the wisest of men. The student of nature is like a traveler climbing the sloping sides of a mountain with its snow-mantled peak far above and beyond him. At the base, as he girds himself for the ascent, and takes up his alpenstock, he looks out and his eye takes in a beautiful but limited landscape, dotted all over with peaceful habitations of men; but as he ascends, the eye ever takes in a wider sweep of landscape. Onward he goes, higher and still higher, and the landscape widens more and more. At last he sets his foot on the loftiest crest, the *pico del fraile*, and the landscape is lost in the horizon which encircles him in dim and hazy outline. From that mountain summit he is fairly entranced by the sight of the magnificent distances which spread out before him, and is awed into silence and humbled into the dust. So is it with God's universe: in youth we are liable to be proud of our acquisitions and to become boastful of what we know; but let us climb higher up the mountain-side of life, and we seem to know less and less. Nay, but we do know more, only that the field has so wonderfully widened that we are lost, and seemingly dwarfed into nothingness.

The men who have delved deepest into nature, who have gone out farthest along the lines of thought, are they of the least pretension and of the most humble and reverent spirit. All these studies lead to God, who is the author of all the principles which enter into life. This stone book, the earth, teaches us of God, his self, his power, his wisdom, and his benevolence. He who cannot see a plan, a purpose, a means to an end in the unfoldings of this rocky scroll of the long-gone ages gives evidence either of a bad heart or an inability to reason correctly; but let us be charitable.

CHAPTER V.

FACT AND FICTION IN HUMAN LIFE.

WE are perfectly well aware of the fact that the title of this book may, at least to a few people, seem objectionable; for with some the very idea of writing about fiction in Holy Writ would seem to border on the irreverent. But in the light of the foregoing chapters in our opinion there is entire justification in the selection of title.

In an age of ignorance, or among a people who are ignorant, religious thought, like all other thought, is crude. There are two extremes which it is alike desirable to avoid—a religiousness running into downright superstition on the one hand, and on the other an irreligiousness that runs into positive rationalism. We scarcely know which of the two is most to be shunned. The author thinks that he dealt justly with the Scriptures when he said in a previous chapter that the Bible is part human and part divine. It might be better to say divine, with some mixture of the human. No thoughtful person, however orthodox, will deny the existence of at least a small human element in the sacred book.

The Church has always been, and is yet, rightfully jealous of Scripture. The ark is very sacred, and so we do not wish to touch any part of it with violent hands or to utter a word that would make it any less sacred in its claims. And yet to ignore reason in the rendering of Scripture—to say, as we have heard a man say, that if the Bible declared that Jonah swallowed the whale he should believe it, is to be irreverent in another way; to cast down and trample under foot the precious pearl of reason which God has given to us, to be superstitious, and to convert the Bible into a mere fetich.

The reader may call to mind the story of the returned sailor-boy who, when questioned by his venerable grandmother as to what he had seen in his wanderings, told her of fish which could fly in the air almost like birds, and would sometimes actually fall on the ship's deck. This, of course, called down upon him her matronly rebuke. The idea of a fish flying! But the cunning boy made up his mind to tell her something which he knew she would believe, and so related to her that when they were fishing one day in the Red Sea they drew in their net, and lo! what should it contain but a beautiful wheel covered with gold and set with diamonds! This she did not doubt, for "Pharaoh and his host" had been overthrown in the Red Sea, and this was, of course, one of his chariot-wheels. The story illustrates the fact that some people will accept and believe the most contradictory and impossible things in life and yet reject the plainest truths of science. There are skeptical people who discredit Bible teachings and yet believe the various superstitions of the ignorant world. One of the ends held in view by the author in the preparation of this book is to run parallels between the remarkable statements made in the Bible and the equally remarkable things recorded outside of the Bible in nature and human life. If some things in this divine book are, as is sometimes claimed, too great a strain on human credence, there are some things in the natural world and in the history of humanity very marvelous, but we believe them, for they come within our observation and are undeniable; but had they been written in Genesis or John, and so placed beyond the world's present experience, they would be called myths, fables, legends, and declared to be contrary to reason.

Among the superstitions which have governed people some are quite amusing. For instance, one in which it is declared to be "unlucky to weigh a new-born child, for if you do it will probably die."

It is believed by many, even to this day, that cats suck the breath of infants when they are asleep in their cribs; and because of this old superstition many a poor kitty has been ousted from a warm nest at the baby's feet by a ruthless nurse. Again this: "When children first leave their mother's room they must go up-stairs before they go down-stairs, or they will never rise in the world." Most of us must have been carried down-stairs first. "If a grave is opened on Sunday another one will be dug during the week." Quite likely. "If a looking-glass is broken there will be a death in the house within a year." "If you break two things in succession you will break a third;" and so the credulous servant deliberately breaks the third, selecting something which is of no value, and thus breaks the spell. "It is very lucky to put on any article of dress wrong side out, but if you wish the omen to hold good you must continue to wear the reversed portion of your attire in that condition until the regular time comes for changing it; otherwise you will have no luck."

It was believed by these same superstitious people that ague could be cured by swallowing spiders and their webs. When these objects were put into goose-quills and hung around the neck it was considered to be a sure cure for the malady. It was generally believed by people living on the sea-coast that the going out and coming in of the tides had an effect for good or evil upon the sick. It will be remembered that Dickens tells us that "Barkis lingered in his dying until the turn of the tide. When the tide was going out Barkis went out with it."

"Water in the dinner-pot evaporates more rapidly when the tide is low." "It is unlucky to eat fish from the head downward; it drives away the fish from the shores." "To tell the stage of the tide without going to the beach look into a cat's eyes; the pupil of every intelligent cat's eye is elongated when the tide is at the flood." "Never count a catch of fish until the day's work or sport is done; otherwise the sport is spoiled." And so on *ad nauseum*.

It is not alone among the people who live on the sea-coast that superstitions are believed. Not very long ago the author was in the company of a number of people gathered to witness a very common but very interesting ceremony in which as a clergyman he had some part. It was a very genteel sort of place, and the people were all members of what the world calls "good society," which means, first, that they were well-dressed, and, in the second place, were tolerably well educated. With some dress comes first, culture and piety afterward. At one of the tables it happened that there were thirteen seats, and after all had taken their places and thanks had been returned one of the guests—a young lady of eighteen—arose quickly and left the table, remarking that she would not under any consideration be one of a party of thirteen at a dinner-table. At first we were quite amused, then shocked, and afterward disgusted, to think that in this age of high schools, newspapers, and science any one pretending to have even ordinary intelligence should be guilty of such great folly as to be governed by the merest superstition. But there are superstitious people almost every-where, even in tolerably well-cultivated communities. There are superstitious notions in the minds of people even where we would least expect to meet them. They constitute a curious study, and to understand them is to possess the key to a great many wrongs which have cursed humanity in all ages.

There are some superstitious beliefs, as has been said, that are only amusing, while some others have been deadly in their effects on life. Some of them have led to the severest persecutions. Men, women, and even innocent children have been tortured and put to death because of their supposed complicity with evil spirits. But that day has passed away, let us hope, forever. Science and reason have dispelled from human society some of the dreadful things which once hung like a dark cloud over the world. Let us thank God for this.

Mr. Leckey, in his work on *Rationalism in Europe*, draws this picture of the horrors of witchcraft:

"The legislators of almost every land enacted laws for its punishment. Acute judges, whose lives were spent in sifting evidence, investigated the question on countless occasions and condemned the accused.

Tens of thousands of victims perished by the most agonizing and protracted torments, without exciting the faintest compassion; and as they were for the most part extremely ignorant, extremely poor, sectarianism and avarice had but little influence on the subject. Nations that were completely separated by position, by interest, and by character on this one question were a unit. In almost every province of Germany, but especially in those where clerical influence predominated, the persecution raged with a fearful intensity. Seven thousand victims are said to have perished at Treves, six hundred by a single bishop at Bamberg, and eight hundred in a single year in the bishopric of Würzburg. In France decrees were passed on the subject by the parliaments of Paris, Toulouse, Bordeaux, Rheims, Rouen, Dijon, and Rennes, and they were all followed by a harvest of blood. At Toulouse, the seat of the Inquisition, four hundred persons perished for sorcery at a single execution, and fifty at Douay in a single year. Remy, a judge at Nancy, boasted that he had put to death eight hundred witches in sixteen years. The executions that took place at Paris in a few months were, in the emphatic words of an old writer, 'almost infinite.' The fugitives who escaped to Spain were there seized and burned by the Inquisition. In that country the persecution spread to the smallest towns, and the belief was so deeply rooted in the popular mind that a sorcerer was burned as late as 1780. In Italy a thousand persons were executed in a single year in the province of Como. The same scenes were enacted in the wild valleys of Switzerland and Savoy. And these are only a few of the more salient events in that long series of persecutions which extended over almost every country and continued for centuries with unabated fury. . . . It spread with Puritanism into the New World, and the executions in Massachusetts form one of the darkest pages in the history of America."

Every age and every nation has had its superstitions, but not all so dreadful as those just recited. Dr. Russ tells the story of a Hungarian officer who was severely, though by no means fatally, wounded in the field of Sadowa. He was fast bleeding to death, however, when the surgeon came to him, but might have been saved had he not obstinately refused all aid. The surgeon noticed that he held something very tightly in his hand which he pressed convulsively to his breast. Presently he began to tremble violently, and crying out, "It has done me no good!" threw away a piece of paper and the next moment expired. The paper was found to be a talisman, bearing some written characters which were quite unintelligible. The poor fellow trusted in its supernatural power until aid by natural means was out of the question, and then cast it away with a pang of despair. Many a similar agonizing discovery was made during the war of 1870–71, too late for the learner to profit by the experience. After the battle of Woerth, in particular, a great number of talismans, charms, and the like were picked up close to the corpses of those who had clung to them until in their last agony they had lost faith in their healing virtue and had flung them away. It must not be supposed, however, that the German soldiers as a class are given to this kind of superstition. It was found, on investigation, that there was a close relation between education and the existence of such beliefs. The provinces which were in the lowest state as regards education gave the largest contingent of those who were thus credulous. Talismans, charms, letters of exemption, etc., were found in the largest proportion among recruits from the Polish provinces, and in those provinces education is at the lowest point.

From time immemorial it has been believed that horseshoes keep away evil spirits. Even Lord Nelson had a horseshoe nailed to the mast of his flagship. It is maintained that the origin of this belief goes back to the old Scandinavian mythology. The horseshoe was supposed to be sacred to Odin or Woden, as the Anglo-Saxons call him, and it was especially lucky to find one on Wednesday. Odin was considered to be the destroyer of giants, witches, and all powers of evil, and so perhaps the horseshoe came to be considered as a protector against witches. It is claimed that this superstition is only found among the descendants of the Saxon and Scandinavian nations. Some antiquarians assert that the practice of nailing horseshoes to thresholds resembles that of driving nails into the walls of cottages among the Romans, which they believed to be an antidote against the plague. For this purpose L. Manlius, A. U. C. 390, was named "Dictator to Drive the Nail." Apart from this old belief in the exorcising virtue of cold iron the horseshoe appealed to superstition in an astrological age as being moon-shaped. The Greek name for it has reference to its shape. The sickle for this reason shared its virtue.

Many superstitions have vexed the world, others

have amused it, while a beautiful romance has gathered about some of them. Among the ancient Greeks and Romans it was a common custom for the bridegroom to give his bride on their wedding-day a considerable sum of money for the purchase of her person. From this usage, no doubt, has come the modern custom of making wedding-presents, under which so many people groan. The ancient Saxons gave a betrothal ring or other gift, which was called a "wed," and from this we have named one of the days of our week—Wednesday. Now we throw an old shoe after the married couple. This custom, we suppose, came from our stern forefathers, who ordained that the bridegroom should tap his new-made wife on the head with his shoe as a token of her submission to her lord.

There are a great many superstitions about the supposed effect of the moon upon the weather, etc. There is a very prevalent belief in some sections that the general condition of the atmosphere throughout the world during any lunation depends on whether the moon changed before or after midnight! You are told that you must not kill a pig in the wane of the moon, for if you do the meat will shrink in the cooking. Often has poor piggy's death been delayed or hastened so as to happen during the moon's increase. This same luminary has been an object of worship in some lands, and even yet in some portions of Europe many persons will courtesy to the new moon on its first appearance, and at the same time turn over the money in their pockets, if they have any, for luck. Then, again, you are told that you must not look at the new moon for the first time through glass; it is unlucky. And if the new moon happens on a Saturday the weather will be bad for a month to come. Another weather-guide connected with the moon is that to see the old moon "in the arms of the new," as it is expressed, is reckoned a sign of bad weather. So also the turning up of the horns of the new moon has its meaning. In this position it is supposed to retain the water which is imagined to be in it, and which will spill out if the horns were turned down. There are many people who when they see the streaks of light caused by the sun shining through broken clouds believe them to be veritable pipes reaching into the sea, or somewhere else, and through which water is drawn up into the clouds, ready to be sent down in rain-showers. Truth is sometimes contained in popular errors, as gold is hid in quartz rock. These streaks in the sky, while they are not real pipes, are yet visible signs of the sun's action, showing that evaporation is constantly going on over earth and sea, by means of which the rains and snows are formed. It would be a difficult task to report all the superstitions and unscientific notions so often cherished concerning the moon's influence on life in general, and inasmuch as they are so harmless it may be as well to let them alone. In time they will die a natural death. That the "lesser light" of Moses does exert some influence on the earth is not questioned. But Luna has legitimate work to do, and should not be charged with too many trivial affairs. It is not at all likely that she exerts a particle of influence on the weather, or the killing of pigs or poultry, or over the planting of beans, cucumbers, turnips, etc. The moon is a secondary planet two hundred and forty thousand miles away from us. She is constantly changing in appearance, and yet she never changes a particle. She does exert some attractive power on the ocean, and in fact helps to cause the tidal waves; but she does not concern herself a rush about the aspiring youth who turns over the few nickels in his pocket for luck when he happens to first get a sight of the new moon.

Another popular superstition is that concerning Friday, which day has been almost universally considered a day of ill omen. At a time when superstition had full sway almost every-where, say about two hundred years ago, it was not to be wondered at that such notions should have gained currency; but now they seem puerile, and ought, like other childish things, to be put away. Like the young lady who would not sit at a table of thirteen, so there are even in this matter-of-fact age some who would hesitate to begin any sort of work of importance on a day so inauspicious as Friday. Sailors, as a class, are proverbially superstitious, and many a brave tar whose heart would not quail before the fury of the wildest storm would never think of leaving port on Friday under any consideration. His cheek would blanch at the very thought of binding a sail on that day, a day fraught in his imagination with so much evil.

Friday has played rather an important part in the history of our own country especially, and it serves somewhat to show how very unreasoning is the superstition of so many concerning it. "Let us remember that it was on Friday, August 3, 1492, that Columbus sailed from Palos in Spain in search of the New World. On Friday, October 12, of the same year, he first sighted the Bahama Islands, the door-way to the American continent. On that same much-dreaded Friday, January 4, 1493, he sailed on his return to Spain; and surely no evil overtook him, for if it had the results of his explorations never would have been known. On Friday, March 15, 1493, he arrived back at Palos in safety. On Friday, November 22, 1493, he arrived at Hispaniola in his second voyage to America. On Friday, June 13, 1494, he discovered the main continent of America. Friday, March 5, 1496, was the day on which Henry VII. of England gave to John Cabot his commission which led to the discovery of the northern part of the American continent. On Friday, September 7, 1565, Melendez founded St. Augustine, Florida, the oldest settlement in this country by more than forty years. On Friday, November 10, 1620, the *Mayflower*, with the pilgrims on board, made the harbor of Provincetown, and on the same day they signed the compact which laid the foundation of the American Republic. On Friday, December 22. 1620, the final landing of the pilgrims took place on Plymouth Rock. Our great Washington was born on Friday, February 22, 1732. The surrender of Saratoga by the British occurred on Friday, October 7, 1777, which led France to declare herself in favor of the American colonies. It was on Friday, September 22, 1780, that the treason of Benedict Arnold was brought to light, which saved the cause of the Americans from ruin. The final surrender of the British army under Lord Cornwallis took place at Yorktown, Va., on Friday, October 9, 1781, at which time the American army was victorious over a then haughty and powerful foe." Rather unlucky for Cornwallis, we will admit. And so one might go on at almost any length to disprove by facts the folly of the superstition about Friday. And yet there are some people silly enough to believe that Friday is an unlucky day.

Christian people are now and always have been censured and criticised by skeptics for their belief in the Bible. And yet their faith has not been a blind, unreasoning credence; but a rational one. This cannot be said of the beliefs of the world. As an illustration of what has been believed we will relate this curious story concerning a species of the cocoanut once called the "nut of Solomon," or the "fruit of the tree of Solomon."

During the Middle Ages the countries of the eastern hemisphere were enveloped in a great many mysteries and superstitions. Certain drugs and chemicals were supposed to possess miraculous properties, and almost any fable, no matter how ridiculous, was readily accepted by the common people as the truth. Just then the cocoanut came into great demand. The rulers of the East held it in such high esteem that it seldom found its way into Europe. It was exceedingly rare, and was declared to possess curative properties of such extraordinary potency that Christians and Mussulmans vied with each other in lauding it. Then it was that it was named the "nut of Solomon." These nuts were occasionally found floating at sea or wafted by the waves to the Coromandel coast and the Maldive Islands. But these occurrences were so rare that the fruit found was estimated at an incredible price. Various theories sprung up concerning this strange nut. By some it was thought to be a submarine production, and human imagination at once ascribed to it the most wonderful virtues. The story of the prices paid for these nuts can scarcely be credited. One of the Indian monarchs, we are informed, sold one nut for which was paid as the price a ship and her cargo. The Emperor Rudolph offered four thousand florins for one of these wonderful nuts, and his offer was refused. Two thousand dollars was no uncommon price for a single cocoanut.

Time is a great revelator as well as healer. Men began to think, and knowledge increased; consequently the "nut of Solomon" began to suffer in its reputation as a curative agent. Nevertheless it still continued to be considered a great curiosity, and in the far East retained some of its supposed medical virtues and commanded a high price, though that price came down and the nuts came to have a value corresponding with their size. A small one would bring about one hundred to one hundred and fifty dollars, while a large one would be worth five hundred dollars. Some extraordinary nuts in point of size would bring as high as seven hundred dollars. Think of it! For two hundred years this nut was held in such high esteem that ships were fitted out to search for it in distant seas, very much as men are now hunting for the North Pole.

The "nut of Solomon" at once became famous as a remedy for poison. In those days poisoning was the crime of the great, and any thing that would prove an antidote for poison in the human system would command any price. Cups were constructed out of it for drinking purposes, for it was believed that even drinking water out of one of them would effectually cure certain maladies.

The history of the nut, as it was told, helped to keep in mind the delusion. The stories were very fanciful, but they were believed. One was that there was but one tree in the world that produced it, that the roots of this rare tree were fixed at the bottom of the Indian Ocean so far down that no fathom-line could ever reach them, but that its branches, rising high above the placid waters, flourished in the bright sunshine, serene sky, and pure air of heaven. So when the nuts matured they fell into the sea and were wafted by winds and waves until they were cast upon some distant shore to be picked up by man.

The tidings of this wonderful discovery in time reached Europe. The Portuguese fitted out a vessel which sailed around the Cape of Good Hope and entered the Indian Ocean for the purpose of finding some of these wonderful nuts of the tree of Solomon; but they were unsuccessful. Still the story spread, and the English and Dutch followed in the path of the Portuguese and made their way into the same sea, and with great energy carried their enterprise forward, hoping to find the source of the wonderful nut; but they, too, failed.

A French naval officer, whose name was Picault, was sent to explore the cluster of islands known as the Seychelles. He was a careful navigator, and discovered some islands formerly unknown. One of these he named Palmiers, on account of the abundance and beauty of the palm-trees which grew upon it. Then in 1768 a subsequent governor of the same island sent out another expedition for a similar purpose. Barre, the hydrographer, on landing upon Palmiers, at once discovered that the palms from which the island had been named a quarter of a century before produced the famous and long sought-for "cocoanut of the sea"—the "fruit of the tree of Solomon." The explorers returned home to the Isle of France, fitted out a vessel, and sailed for Palmiers and loaded it with cocoanuts. Then they set sail for the East, landing at Calcutta, where the vessel arrived with her cargo in 1770. What was the astonishment among the people that thronged about the ship when to their eager inquiries they were informed that the cargo consisted wholly of the invaluable "fruit of the tree of Solomon." They could scarcely believe the evidence of their own eyes, as upon opening the hatchway of the ship it was found to be actually filled with the precious commodity. Rare no longer, precious no more! Down went the price, and persons who had paid fabulous sums for a single nut were ruined. The French captain expected to make a fortune out of his cargo, but failed. Had he been financially shrewd he would have sold them one at a time and made a fortune. Cocoanuts were entirely too plenty. The mystery was solved, the secret was told, the spell was broken! An English mercantile house landed another cargo the following summer at Bombay, thus completely solving the mystery of the remarkable nut and reducing the price to zero.

CHAPTER VI.

FACT AND FICTION IN HOLY WRIT.

THERE is a right way and a wrong way to read the Bible. The wrong way is to approach it with a spirit of irreverence and with undue criticism, demanding of it that which it is not pledged to give. The right way is to approach it precisely as we would any other book worth reading, as earnest seekers after the truth.

If it were a book limited in its scope, treating of a single topic only, and doing that superficially, like so many human productions, it would not command the thought of the world as it does and has done for ages. The facts taught by the Scriptures, such as the existence of God, an overruling Providence, sin, redemption, and so on, need no defense or argument here.

But what is fiction? It has been defined as the act of feigning, inventing, or imagining. A story may be related or written in which the imagination has been drawn upon for the facts; facts, real or supposed, constitute the base of any story. Fiction is sometimes used to deceive, but is more frequently employed as a convenient method of passing rapidly over what is not disputed, or of reaching points which are easily apprehended.

Fiction differs materially from fabrication; the latter is always intended to deceive; but the two sustain a close relation to each other. We know that one of the grandest gifts of God to man is this power of imagination. A volume could not tell of all its benefits. Fiction, as distinguished from fabrication, has its legitimate use in both literature and life. It narrows the circle of description and enables one to compass in a shorter way a wide field of thought; and so it may be called a species of literary crystallization. By means of it instruction is often rendered more palatable than it otherwise might be by a coating of figures and strophes. The conveyance of moral teaching by means of the fable used so freely in former ages is of this nature inasmuch as it puts truth in a pleasant garb, while from the bare presentation of it the mind might turn away in indifference or disgust. Of this we have abundant biblical precedent. There is fiction in the Bible. The parables, whether in the Old Testament or the New, are fiction. The great Teacher used parables for the reason that the "common people" who "heard him gladly" would not have been able to comprehend abstruse reasoning; but they could understand a story. A child always relishes a simple story. These children of a larger growth feasted on the stories—the parables related by our Saviour. Thus he made use of fiction in the conveyance of instruction on all the subjects which he brought before their minds.

Take, for instance, the beautiful parables of the "talents," the "ten virgins," the "fig-tree," or the "grain of mustard-seed." How else could the Master have presented the truth so forcibly to the simple-minded people about him as in this way? The Bible is a book that chronicles great facts which constitute the bed-rock of all its moral teachings. We need not name them or attempt their classification in full. But it is a fact that God is, and that he did create all things. He is not a mere force or law in nature, which men call God; but a personal Deity who upholds all things; a wise, holy, and benevolent Being who rules in the heavens and in the earth.

Is there such a God? The Christian answers, Yes. The whole world of mankind says in one speech or another, "I believe in God the Father Almighty, Maker of heaven and earth." We have never seen him; "no man hath seen God at any time." And yet it has been stated that certain men of old "saw God face to face." But how? It is answered: "The only begotten Son which is in the bosom of the Father, he hath declared him." We have never heard his voice, and yet we believe in this supreme God. Among the Egyptians he was called Kneph; among the Persians, Zeruane Akerene; among the Hindus, Para Brahma; among the Phenicians, Greeks, and Romans he was called Chronos, or Saturn, who was held to be the absolute in the fathomless immensity of time. Among the Scandinavians he was known as Surtur. Thus through the literature of all the nations there are found traces of the supreme God. In Paul's day, upon Mars' hill, there was one altar bearing the inscription, "To the Unknown God." Was not this altar erected to the God who could not be represented, whose mysterious depth of being could not be laid open to the human understanding, and therefore must ever be "The Unknown?"

It is impossible for the finite to comprehend the Infinite; but we may apprehend him. There are two circles, one not larger than the ring on a lady's finger; the other may have a diameter of leagues, and yet the smaller may touch the larger, and a line drawn through the center of the one may pass through the center of the other. They have something in common. Thus may we touch God as we sing with Faber:

> "Great God, our lowliness takes heart
> Beneath the shadow of thy state;
> The only comfort of our littleness
> Is that thou art so great.
>
> "Then on thy grandeur I will lay me down;
> Already life is heaven for me;
> No cradled child more softly lies than I;
> Come soon, Eternity!"

Whoever will attempt to interpret nature without recognizing God will find himself involved in inextricable mazes. The first chapter in Genesis may be, as some claim, a grand anthem of creation, or a scenic representation—a panorama passing before the eyes of Moses the Seer; or it may be history condensing into a few lines the processes of world-building, enabling us to read in a few moments an epitome of the history of cycles of creative energy.

One thing is sure, the heavens do exist, and God created them. Does any one ask, When? How? Who knows? It does not matter much to us now. We can study the philosophy of creation in the constant unfolding of science, or wait until we reach the immortal state, where our vision will be clearer and our capacity larger. There are some more important subjects to contemplate at present.

Yet no harm need come from attempting the solution of the problems of life and being; and whatever view we take, whether that of La Place or the simplest interpretation of the most unlettered and unphilosophic plebeian, our highest spiritual and moral good do not hinge on a correct understanding of incomprehensible mysteries. On the other hand, some good may come from the attempt; it may teach us our littleness, and thus not only humble the haughty spirit of man but create in him a longing desire to reach a perfect state, where we shall see as we are seen and know as we are known.

The creation of the human race is another great fact. We accept the Bible statement of the origin of our species as more dignified and reasonable than any other account given by man. The earth was prepared for man's coming, and every thing pointed to him. He, too, began to be; there was a time when he was not. All agree in this. But how did he come into existence? Did nature in some accidental way work out this superior being and endow him with the power of reason? If so, why did not these atoms and molecules about which the materialists talk so glibly come together ages before? Why did they move so slowly? Why waste themselves on infusoria, tadpoles, and lizards through countless eons of time, when man, the monarch, was so much needed? Can it be that George Washington and Julius Cæsar were only developed monads? A noted writer, and a preacher at that, stated in a sermon recently that according to Moses "man is the child of a clod," while science affirms that he is the "child of an ape;" and he would just as soon be the child of an ape as the child of a clod. The statement only shows the tendency of some minds to run in eccentric grooves, as well as to repudiate facts in the Bible simply because they are in the Bible.

We all believe in development, in a qualified sense. No doubt the life-processes of past ages have worked out some very remarkable changes. Here is one out of many which serves to illustrate what we mean: On the French and Italian shores of the Mediterranean grows a wild and neglected grass known by the name of ægilops. The seeds of that wild grass were taken up and transplanted into new fields in remote parts of the earth, where it was fed by a new soil, and after a few years was changed over into the perfect and productive wheat which enters so largely into our industrial and commercial life. From similar wild weeds have come our oats, barley, corn, and other valuable grains. The nutritive potato of to-day is but the cultivated bitter root which was indigenous to some of the wild mountain districts of subtropical America. Concerning the development hypothesis of Lamarck and Darwin we shall have more to say in a subsequent chapter.

The intermixing of varieties of the same species is endless, and is not unlike the law of permutation in numbers. But species do not mix voluntarily. This very fact was foreshadowed by Moses when he wrote of vegetation in the beginning, "whose seed is in itself after its kind." How could the fact of the persistency of species be more strongly put than the writer of the book of Genesis puts it? Hence it is that acorns produce oaks, and thistles generate thistles. So in the animal world apes produce apes, and man produces man. This law was stamped on creation in the beginning; had it not been so there would have been no stability to any thing; there would have been "confusion worse confounded" long ago, and the world would be a strange medley. And if a few exceptions are named they but give emphasis to the law.

Still there is such a thing as development. The ocean steamer gliding majestically over the waters of the great deep, carrying a whole village safely, is the developed dug-out or raft on which a savage first floated across a stream in the chase or in pursuit of an enemy. The first tree bower, hut, or tent of some kind in which a human being found shelter from the storms was the beginning of the architectural piles upon which we gaze with wonder and admiration. Here has been development in the human sphere, resulting from the operations of the laws of mind, and not as a result of some force resident in matter. But there is a higher sphere, that of nature, in which God alone reigns. The eagle has developed from a germ in the egg, the oak from an acorn, the crops of all kinds from seeds which have rotted in the ground. The human intellect is a developing force in the one sphere, in the other the results have come through certain specific laws formulated in the beginning by infinite wisdom.

The greatest of all facts are those of human nature, human life, human sin, and how to escape evil. Great disputes have arisen over the "tree of life" and the "tree of the knowledge of good and evil." Many have been the discussions as to how evil came to be. There have been various opinions held among men concerning the freedom of the will, the location of the garden of Eden, the part played by the serpent, etc. The main facts have been at times quite lost sight of in these discussions. Sin and redemption are the central facts of the Bible. To impress these on the minds and hearts of the race is the principal object of Scripture revelation. To effect this the writers have used plain historical statements, but often under cover of strong figures of speech, which the eye itself could discern.

The story of the first woman's creation is regarded by many as mythical or legendary, and the question has been raised in many a Bible-class, "Was Eve really created out of a rib taken from the side of Adam?" Well, who can say positively that she was not. Suppose you attempt to argue the case on the negative side. Where would you obtain your data? It is easy to laugh and ridicule an idea and call it preposterous, and all that; but ridicule is not argument. If she came into being in the manner described, though it may seem a strange method of procedure, is not the whole universe full of strange things? Can we explain all things? There is a very small animal or animalcule known to natural history which is very curious. If one of them is cut in two each half in a very few minutes becomes as perfect as the original. Cut each of these in two in the same way, and the process goes on; four become eight, eight become sixteen, sixteen become thirty-two, and so on. A million will be produced in twenty-four hours, and a hundred and forty billions in less than a week. They are microscopic, to be sure, but they are nevertheless living beings. Do not smile or ridicule this, for it is science. The Bible says nothing about it. The result is worked out by the law of nature, which is the law of God.

Then there is that loathsome worm that crawls across your pathway. In the autumn it creeps into some nook or cranny, and in the most ingenious way conceivable weaves about itself a little house, impervious to wind and water, and in the spring-time comes forth a beautiful butterfly which flits about us on airy wing. Is it not marvelous? Can you explain it? Here lies before us an egg; let us examine it; we see no sign of life in it; it is food. But place it under the warm feathers of the mother-bird, and that shell soon incloses a living being, and then in time discloses a perfect organism with eyes as perfect as a man's, with a bony frame to support the flesh, with joints, cartilages, muscles, veins, arteries, nerves, with a heart which at the first trembled almost imperceptibly, but which increases as the days go by, until that tremulous motion turns into rhythmic throbs, sending the blood through its whole body. But look at it again, and here are wings to cleave the air, the feathers of which are placed at such an angle of obliquity that though the stroke as it flies is vertical the bird is propelled forward horizontally, or in sweeping curves, up or down in any direction which it may choose.

What first moved that heart and set it to beating? There is only one answer—God. There is nothing in the natural world which presents a more striking instance of design than the plumage of the birds.

"Take the fact that their feathers themselves are composed of small parts having barbs or hooks to fasten them together where tightness is necessary, and the other fact that the inner coating is often of loose fine down, as in the eider-duck, to secure warmth. It is interesting, too, to observe that the feathers all lie smoothly in one direction, so that in passing through either the air or water there is no obstruction.

"But a wonderful provision for the water-fowl, in particular, strikes us very forcibly as a proof of a superintending Providence in the creation of all animals. A goose or duck, for instance, being so much in the water, would soon be soaked through all its feathery garments and be loaded down and unable to swim; and so those water-fowl that make long journeys on the wing through rain-storms and mists would for the same reason be unable to fly. But here Providence meets this difficulty by giving to these birds small oil-sacks, and the apparatus also for making the oil and always keeping them full, and then placing them within reach of the bill of the bird, so that it can draw out the oil and spread it through and over the whole of its garment of feathers; and thus is the bird clad in a first-class water-proof suit which no India-rubber manufacturer could improve, and which adds nothing whatever to its weight. This water-proof suit can be worn every day without inconvenience, and is always on hand ready for use. By watching the fowl the oiling operation can often be seen; and how very dexterously it is performed! This explains why water runs so easily from the duck's back."

Let us not rule the Almighty out of his own dominions, for his ways are not our ways; his footsteps are seen every-where, in the rocks and among the beasts and the birds. All nature sings his praise, whether it be in the babbling brook, the blooming flower, or the rolling planet.

"I tossed a little dried-up root," wrote the Rev.

Robert Collyer, "into a dark corner once, where I was doing a bit of gardening. 'You are of no use,' I said, 'and might as well rot.' But the little thing knew better than that. I had given it up; but then it fell back on the only God it knew of—our blessed mother, Nature. It ran rootlets into the tilth of May, and began to sprout. Then June came along and said, 'You must flower.' But there was no flowering in that dark hole; so what should my brave little root do but creep out of the hole on a long stock, find the sun, and unfold a blossom as blue as heaven, and beautiful, and then turn up its cup to drink the dew. And so it was that one day, when I went to hunt up an old rake or something in the hole, there was my blossom—no, not mine, God's blossom—bowing to me in the sweet south wind, and seeming to say, 'Good-morrow!' And I lifted the bonnie blue-bell and kissed it tenderly on my knees. I have never heard such a sermon as my blue-bell preached that June day."

But to return to the creation of Eve; suppose all this to be a figurative or allegorical representation. Some most beautiful truths are among them: first, that the woman was created after the man. He is to go forth and battle with the elements, while her mission is to garnish things into beauty. Adam was made of the raw material, "red earth," she of the same material after it had gone through a refining process. She was destined to walk by his side, his equal, not his slave nor his drudge. She was by God's appointment made to be a potent factor in the life of the world.

Is she not so, and do we not all receive our first

impressions from woman? In school, in church, and in society she is any thing but a cipher. She does exist as wife and mother; and if there is any thing mythical in her creation or origin one thing is evident, she is not a myth. Let us cling to the plain scriptural account at least until the world can find something better, which it never will.

By way of contrast with the Scripture, I wish to introduce here from Greek sources the account of the creation of the first woman.

The attempt has been made to trace an analogy between this more ancient tradition and the account of the fall as detailed in the sacred volume. But the words of the writer who furnished the legend do not warrant such a relation. According to this story, "Jupiter, it seems, became incensed at Prometheus for having stolen fire from the skies, and resolved to punish men for this daring deed. He therefore directed Vulcan to knead earth and water together and give it human voice and strength, and to make it assume the fair form of a virgin, like the immortal goddesses. He desired Minerva to endow her with artist knowledge, Venus to give her beauty, and Mercury to inspire her with an impudent and artful disposition. When formed she was attired by the seasons and graces, and each of the deities having bestowed upon her the commanded gifts, she was named Pandora — All-gifted. Thus furnished, she was brought by Mercury to the dwelling of Epimetheus, who—though his brother, Prometheus, had warned him to be on his guard, and to receive no gift from Jupiter—dazzled with her charms, took her into his house and made her his wife. The evil effects of this imprudent step were speedily felt. In the dwelling of Epimetheus stood a closed jar which he had been forbidden to open. Pandora, under the influence of curiosity, disregarding the injunction, raised the lid, and all the evils hitherto unknown to man poured out and spread themselves over the earth. In terror at the sight of these monsters she shut down the lid just in time to prevent the escape of Hope, which thus remained to man, his chief support and comfort."

Long ago we read in an old book something far more worthy of woman than this mythical extract from a Greek author: "Woman from her infancy to old age is an object of constant interest, and it is not strange that a being so tender, and yet so full of endearments, should call forth the admiration of the philosopher and the fervid praises of the poet. Her history is the narrative of good deeds; in health she is our pride, in sickness our solace, and in the faithful discharge of her duty she is the idol of all hearts. Like a ministering angel she soothes us in our afflictions, in adversity she inspires hope and invites us to new efforts. Who has not felt the cheering influences of her smile and the encouragement of her eloquence in the dark hour of despondency? Abandoned by friends and left to the cold charities of a selfish and heartless world, the husband then, if not before, knows how to appreciate the depths of a wife's love and the sincerity of a wife's vows.

> "God fashioned man from out the common earth,
> But not from earth the woman ; .
> So does she even when fallen bear with her
> Some sign of heaven, some
>   Mystic starry light.

> "Most gentle is she in all gentle deeds;
> In all sweet offices in fireside life;
> A touch to cool the fevered brow of pain,
> A voice to ease the heavy heart of care."

Another point in this Bible account relates to the personating of Satan by the serpent, in the conversation with Eve. But was it a serpent? On this question the most learned scholars differ, some holding that it was a real serpent, bringing forth as an argument that some serpents even to-day have rudimentary legs, the use of which they have entirely lost. It is a fact, we think, that all serpents have these same rudimentary legs; but that does not prove that they ever walked like quadrupeds; nature is full of strange types. Another class of writers holds to the belief that the word translated "serpent" might equally well be rendered ape, and therefore it was not a serpent. That which so divides the learned world cannot be of very much importance; and, whether serpent or ape, the miracle would be the same. But for the sake of argument let us conclude that this was an allegory designed to set forth the stealthy creeping in of sin. The word Eden signifies delight. The sinless inhabitants were happy when they were obedient and pure. Wherever this garden of delight was located, whether in Assyria or at the North Pole, as a recent writer [*] claims, matters but little save as a question appealing to our curiosity.

The Eden was in them because they were happy. But temptation came; sin, serpent-like, crept into the garden; they ate—that is, they disobeyed God. All discussion about what they ate is the merest

[*] President W. F. Warren, *Paradise Found*.

waste of time. It was the disobedience, not the apple, that disturbed the harmonics of Eden. They fell—that is, they became consciously guilty. They were driven out of Eden—that is, they lost their innocence and were rendered unhappy; in other words, Eden was banished from their hearts. This whole account has a meaning deeper than the mere wording. The reader may see in this a literal history, or he may read it as an allegory or fiction, so far as the tree and the serpent are concerned; but so far as the great fact of human transgression of divine law and the resulting misery to mankind are concerned there is no room for doubt. Sin is in the world, its most prevalent and most awful fact.

CHAPTER VII.

FACT AND FICTION AMONG THE HEATHEN.

THERE is one other phase of this subject of which I wish to speak, namely, fact and fiction among the heathen, and especially in ancient times. Their system was full of fiction along the lines of the supernatural. But there was this difference between the heathen or Gentile world and the Jewish, that while the writings of the latter contained fictions appealing to us in symbols, metaphors, allegories, and parables, they were intended to teach mankind spiritual truths which should uplift and purify the soul. On the other hand, the fictions of the pagan world were rather explanatory of nature. That they were founded on facts or phenomena of the natural world is most apparent. There is a pathetic side to this subject; our deepest pity is awakened as we peruse this story of the world's effort to understand the mysteries of the universe. That there have been honest seekers after the truth among pagans let us cheerfully admit. While among savage peoples the symbolisms were coarse, crude, and often bloody, among the cultured Egyptians, Greeks, and Romans they were often characterized by great refinement, running into the beautiful and poetic. But they all failed to reach the height gained by the descendants of Abraham.

A veil of mist overhung their theories and their theologies, and sometimes they were shrouded in deepest gloom. They only caught glimpses of light as it darted through the cloud-rifts about them. Nothing seems to us more certain than that mankind in the beginning were monotheists—believers in and worshipers of the one true God. That in every land and in every age man has been a religious being is as certain as that he has a physical nature. The altars and gods of universal heathendom are witnesses of this fact in the world's life. This subject is introduced at this time for the purpose of showing the difference between the pagan world, with its innumerable myths, and the true people of God.

The Bible tells us that God stamped upon the first man his own image, and, though it has been blurred by ignorance and so defaced by sin as to be almost invisible, nevertheless it does exist. No one thing, furthermore, is more distinctively characteristic of the human race, as a whole, than the omnipresence of religious ideas and forms of worship. That they are crude, and often cruel, we know. Perhaps the lowest tribe of men on earth are the Orang Kooboos of Sumatra. A traveler relates that he once saw a group of male and female worshipers sitting around a buluh batang, or species of bamboo which attains a great size, and all of these poor devotees would, as many as could, strike their heads in concert repeatedly against the trunk of the tree and simultaneously utter in a monotonous tone some rude grunting ejaculations. This he observed took place when any one of the number was hurt or received any special gratification, but mostly when injured. The same author informs us that a large portion of the semi-civilized, semi-pagan Sumatrans believed that in the enormous tufts of the buluh batang, as well as in some other varieties of trees, there exist good and evil spirits. The claim has been set up that some tribes of men have been found without any religious notions or forms of worship of any kind whatever. But that which is common to ninety-nine one-hundredths of the whole population of the earth will, we think, be found upon more careful investigation to belong to the remaining one one-hundredth. Whence came this universal impulse? Not from the teachings of the priest nor from a revelation to the race in the beginning perpetuated by an ever-widening channel of tradition; no, but by a supernatural endowment.

Thomas Carlyle has remarked that "Quackery and imposition have fearfully abounded in the later and corrupt period of the pagan religion; but quackery was never the originating influence of such things, but their disease, the sure precursor of their being about to die. Let us never forget this. It seems to me a most mournful hypothesis that, of quackery giving birth to any faith even in a savage. Quackery gives birth to nothing; gives death to all."

Religion, however debased, is the result of a supernatural endowment, which may be traced to a fertile germ which was originally implanted in the human breast by the Creator, and which manifests itself among men in all ages and races. The great apostle writes: "For when the Gentiles"—the heathen—"who have not the law, do by nature the things contained in the law, these having not the law are a law unto themselves." That is to say, they have a spiritual nature bestowed upon them in their creation. Mankind fell into idolatrous worship as they lost acuteness of perception and spiritual sensibilities, and became sordid and sinful. So long as primeval man worshiped the true God he was pure, but as he grew out of these early conditions he reached a point where the universe could not be contemplated by his untutored mind as the sole production of one supreme God. It was then that he became intellectually and spiritually debased, almost losing the image of God from his soul. Had Bacon lived earlier, or if all men had been Bacons, it would have been otherwise; for it was he who, in the *Novum Organum*, taught the world more than any other man who ever wrote to reason from effect to cause, a process that must always lead the mind "through nature up to nature's God."

With the idea of God implanted in the mind of man, his inherent religious nature will develop in some manner. If a savage, it becomes grotesque; if civilized, his religious forms become æsthetic. The wild Sumatran is an illustration on the one hand, the cultured Greek and Roman on the other. It must not be forgotten that imagination claimed the ownership of the world long before science attempted to establish her empire. We have spoken of man as naturally a religious being, but he has not always been made good by his religion, for in all ages and lands his altar-fumes have intensified his passions and given him the greater power to do evil; he has often gone forth to rob and murder and commit all other crimes in the name of his divinity. To this child of God—for such he has ever been by nature—wandering in the shadows of moral night, the stars above were the eyes of heaven. While darkness shrouds the earth they act the part of sentries, keenly surveying the actions of mankind.

The moon was held to be a female deity, and, having an apparently human face, she was believed to be in a pleasant mood so long as she presented her lustrous countenance toward the earth ; but if she veiled her face under an eclipse she was thought to be angry at her votaries. Rain-drops were the tears heaven shed upon the earth. The clouds were easily transformed into mailed warriors of the skies. Hail-stones were the algid missiles of some angry frost-king. The earth, under the name of Ceres, was a mother producing a numerous progeny. Did the rainbow throw its arch across the sky, belting the thunder-cloud with beauty, imagination at once transformed it into the "bridge of the gods," down which the spirits of a brighter sphere came to hold soothing converse with the fallen, world-battered sons of men. We may call all this fancy if we will, yet there was a beautiful and even an elevating philosophy in the thought ; it taught men that the benevolent "All Father" watched over his children and would sometime come down to sympathize with the sorrows and gladden with his presence the world.

"Under this apparently primitive habit of mind," says Dr. Horace Bushnell,* " we find men readiest, in fact, to believe that which exceeds the terms of nature—in deities and apparitions of deities, that fill the heavens and the earth with their sublime turmoil, in fates and furies, in nymphs and graces, in signs and oracles and incantations, in 'gorgons and chimeras dire.' Their gods are charioteering in the sun, presiding in the mountain-tops, rising out of the foam of the sea, breathing inspirations in the gas that issues

* *Nature and the Supernatural.*

from caves and rocky fissures, loosing their rage in the storm, plotting against each other in the intrigues of the courts, mixing in battles to give success to their own people or defeat the people of some rival deity. All departments and regions of the world are full of their miraculous activity. Above ground they are managing the thunders, distilling in showers or settling in dews, ripening or blasting the harvests, breathing health or poisoning the air with pestilential infections. In the ground they stir up volcanic fires and wrestle in earthquakes that shake down cities. In the deep world under-ground they receive the ghosts of departed men and preside in Tartarean majesty over the realms of the shades. The unity of reason was nothing to these Gentiles."

The religious sentiment ran like a vein of gold through the fictions of the early world. Philosophy had not laid bare the laws and operations of nature as it has to us; and in their simpler faith they traced the immediate finger of the Deity in all the mysterious phenomena around them. They heard his voice in the rolling thunders and in the mysterious winds, chanting their anthems in the forests at night. They felt his presence alike in the hot silence of a summer noon and saw it in the solemn splendors of the midnight sky. All music was but the echo of his voice; all beauty was but the shadow of his smile. The poetical mythology which confided the fountains to the naiads, the flocks to Pan, the harvests to Ceres, and the thunders to Jupiter taught its disciples that the universe itself was the spacious temple of divinity; and we must see that divine dogmas ran like silver threading through the weft of the ancient nations.

"As in the individual sentiment is manifested before intelligence and imagination precedes reflection, so in nations the literature of the heart has always preceded that of the head. Hence the vagaries of fiction, if not based always on substantial facts, have yet heralded, though sometimes at a distance quite remote, the footsteps of philosophy." Plato, in his *Reminiscences*, shadowed forth the doctrines of the soul's antenatal life, and so the Greeks fancied that it was the milky way down which the spirits, exiled from their heavenly home, descended on their tearful pilgrimage to dwell in human flesh, and as they gravitated toward this lower world, and came in contact with the grosser forms of nature, became stupefied, and, waking up to their earthy nesting, had but a confused memory of their former history. This, like most of their philosophy, was borrowed from Egypt, land of symbols as well as the earlier home of philosophy. There was in all the ancient world a religious sentiment, based on the original idea of the one true God. This was followed by the deification of single attributes, or cosmic manifestations of the Supreme. These were personified, or considered as so many little gods or divine hypostases.

Their reasoning must have been after this manner: The Supreme Being has attributes or qualities which collectively make up his being; hence, he would not be the Supreme if any one of these accessories were wanting, and so it follows that each one of these must be a supreme being, because each one includes or requires all the rest to complete the idea of such a being. In their pantheistic faith the atmosphere, ether, light, fire, the sun, winds, storms, fear, virtue, all were deities. Surely theirs was a spirit of reverence, and beautiful indeed were many of the fictions of the early world. We do not say that they were based on truth wholly, but that there was a grasp and a grandeur in them which later ages have scarcely been able to understand is equally true.

The imagination of these early peoples was bold and vigorous, and besides was characterized by a greater freshness than we of this practical utilitarian age can well comprehend. All this was only mythology after all. These meant nothing to man's inner life. They possessed no soul-searching power which resulted in faith, love, duty. The foundation of all religion is in the natural heart, in the belief of one God and Father. Blot this out even partially, and mankind will turn to the planets, the mountains, the grottoes, and the groves. Destroy the Bible, raze the churches, scatter the Sunday-schools—demolish all these evangelical agencies which exist for the world's welfare, and our posterity would worship serpents, paint their faces with hideous figures, brandish the savage war-club, believe in witches, and in a word walk just where mankind through the ages of paganism have walked.

CHAPTER VIII.

MAN THE MONARCH.

IN no one thing do the two books—the rocky scroll we call earth, nature, and the written scroll we call Bible—come together more certainly and closely than in the position given by each to the human species. In both man is placed at the head—the monarch of the world.

We are aware of the fact that some writers claim that the human race, instead of having come upon the stage recently, has existed upon the earth for the space, possibly, of one hundred thousand years, more or less. This claim is based on the finding of human remains, notably skull-bones, in such geological relations as to argue for a much longer residence than has generally been allowed. We are not in possession here and now of sufficient data by which formally to disprove this claim of a certain school of scientists. It may be that he has lived, moved, and had his being on the earth through as many ages as some have tried to show.

We would not leave unnoticed the fact that an argument for his development from some lower order of being—remotely, the monad or tadpole, more recently, the ape or monkey—has been made for the purpose of forcing upon the world this theory. Great periods of time have been drawn upon in order that this monad or original protoplasm might graduate through fishes and other animals into a man.

It is not the author's purpose to enter into a close or extended discussion of the development theory at this time. It has really become too much of a commonplace topic and has too small a hold on the thought of the Christian world to merit here an elaborate treatment; and yet a professor of Harvard University has recently prepared a *First Book on Geology*, for beginners, in which there is a chapter telling us how "species are made." "It is worthy of note," says a reviewer of the book, "that the chapter appears with no apology for being presented—a circumstance that would have been hazardous a decade ago." This teacher of science [*] goes on to say:

"Among the questions which the student of the earth finds always before him in the study of its history are: how animals and plants have come to be; how this life began; how, from time to time, these living creatures have disappeared and been replaced by other kinds. These are all hard questions, and we cannot yet give them full answers. Until modern times students did not know there had been a very long history to life, in which all the kinds of beings had often been changed, giving place to other kinds. Therefore, until our own day, the general opinion was that all the kinds of animals and plants now on the earth had been created from the dust in the shape we find them. But when in this century it was found that before the coming of each of these living animals and plants there were other forms closely resembling them, yet of different species, and that this chain of beings stretched clear back into the past, the animals becoming more simple as we went toward the

[*] Professor N. S. Shaler.

time when life began, it was gradually learned that these animals had in some way sprung from each other. For we cannot well believe that the Creator would make such relationships between creatures, creating each like that that went before, yet with a difference. It is far more reasonable to believe that the living forms have sprung from the kindred forms that have passed away. So strong is this argument that there is probably not a single person living who has been a careful student of animals or plants who doubts that the life now on earth has sprung from species or kinds that have passed away. The only doubt is as to the means by which the change from one to the other has been brought about. This is the question to which students of nature are now giving the most of their attention.

"So far but one clear way has been found in which the change can be accounted for, and while it cannot explain more than a part of the puzzle it is an important help to our knowledge of life. This partial explanation is known as the Darwinian theory, taking its name from the student who first suggested it."

It is only in a modern sense that Darwin can be called the originator of this "theory." It dates farther back, and is a godless theory, in fact. But does not the author of this quotation make rather a bold charge when he affirms that there is probably not a "single person living" who has been a careful student of animals or plants who doubts that the life now on the earth has sprung from species or kinds that have passed away? It is true Hugh Miller is not "living," neither is the great Agassiz; but they, "being dead," yet speak. And this is the way the great Scottish Christian geologist, whose writings have been read around the world, puts himself on record: "The perished tribes and races ... all *began* to exist. ... There is no truth which science can more conclusively demonstrate than that they all had a beginning. The infidel who, in this late age of the world, would attempt falling back on the fiction of an 'infinite series' would be laughed to scorn. They all began to be; but how? No true geologist holds by the development hypothesis. It has been resigned to sciolists and smatterers; and there is but one other alternation. They began to be through the *miracle of creation*. From the evidence furnished by these rocks [the Old Red Sandstone] we are shut down either to the belief in something infinitely harder of reception, and as thoroughly unsupported by testimony as it is contrary to experience." *

The learned Agassiz says: "It is evident that there is a manifest progress in the succession of beings on the surface of the earth. This progress consists in an increasing similarity to the living fauna and among the vertebrates, especially in their increasing resemblance to man.

" But this connection is not the consequence of direct lineage between the faunas of different ages. There is nothing like parental descent connecting them. The fishes of the paleozoic age are in no respect the ancestors of the reptiles of the secondary age. Nor does man descend from the mammals which preceded him in the tertiary age. The link by which they are connected is of a higher and *immaterial* nature, and their connection is to be sought in the view of the Creator himself, whose aim in forming the earth, in

* *Footprints of the Creator*, p. 301.

allowing it to undergo the successive changes which geology points out, and in creating successively all different types of animals which have passed away, was to introduce man upon the surface of the earth. Man is the end toward which all the animal creation has tended from the beginning."

Professor Joseph Leconte writes : * " Geology, then, teaches, and, as it seems to me, unmistakably teaches, that the law of succession of animals and plants is that of progressive development in time of these two kingdoms. But although there has been a development it is not the development of the Lamarckian, or that of the author of the *Vestiges of Creation* and the Pantheists. The development which geology teaches is not a development which is the result of physical laws and physical form. If there is any thing which geology teaches with clearness it is that the animal and vegetable kingdoms *did not commence as monads*, or vital points, but as organisms so perfect that even the maddest Lamarckian must admit that they could not have been formed by agency of physical forces; that species *did not pass into one another by transmutation*, but that each species was introduced in full perfection, remained unchanged during the term of their existence, and died in full perfection; that physical conditions cannot change one species into another, but that a species will give up its life rather than its specific character.

"In traversing from the equator to the poles we pass from one geological fauna to another, from one set of species to another; but observe there is no transmutation. So also in passing from the oldest geo-

* Lecture, Smithsonian Institution.

logical to the present fauna we pass from one set of species to another, not, however, by transmutation, but always by substitution. This has been repeated so many thousand times in the geological history of the earth that there is no room for doubt on the subject. As far as the evidence of geology extends each species was introduced by the direct miraculous agency of a personal intelligence.

"As to varieties among the different species there is no question of doubt. There are over three hundred varieties of humming-birds, hundreds of varieties of dogs, horses, swine, sheep, etc.; but species do not mix, dogs do not grow into horses, nor humming-birds into eagles. The ingenuity of man has been taxed to produce varieties, and here there is scarcely a limit. But the laws regulating species were formulated in the very beginning, and hold sway to-day over all the earth."

So we prefer to accept the simple statement of the great fact we call *man*. No matter how he began, when he began, nor where he began, his existence with all the powers with which he is endowed constitutes a fact of overwhelming magnitude. But even if he has been here for one hundred thousand years his advent, geologically speaking, was relatively recent. The age of the world itself has never been settled, and cannot be, though attempts have been made to ascertain exactly how old the earth is.

While it does not matter so much practically about the origin of man, it does matter greatly what he is and where he is going. It is the man of to-day, and not the man of prehistoric times, in which we are interested. That this wonderful being bears some resemblance to the animal world is not to be denied.

That he has a spinal column molded after the fashion of the first spinal column owned by a fish that sported in primeval seas is true; but this does not argue that man is a developed fish!

Position is not parentage. We have actually heard it rumored in recent times that some men were without spinal columns, and may be they descended from the original protoplasm and have remained protoplastic ever since! But man is more than a mere bodily organism; he has all the instincts of animal nature; but these are surmounted by the higher powers of reason. Plato said: "Man is a two-legged animal without feathers." Socrates turned the laugh on Plato by bringing in a fowl clipped of its feathers, exclaiming, "Behold Plato's man!" Man has been called a "laughing animal," a "cooking animal," a "lazy animal," a "tool-making animal," an animal that "makes bargains;" for no animal does this; dogs never trade bones; they sometimes exhibit a good deal of human nature, and adopt the maxim that "might makes right." He has also been called a "dupable animal," who loves quacks in medicine, politics, and religion. No definition which includes the animal merely sufficiently defines man, for by his reasoning faculties, his spiritual endowments, he is as far removed from mere animalism as the sun is above the glow-worm.

The universe was created for a purpose; and what was that purpose? To show forth the power, wisdom, and glory of God. "The heavens declare the glory of God, and the firmament showeth his handiwork." But in whose eyes do these glories shine?

Does any one imagine that the fishes that sport in the depths of the lake or ocean ever turn their eyes to behold the wonders of the elements in which they swim, or that the birds that cleave the air on pliant wing have any admiration for the landscapes that undulate in beauty beneath them in their flight? Is it at all supposable that the myriad beasts of the field and forest are ever moved to feelings of rational delight, or awed into reverence by the light which streams upon them from sun or star? The sea, the earth, the heavens, declare the glory of their Author only to man, who possesses the power of reason, and whose soul, like a harp-string, is responsive to the touch of divinity. Take man out of the field of vision—man as we see him, developed into sensitive rational life; man as we behold him wresting the secrets of Nature from her grasp, going forth to publish the mystery of the stars—take him away and fill the earth with every thing else, animate and inanimate, and the blank would be oppressive.

It is a fact that as the present order of things in the earth was approaching its completion old forms began to disappear; the hideous and frightful monsters that sported in primeval seas or roamed over the virgin earth became extinct, and the violent changes in the earth itself all subsided. "Not only the uses, but the beauty, of created things gradually increased with the progress of time. The gorgeous plumage and the musical warblings of birds, the brilliant hues of the insects, the delicate tints and fragrance of flowers, all have been increasing. The same is true of the inorganic kingdom. By physical agencies which are well understood the surface of our earth has been sculptured into higher and still higher forms of beauty. Indeed, currents of air and water, sunshine and shower, blue sky and snowy clouds, mountains and valleys, crag and cliff, all that gives beauty and variety to this our beloved earth, has been steadily increasing with the lapse of geological time." *

"Nature," wrote Emerson, "is sanitive, refining, elevating. How cunningly she hides every wrinkle of her inconceivable antiquity under roses and violets and morning dews! Every inch of the mountains is scarred by unimaginable convulsions, yet the new day is purple with the bloom of youth and love. Look out into the July night and see the broad belt of silver flame which flashes up half of the heavens, fresh and delicate as the bonfires of the meadow-flies. Yet the power of numbers cannot compute its enormous age, lasting as space and time, embosomed in time and space."

Why all this change? The answer is plain. When this God-appointed ruler came upon the scene the earth was no longer without its proper governor under the supreme Governor of the universe. To him it was said, "Thou shalt have dominion." Does he rule? Is he not a master? What matter or what force does he not control? The storing away in the earth's deep beds these varied elements was but the preparation for the advent of the "lord of this lower world." Vast mechanical power was packed away for his use. For ages uncounted it lay there awaiting his coming. At last his hand has touched it, and out from the deep he exhumes the buried past, and spindle and wheel and throbbing engine on land and sea disclose the purposes of God formed ages and ages ago.

* Professor Leconte, *Science and Religion.*

Man is here, but how did he come? By the fiat of God.

It is written, "Let us make man." From this simple and dignified statement of the old book a class of men dissent, claiming that this lordly being is but the last link in a chain, the end of a long series of changes culminating in himself. It is marvelous how some people will disbelieve the possible and affect to believe the impossible.

As a specimen of the reasoning of the materialist, note this from Professor Lorenzo Oken: "There are two kinds of generation in the world—the creation proper and the propagation that is sequent thereupon, or the *generatio originaria* and *secundaria;* consequently no organism has ever been created of larger size than an infusorial point. No organism is nor ever has been created which is not microscopic. Whatever is larger has not been created but developed." Hugh Miller says:* "God might as certainly have originated the species by a law of development as he maintains it by a law of development; the existence of the first great cause is as perfectly compatible with the one scheme as with the other. But," he continues, "there are beliefs in no degree less important to the moralist or to the Christian than even that of the being of a God, which seem wholly incompatible with the development hypothesis. If during a period so vast as to be scarce expressible by figures the creatures now human have been rising by almost infinitesimals from compound microscopic cells, minute globules within globules, begotten by electricity on dead gelatinous matter, until they have at length

* *Footprints of the Creator,* pp. 37, 38.

become men and women whom we see around us, we must either hold the monstrous belief that all the vitalities, whether of monads or mites, of fishes or reptiles, of birds or beasts, are individually or inherently immortal and undying, or that human souls are not so."

As a further specimen of the reasoning on the other side I again quote from Professor Shaler: "Nearly every living thing has two sorts of enemies in the world—passive enemies, which occupy the place in sea, on land, or in the open air which the new-comer needs, and active enemies in the creatures that prey upon it and try to make food of its body. We see that these creatures are constantly trying new plans to make themselves better fitted to win success out of their difficulties; they become swifter of foot or wing, they get stronger defensive weapons, they invent new habits that will elude their enemies; in a thousand different ways they change to meet their needs. It is certain that to these changes, which serve to help the creatures in the long battle for life, we owe a great part of the changes that are constantly rising in the forms of living things. The only trouble arises when we try to see just how the change is brought about. We may in part explain it in this way: Among all the young of any animal or plant each differs somewhat from any other. These differences are generally slight, but they may be enough to give the particular creature a better chance to live; it may be stronger limbs for flight or chase, or some difference in habits or any other profitable quality of its body or mind. In other words, those that vary in the direction of profit will be more likely to survive in the struggle for existence than those that vary in other directions. Next we must notice the fact that each living creature is likely to give its peculiar traits of body and mind to its descendants, so that they will have a share of the same peculiarities that the parent had, and on these creatures the same principle of survival of those that are fittest for success will again act, making the profitable feature stronger than it was before. If longer legs or stronger wings saved the parent, it is likely to give those longer legs or stronger wings to its offspring which will give them an advantage over the children of those other members of the same species that have not this peculiarity. Some of these descendants of the long-legged or strong-winged animal will probably have these parts better developed than the parent, and so its children will get the advantage of its cousins and thus prevail over them. From generation to generation the wings become stronger or the legs larger until a race is made that differs very far from the creatures from which it originally came, so that we call it a different species. In time all the individuals of the species that have not changed in this way will be destroyed by their enemies, so that the old species will disappear and the new take its place."

The African giraffe then was not originally a giraffe, but a plastic monad, a microzoon; then at length becoming dissatisfied with its lowly condition it concluded to become something else, and then after infinite ages still something else, until it conceived the idea of locomotion, and so tried a "new plan," and created for itself legs with bones, muscles, nerves, arteries, joints, and thus in time became a quadruped. But in some way this quadruped, unlike all others in existence, was seized with a desire to feed on tree-tops, and all it had to do was to desire, and in time this desire, persisted in, gave it enormously long fore-legs and a prodigious length of neck. The Creator had nothing to do with the origin of the giraffe species. Like the oft-quoted Topsy, it was not born, it "jes' growed."

So the duck, swan, goose, loon, and all other aquatic birds belonged to no species in particular; they were mere lumps of animated matter, but from some cause unknown to themselves they were seized with a desire to swim in the ponds, and so they "invented" oil-sacks with which to fill their skin, that they might not become water-logged, taking great care to place them just where they could easily reach them with their bills, and then all they needed was web-feet. This required only a few millions of years, but they persisted and won. This is how we have ducks and geese. By the same process the elephant came into possession of his trunk, the camel his series of stomachs, so that he could make long marches through sandy deserts, the turtle his shell, the serpent his venom and rattles, and the Darwinians their hypothesis! We are actually taught by this school of philosophers that "the sperm-whales come from creatures nearly like our bears that were pretty well up in the world, but their ancestors took first to living partly in the water and partly on the land, then finally to an altogether water life, so they have lost their hair, their hind legs have shrunk away, their fore legs become reduced to paddles, and the whole body has taken on the outside form of a fish!"

Admitting that there are some considerations along

this line which are worthy, yet the structure as a whole is not only unphilosophical, it is visionary and irreverent, if not positively absurd.

Science is ever extending man's intellectual vision, and the universe seems to be enlarging its boundaries. On the one hand the telescope is bringing before us new star wonders, while on the other the microscope is an equal revealer of living wonders in nature all about us of which our ancestors never dreamed. The yawning gulf that divides living protoplasm from dead matter is just as impassable now as it was before the invention of the microscope. If the theory of evolution be true, it ought as certainly to become apparent in the microbe world as anywhere else, for these microbes are living beings which propagate their species and die. We can start on our argument to-day with the axiom, *Omnia vivum ex ovo* (every living thing has sprung from an egg or germ), with just as much assurance on our side as when the principle was first enunciated. Time and increased knowledge of nature have only accumulated evidence of its truth.

A recent writer [*] puts the question thus strongly: "There is a dazzling simplicity in the hypothesis of the genesis of all organic forms that is very attractive to the imagination. To believe that all living organized existences have been produced from a few masses or particles of living protoplasm by forces of natural selection, and the conditions of their environment seemingly solves the mystery of the universe as easily as a child, by the aid of the letters of the alphabet, masters the words of his mother-tongue. But when in a spirit of calm and scientific inquiry we proceed to

[*] Dr. R. Reyburn.

study these problems, we do not find them quite so easy of solution as the theory of evolution would seem to indicate. Difficulties and doubts arise that must be overcome before we can accept it.

"The life-history of micro-organisms should throw light on these questions; many of them are composed of small particles of germinal matter or protoplasm, without either the nuclei, cell walls, or cell contents that are found in what are ordinarily known as cells in living organisms. Before our eyes and on the stages of our microscopes we can study them to our heart's content. We can watch them multiply either by the development of ova (or eggs), by germination (or budding), by fission (or division), or by the production of alternate or successive generations.

"When the biologist of to-day makes a pure culture of a living organism and places it with the proper precautions in a pure medium or soil fitted for its growth, he invariably finds, and expects to find, the same organism growing under his eyes, or on the stage of his microscope. He no more finds, or expects to find, a different organism resulting than a horticulturist would expect to find grapes growing upon an apple-tree, or thistles upon a plum-tree."

The first question to be answered concerning these microscopic organisms is the natural query, Whence came they? To this question evolution gives no answer. The microscope certainly disproves the Darwinian theory of evolution in the animal world.

To see how from the merest vegetable cells, microscopic in their size, have been derived all the species is passing strange. But then that would be no argument against it; but we are confronted with difficulties. In one case these cells grew into oaks that have preserved their identity unimpaired for countless ages; in another case the cells grew into mere shrubs, here a mushroom, there a cedar. Here they became apple-trees, there grapes, now vegetables for food, and then blossoms on which to feast the eye, and all without God, only by a blind law of nature!

If the evolutionists would put the divine Ruler into the account we should not object, for "with God all things are possible." It can be but necessary to state that the great points of antagonism in the opposite lines of belief are simply the law of development *versus* the miracle of creation. How shall we get rid of God? is the cry of the materialists. The task will be a difficult one.

It is estimated that there are on the earth about fifteen hundred millions of human beings. Those who imagine that the conditions of savage life are unfavorable to density of population may be surprised to learn that the latest estimates give to Africa a population of sixteen, and to North America only about nine, to the square mile. While the latter continent is known to contain only about eighty million people the population of Africa, according to Professor Levasseur, approximates two hundred millions. Nearly two thirds of the human race are grouped on about one twelfth of the land area of the globe. At this rate a population of twelve thousand millions, instead of fifteen hundred millions, is possible on the earth. They speak more than three thousand languages and dialects; they are civilized and barbarous; in the extreme north they are clad in fur, in the tropics they often live in a state of nudity. All are not alike capable; some are very low down in the scale of being, others high up.

But what a contradiction man is in himself. He is either rising up toward angelic life or sinking down toward that of the demon. Both extremes are reached. On the one side he is actuated by combativeness, his mission seeming to be to foment quarrels and stir up strife, to divide friends and convert love into hatred, to bring war instead of peace.

Long ago Dr. Thomas Dick wrote: "Since the creation of the world fourteen millions of human beings have fallen in the battles which man has waged against his brother-man. If this amazing number of men were to touch each other by the hand at arms'-length they would encircle the globe on which we dwell six hundred times." Dr. Prideaux states that "in fifty battles fought by Cæsar he slew 1,122,000 of his enemies. If we assign an equal number to Alexander the Great, and the same to Napoleon Bonaparte in his numerous wars, we may ascribe the untimely deaths of six millions of human beings who had no knowledge of the true reasons why they were led to battle, the truth often with much artifice being kept from all but those who were parties to the designs."

We have not verified these startling figures; but all men know that war is a terrible waste of life.

But there have been other conquests that were bloodless; human power has been victorious over the elements; man has subordinated the forces of nature to himself and thus increased his powers many fold. The echoes of his footsteps are heard in every part of the earth, from tropic to polar region. He is an explorer, an adventurer, an autocrat. Does he covet the treasures hid away in the earth itself? He contrives methods of finding them. He has mapped out the ocean and ascertained its configuration with almost as much ease and accuracy as he can survey a farm and compute its acreage. Does a mountain lift its frowning summit in his pathway? He scales its crest, or burrows his way through its heart.

The Mont Cenis Tunnel between Savoy and Piedmont in the Alps is more than seven miles in length. Two companies of workmen cut their way through the entire distance, beginning on opposite sides, and when they met mid-mountain their lines did not vary an inch.

We are living not only in a wonderful age, but in the very best age of the world so far. Society is not as good as it will be in the time to come, but it is far better than ever before. Some honest people do not believe this; they are ever telling us how much the human race has fallen behind; how much virtue and skill and knowledge there were in the world several thousand years ago. Even that very erudite lady, Miss Martineau, remarks in her book of *Travels in Egypt and Palestine* that the art of lifting such masses of stone as are found in the pyramids of the Nile and in the ruins of the Baalbec is lost, and that the men of this degenerate age could not quarry, transport, and raise such immense weights. In this we think she is in error; and to hold such opinions is calculated to throw discredit upon all the engineering science of the age. The largest block of stone at Baalbec is sixty-eight feet long, eighteen feet high, and fourteen feet deep, which would give a weight of twelve hundred tons. It required great skill and power, no doubt, to raise that solid mass to its place in a temple or pyramid; but look at the great Britannia Bridge which spans the Menai Strait between the island of Anglesea and the main-land of Wales. It is an iron tubular structure erected by that master-engineer Robert Stephenson, and at the time of its completion, in 1850, was regarded as the greatest piece of work of the kind in the world. One of these single tubes weighs eighteen hundred tons, or six hundred tons more than the famous "big rock" of Baalbec. We can hardly imagine that the great stone was any more difficult to put in place than one of the tubes of the Britannia Bridge.

Man invents machines which can work more rapidly and almost more intelligently than he can himself. He invokes the spirit of the waters to propel his ponderous trains, and the spirit of the air to stop them. He has constructed a machine that can talk; the phonograph registers the song or the sermon, which may be reproduced in other lands and in other ages.

But here is a problem which confront us. What is to be the final result to future generations of all this advance in the use of physical force? When a machine is invented by which one man can accomplish the work of ten or twenty, the nine or nineteen are thrown out of some particular kind of employment, but not necessarily out of every kind of service. Facts tell us that the improvement and increase of machinery do not diminish but add to the aggregate labor of a community. Where is there more labor than in the United States and Britain, with their thousands of steam-engines, electric motors, and all kinds of "labor-saving" instruments? Where is there less labor than among the machineless Hottentots of Africa or the sensual islanders of the South Pacific? The machine simply changes the direction of human energy.

When the patent air-brakes were introduced upon the Mexican railroad between Vera Cruz and the national capital the change eliminated a considerable number of men, throwing them out of the positions they had held; and instead of going at something else they sought revenge by stealing about in the dark and cutting the rubber pipes, demanding to be re-instated as brakemen. For a while it was a contest between brain and muscle; but brain always wins in the end, and it did it this case. It is a trite saying that we are living in an age of machinery. We have just entered it, and the future must adjust itself to the modern order.

The Bible speaks of a time when "the earth shall be filled with the knowledge of the Lord," when there shall be a "new earth."

I imagine that in these times there will be no less of industry than now, but far more. The millennium will not be an age of psalm-singing merely, but one of work and thrift. Then industry will banish pauperism; scientific skill will have the mastery over both matter and force. It will be an age of science, when men shall be "kings and priests unto God." We shall not do less, but more; we shall do it by machinery. This will be elevating. The whole race will rise by virtue of the increase of man's power.

As the world grows older there will be greater intelligence; we shall have more time for intellectual and spiritual pursuits. Then will be the long-talked-of and much-dreamed-about "Golden Age." All this machinery, all these numerous inventions, point us to just such a good time to come. We are not describing some fancied Utopia, but rather a land of promise.

All things are put in subjection to the human race; indeed, man stands for God in this world; but it is only when he is pure in heart, noble in soul, wise in thought, benevolent in action, that he properly represents his Father and his God. The truest victory he can ever achieve is over that which enslaves and degrades humanity. A world redeemed is a world of moral and intellectual beauty, a world of industry and thrift, where man is not yoked with the beasts of the field, but where heart and mind reach upward toward God.

The reign of truth will be a reign of peace. Just at present there is a great contest going forward between heavy rifled cannon and iron plating on ships of war; rather it is a strife for the mastery between the angel of science on the one side and the demon of war on the other. The angel of science says ironclad ships can be made impervious to any weight of ball and any charge of powder. The demon of war says, "I will crash through the thickest plating with my steel-pointed shot." Now, this whole question of war is destined ultimately to be resolved into another question: Who can make the best machine? The nation which can produce the best mechanics will bear away the palm of victory. Thus science, by making war engines so very deadly, will virtually abolish war. Long ago an old prophet wrote: "The wilderness and the solitary place shall be glad for them, and the desert shall bud and blossom as the rose." Nor is this all a mere figure of speech.

Science applied will make the earth more productive; it will drain the marshes and irrigate the desert places; it will analyze the soils, supply their lack of essential ingredients, and check their waste. It is now detecting great values in many places in that which has been deemed useless. Our most choice fruits and cereals have come from wild progenitors which would not be recognized by us were we to see them in their native state.

The greatest fact in the history of the world is the existence of man, the monarch.

CHAPTER IX.

WHAT IS LIFE?

WE do not mean by this heading what is the Christian life, or the animal life, or the life of man, but what is life in itself—its extent, its results—whether of man or beast, insect, vegetable, or monad? There are some things which are quite difficult to define, and life is one of them. Dictionary-makers, scientists, philosophers, and theologians alike have endeavored to state in a few words, and as comprehensively as possible, the meaning of life, but with what success the reader must judge for himself. Our great standard lexicographer defines it to be "the state of an animal or plant in which the organs are capable of performing their functions." He then gives us as equivalents the words, "animate existence," "vitality," and also the "time during which this state continues, either in general, or in an individual instance; as in the life of a tree or a horse." But it may be said that this definition applies with equal pertinency to decay, which goes on after life is extinct.

According to Professor De Blainville, "Life is the twofold internal movement of composition, at once general and continuous."

Herbert Spencer, in seeking a definition of life, says, "It is difficult to find one that does not include more than is necessary, or which does not exclude something that should be taken in." He also tells us that it is the "co-ordination of actions," but he furthermore observes, "Like the others, this definition includes too much, for it may be said of the solar system, with its regularly recurring movements and its self-balancing perturbations, that it also exhibits 'co-ordination of actions.'"

Professor G. H. Lewes defines life to be " a series of definite changes, both of structure and composition, which takes place within the individual without destroying its identity."

Dr. Carpenter tells us that "the life of man or of any of the higher animals essentially consists in the manifestation of forces of various kinds, of which the organism is the instrument."

If the reader does not know what life is from the foregoing definitions the following will not help the case any, though it comes from a very high scientific source. This learned definition is as follows : " Life is the definite heterogeneous combination of definite heterogeneous changes, both simultaneous and successive, in correspondence with eternal co-existence and sequence."

Thomas Carlyle calls life an " infinite mystery."

We are not going to undertake a task in which so many have failed, namely, to define life. The great Teacher asked, "Is not the life more than meat?"—more than the food which sustains it—"and the body than raiment?"—more than the clothing that covers it. Suffice it to remark that life is the most wonderful thing in the universe. Let us ask the reader to consider some of the many forms which life puts on—its universality and some of its characteristics.

We know that the time was when there was not on

this whole earth a solitary living being of any size, vegetable or animal—a time, as we have shown, when the earth, if not a cloud of fire-mist, was an incandescent globe of matter. Then all the waters now on the earth, in rivers, lakes, and oceans, were floating around it in thick cloud-masses through which the rays of the sun could not penetrate.

Then it was that the earth was "without form and void, and darkness was upon the face of the deep." But it cooled off, and in the cooling-off process the crust was formed, and as it shrank its wrinkles became our mountains and valleys; then the rain descended from the clouds and formed our rivers, lakes, and oceans.

But when did life begin, and how did it begin? There was a distinct beginning of life. Mere nature had not the power to generate life. We hear much said in these times about germs, vital points, and so on, as if all things had been developed up from these so-called beginnings of life. Suppose we admit it all, and conclude that the present order of creation began away back with these germs, atoms, and molecules; nevertheless, who created the molecules? They, too, must have had a beginning. When God interposes directly in the affairs of this world, or in human life, we call it a miracle. Creation, therefore, is a miracle, and yet a miracle may be but some manner in which God works of which we know nothing, only a higher form of nature. To say that life began spontaneously is no answer. It could not have caused itself, for nothing can act before it exists; therefore it must have been caused.

Life began in a very low form. The first living

being was, undoubtedly, a mere vital point; but it did not create itself.

This is not a treatise on exact science, and therefore we shall not discuss the subject of protoplasm and attempt to explain the mysterious Eozoon of the Laurentian granites. But I desire to bring before the reader some of the great *facts* of life simply. We find in the earth, in the waters, and in almost every thing microscopic beings called infusoria, or, to use a better term, *microzoa*, known to have been the very lowest forms of animal existence. Yet even in this world of invisible things there is a difference; they are all small beyond the ken of the naked eye, possibly, and yet there is often as much difference of size between varieties of animalcules as there is between a mouse and a horse or elephant. There are beings so minute that, placed in the most delicate scales which human ingenuity can construct, tens of thousands of them would make no impression of weight whatever.

Let us look at some of those that inhabit a drop of stagnant water. They will be found to range in dimension from the twenty-thousandth to the forty-thousandth part of an inch. But for this wonderful instrument, the microscope, these creatures never would have come within the range of human vision. There is one very remarkable species to which the scientists have given the name *Navicule*.

Upon examination it appears to be incased in an armor of flint, and though so cumbered can walk about on its twenty or thirty legs with as much ease as a soldier on dress parade or armed for battle. If it be watched for five or six hours, which is a large part of the whole life of an animalcule, we shall discover a very thin transparent line spreading across it in some direction or other. The line becomes more and more visible and grows wider every minute. At last the little fellow begins to manifest violent convulsions; the body splits asunder, and two new beings are formed out of the one. This curious animal has something like a hundred stomachs, and its mouth, which is situated near one extremity, is surrounded by a number of almost invisible tentacula, with which it grasps its food; but as soon as the transparent line appears, which denotes its approaching dissolution, or rather division, into two, as another mouth will be needed, another is seen sprouting from the other extremity, and is ready to perform its functions as soon as the separation is effected. The navicule comes to maturity at the age of twelve hours, and under ordinarily favorable conditions divides itself into two every twelve hours. It propagates its species according to a geometrical ratio, and at the end of one month such is the result of geometrical progression that were there no checks to their increase a single navicule would have produced over eight hundred millions of living beings. There are other species of these infinitesimal creatures that split themselves into sixteen instead of two in the same space of time, which would give us sixteen times eight hundred millions in the same length of time. What wonderful processes are going forward all about us in this universe of living organisms, and all employed by the great Architect!

A Brahman, whose religious faith forbade him to destroy animal life in food, was shown by means of a microscope that in every drop of water and in every grain of rice he necessarily consumed hundreds of living creatures. Seizing the instrument, he dashed it upon the earth, breaking it into fragments and exclaiming, "Where is your theory now?" But the shattering of the wonderful instrument did not annihilate the life it brought to light.

Life is emphatically the law of nature, life in inconceivable profusion and infinite variety. It is more than fiction or poetry to say that there is a world of life in each forest leaf.

Every step we take, every cup of water we drink—nay, in every breath of air we inhale—it is said we unavoidably destroy countless thousands of lives, and if so it only proves that the great globe is a vast warehouse packed to overflowing with living organisms, and with scarce an inch to spare. Wherever there is matter there is life in endless, exhaustless—we had almost said reckless—profusion. Life is every-where. The stagnant pool in the woods is a world in itself filled with fascinating interest. Its waters teem with myriads of living beings of varied and curious forms which only the microscope can reveal. Some are naked, others are protected by shells. They resemble stars, boats, trumpets, wheels, rods, etc., and sometimes they look like fruits, necklaces, flasks, and so forth. There is one which resembles a cup, and is called the "Flower Cup," being in the likeness of a crystal vase containing what looks like the blossom plant. So small is this living organism that *thirteen millions* may swim in a drop of water! They have eyes, a muscular structure, and nervous system. They move about independently, and some have been seen with claws with which to grasp objects. A few species are large enough to be seen by the naked eye, and one such, called the Stentor, because of its trumpet shape, is particularly ferocious, ever devouring the weaker kinds about it. It is not mere poetry to say that these microscopic beings are, in fact, "more numerous than the sands upon the sea-shore." Man has only just begun to invade the dominions of the bacilli and learn of their habits. The different species may be numbered by thousands. Some are *pathogenic*, or disease-producing. Ulcers, boils, and other diseases are caused by different species. There is the bacillus of typhoid fever, now well understood; the bacillus of pneumonia, tuberculosis, cholera, lockjaw, etc. A French physician, to test their genuineness, took a mass of a certain kind and rubbed his arm thoroughly with it. He was rewarded in a few hours with a field of pus which covered his whole arm. Billions of these little living creatures are present every-where in all flesh, earth, water, and air; but only a few are the foes of animal life. They play an important part in all animal organisms either for good or evil. Many of them are *non-pathogenic*—their existence is necessary to health in the same way that some insects are serviceable to farmers and horticulturists. Among them are many beautiful growths. Viewed in masses as the pure cults are grown and stained, they are visible to the naked eye, so abundant do they become after a few hours. One of the prettiest of the *non-pathogenic* bacilli is that of the "bleeding heart." It forms a growth of a bright red color and owes its name to superstition. The early churchmen often found that bread left on the altar after being blessed became red. They imagined that this was the blood of Christ dropped there by divine grace, and regarded it as a good omen. When milk turns blue in an hour or two it is due to a species of bacilli, a swarm of which will enter a creamery and attack all the milk in sight at once. The German peasants a few years ago were greatly alarmed at this phenomenon, and threw all the milk so turned away, thinking it diseased. It was as harmless as any.

More interesting even than these are the swarms of minute diatoms—creatures of a vegetable nature—which are chiefly remarkable for the elaborate beauty of their shells. The latter are bivalvular, like those of a mussel. Some are like little boxes exquisitely made; others resemble boats, hearts, dominoes, etc. There is one sort that has been called the "Shield of Achilles," because each half of its disk-shaped shell is cut in concentric circles, with a complicated tracery of designs. In many varieties the valves seem ornamented with so fine a lace-work that to distinguish the patterns is considered the best possible test of the power of a microscope. Great and fathomless indeed are the mysteries of nature!

And hardly has our reason recovered from the effects of these astounding disclosures when it is again overwhelmed by the endless variety of genera and species with which organic nature abounds.

"When natural history completes her catalogue of living organism and confesses in despair that her rude skill cannot classify the finer distinctions of being, that her grasp cannot compass the great circle of life, then geology comes forward to add to our bewilderment, and, opening the thickly packed laminæ of the Stone volume, reveals to our view numberless fossil forms of beings ranging from mere infusoria to the gigantic monsters whose remains are preserved in the rocks and have long been extinct, and of which the very types are no more." Who can count what the great God and Father has created? But through all this law of life there runs a plan and purpose most apparent. Nothing has been created in vain; the meanest insect, worm, or polyp, as surely as the most useful and beautiful animal which man has domesticated, lives for a purpose. We may not be wise enough to understand why so many different beings have a place on earth, basking in the same sunlight, breathing the same air with man; but they do exist, they have been formed for some good and wise purpose, and that is often to serve man, who is the image of God.

There are plants as well as animals so minute as to be invisible to the naked eye. They are of uniform and simple structure, and are justly regarded as forming the base of the vegetable kingdom. But notwithstanding their lowly position in the scale of being they display an infinite variety of the most exquisite forms and finely sculptured surfaces, so that their study affords as much scope for the powers of observation as does the starry vault itself, which is patent to our sense of sight. There is the so-called "Red Snow Plant," which long puzzled the explorers of northern regions. This microscopic vegetable gives a blood-red color to Alpine and arctic snows. It was seen by Captain Ross in his first arctic journey to spread over a vast extent of territory. There were also combined with this plant some minute infusorial animals, which acquired the same color from feeding on it.

The Red Sea takes its name, in fact, from the color of its waters, which are filled with animalculæ of a similar species to those just spoken of. Not only the waters and the snow-surfaces of the North, but great masses of rock, are tinged with this same color from the imprisoned dead forms of microscopic beings. Their abundance exceeds all possible human calculation. Think of a living being so small that forty thousand laid in a straight line would not reach over one inch in length! Rocky strata are formed by them in places from twenty to forty feet thick, and covering vast areas of country. We boast of our power in rearing great buildings, pyramids, and monuments; but when we see animals almost atomic laying down great rocky formations that serve as foundations for continents, and rearing walls for harbors of greater strength and greater size than the mightiest structures ever undertaken by man, one is indeed impressed with the works of God. I do not know that I can make more emphatic this idea of minuteness combined with power than I have done in the foregoing statements; but it has been ascertained that seventy-five millions of these creatures would not exceed a grain in weight. The rocks which underlie the city of Berlin, in Prussia, have been ascertained to be a vast deposit of infusorial shells. These atomic creatures are in the ocean and in the earth. They enter the bodies of men and of other animals—circulating in the blood, accumulating on the teeth in the form of tartar, and as *trichina spirales* devouring the flesh and causing death.

Rocks that belong to the most ancient epochs of the globe, and which contain strata of vast magnitudes, are but the sepulchers of these dead forms. Every grain of dust almost may be said to have been once endued with life.

But all are not infusoria. We have a species of mollusk known as the Nummulite—so named from its resemblance to coin—which are of more ample size. They have combined to produce lofty chains of mountains, and, though very small, they are not altogether microscopic; indeed, compared with those with which we have been speaking they may be called giants. The Arabian chain of mountains which extends along the valley of the Nile was built up by them. They indeed, rather than Pharaoh, built those great pyramids which have been the wonder of the ages. Take the pyramid of Cheops, well called the "great pyramid," or by way of distinction *the* pyramid. It is the oldest, and most likely the largest, human structure in the world, yet it is insignificant when compared with the mountains which God has reared beneath the dome of the skies. There it stands and has stood for four or five thousand years. It was old when Jerusalem was in its glory, when Rome was rising into power, when Homer sang, when David reigned. Its base originally covered thirteen acres and it rose to a height of four hundred and fifty feet. It is computed to have contained about seven million tons of solid masonry before it was mutilated by the hand of the spoiler. Greek, Roman, and Saracen vandals have preyed upon it, stripping off its polished red granite casing with which to enrich their mosques and palaces. Herodotus was informed that a hundred thousand workmen changing every three months were constantly employed for ten years in constructing the causeway for the conveyance of the huge blocks of stone used in its construction, and then another twenty years in building the great pyramid itself. There it stands, a monument to human power, industry, and ambition. The thought impresses us. But back of this there was another power, even more impressive —the power of the infinitesimal nummulite, the little being that under God's direction built the great Arabian chain of mountains. They are so small as to resemble lentil seeds, for which they were sometimes mistaken by the early Greek and Roman travelers. These little creatures often have had more to do in building up the earthy structures than the huge animals. We ask, then, Who built the pyramids? and are answered, Pharaoh; but another answer is, The nummulites; so that the pyramid is at once the tomb of dead nummulites and dead kings. On the other hand, there are mollusks in the sea whose shells are so large that they have been used for bath-tubs.

We cannot go farther in this subject here than simply to say that these living beings have filled the waters of the lakes, rivers, ponds, and seas, from the invisible monad to the great sea-monsters, the shark, the whale, the serpent; they have filled the air and nested and propagated in the sands; they have feasted as parasites on every living thing; they have served God in a way almost beyond our finite comprehension.

CHAPTER X.

LIFE IN LARGER FORMS.

LET us now turn and look at life on the surface of the earth, life in larger form, for all living beings are not microscopic. The world is a great theater for animal activity and display. Of the myriads of the human species we shall speak elsewhere. Vast numbers of wild and ferocious beasts crowd the jungles, roam through the forests, and wander over the plains of both the Old World and the New; but they are destined to become entirely extinct before the on-marching of civilization. The deer of our mountains are fast disappearing, and the buffaloes of our prairies are now never seen where not very long ago they abounded in great numbers. The bear, the panther, the wolf, and many other species of animals, untamed and untamable, are slowly but surely fading out. The elephant, the hippopotamus, and hyena once inhabited the British Isles; but they are all gone, and in like manner will they be exterminated in Africa and in India in time. The birds, too, how vast their numbers! what variety in size, color, and plumage! Here we have the majestic eagle, there the humming-bird; now birds of song, and then fierce birds of prey; they are every-where, in forest and grove, bright, beautiful creatures of God.

What cheer they put into the world! How sweet their vesper and matin warblings! God has sent them with their thrilling notes and gay feathers to serve him and us and to be happy themselves.

"Behold the fowls of the air: for they sow not, neither do they reap, nor gather into barns; yet your heavenly Father feedeth them. Are ye not much better than they?" Let us learn from them a lesson of trust. Then consider, too, this great variety of domestic animals; how they serve us, not only by their labor, but by furnishing us clothing and food as well. That kindly servant, the horse, is ever expending his life-force for man, in turning the furrows to prepare for the harvest, in drawing the loads and carrying the burdens of life. To name all the animal uses would fill a volume. It is enough to say that there is life every-where, on land, in the sea, and in the air.

But let us turn to the sea, the "great, wide sea, wherein are things creeping, innumerable, both small and great beasts." The sea affords scope to uncounted myriads of living beings, ranging from the enormous whale to microscopic polyps, transparent as the water in which they swim, and seen only by the light of the phosphoric gleam which they emit.

It is a well-established principle in nature that animal life is sustained by vegetable life, while vegetable life is supported by the inorganic or mineral. The vegetable is required to change the mineral constituents of the surrounding media into suitable nourishment, hence the "herb" was first created. How, then, is this exuberant animal creation in the sea maintained? God has amply provided for the support of all these creatures in a manner most wonderful to contemplate. In the sea there are fish which are flesh-eating, and indeed they devour each other, for, like the great financiers, the "big fish eat the little ones." The ocean is filled with a species of vegetation called Algæ. They are regular plants which have roots, stems, branches, flowers, and seeds. They are of various colors and sizes. Spread out on paper and preserved in albums they are among the most beautiful specimens in our cabinets. In them God has prepared food for the fishes of the sea, and, though designed for that purpose mainly, he could just as well create them in conformity to the laws of beauty as to give them any other aspect. One often sees in the waters of the ditch by the roadside a green scum or covering, from which it is quite natural to turn away, regarding it as a sort of death-breeder, the begetter of malarial poison. If we examine such a pool filled with a green silken mass it is easy to trace the beads of oxygen on the submerged threads or see the gas collect in bubbles all over it. This "scum," as it is called, is not a scum, but a vegetable growth, a positive benefit to the atmosphere, for it is a producer or eliminator of oxygen. The general uses of these minute plants all over the world are very great in the aggregate, and are worthy of Him who has appointed even the meanest of his creatures something to do for the good of others. There are thousands of species of aqueous plants in the waters of our lakes and ponds on which their inhabitants feed. Whether on sea or land the provisions for sustaining life are equal to the life itself. The great Father cares even for the insect, and why should man distrust him?

But what extremes are seen in nature! On the one hand such minute beings, and then on the other such large ones. This is true especially of the sea, where, swimming in the same element, there are atomic living creatures invisible to the naked eye, and in the same waters whales have been taken measuring from fifty to one hundred feet in length, and weighing in some instances two hundred tons! Living animalcules were found by Sir James Ross on masses of floating ice in the polar seas, in seventy-eight degrees south latitude. They have also been brought up from a depth of twelve thousand feet in the ocean from under a pressure of three hundred and seventy-five atmospheres. Every river and pond abounds with living microscopic beings, while in the ocean they are sometimes so numerous as to create a luminous foam.

The sea is a vast storehouse of life. We have considered the microscopic world, which includes the sea-waters. "The sea has a whole world of life in itself. It spreads its table first of all for its own children. . . . It is said that the life in the sea far exceeds all that exists out of it. There are more than twenty-five thousand distinct species of living beings that inhabit the ocean waters. There are more than eight thousand species of fish, and some of these swarm in such innumerable millions that often they move in columns that are several leagues in width and many fathoms thick; and this vast stream of life continues to move past the same given point for whole months together. Incredible numbers of them are taken from the sea; in Norway four hundred millions of a single species in a single season, in Sweden seven hundred millions, and by other nations number without number! But those that are taken bear only a small proportion to those that remain of the same species, while the whole of these species themselves are but a portion of the entire population of the larger marine life; and this entire population of larger life, again, is but a drop in the bucket compared to the various forms of microscopic and animalcular life with which immense tracts of the ocean are filled. These animalcules are some of them so small that it would take forty thousand of them to measure an inch in length, and so closely crowded together that a large drop of water contains five hundred millions—nearly one third as many as there are human inhabitants on the whole globe.

"It is not necessary to ask whether all this infinitude of life is meant for the use of man or whether it has any thing whatever to do in promoting his comfort or providing his food. It is certain that many of the larger forms of marine life are intended for his benefit and are fitted for his use. Whole tribes of men derive almost their entire sustenance from the sea. The inhabitants of the polar regions draw their support more from this source than from all others combined. The same is true of the savage tribes on many of the islands of the Pacific and along some of the shores of the continents. Even civilized lands levy immense contributions on the life of the sea. Many thousands of vessels are employed in taking fish of various kinds from its waters, and uncounted millions of them are sent into every part of the world; so that the sea is full of God's riches, if we consider it only as a vast store-house of food for man.

"But all the life of the sea does not need to be designed for man in order to explain its use. Life is its own use, and wherever it exists and in proportion as it exists it is in itself considered the proof and illustration of the goodness of God. It is one of the noble uses of the sea, therefore, that it furnishes the dwelling-place for such an inconceivable immensity of life. It is even more full of God's goodness than it is of his power ; for while the latter requires larger masses for its exhibition the former is best seen by examining the minutest portion. Nothing is more powerless than a single drop of water, and yet by placing this single drop under the microscope we discover the character of vast masses of the ocean and learn that in every one of these little globes of inhabited sea-water there is literally a whole continent of happy beings that draw their existence from God, wait upon him for food, and receive their daily sustenance at his hand." *

The earth, we know, is the principal source of food for the vegetable creation, whether it be the microscopic plant or the giant conifer, and, passing through the vegetable process, becomes the indirect source of the animal sustenance. And right here, when we reach the point of organization, do we see the most apparent manifestation of the supernatural. What power is this which takes dead matter, lime, silica, carbon, etc., and lifts them up into such diversified forms? Analyze the woody stem of the tree or shrub, the leaf, the flower, the fruit, and what have we? Only dead, inert matter, but in which there was a something we call life, something so subtile as to elude the most delicate tests of the chemist. Touch it, and it is gone. The tree dies because the ax girdles it or a worm gnaws its heart; some blight

* Dr. Leonard Swain, in *Bibliotheca Sacra*.

comes down on the field and the crop withers; that divine something we call life departs. The animal is equally mysterious. Subject its body to the same analysis, and you find iron, lime, phosphorus, etc., dead, inert matter; but the life-principle is gone. That which filled it, moved it, gave it form and beauty, cannot be brought under the eye—it is invisible only as seen in its results. We see the beauty of the rose, and are delighted with its rich fragrance; we are impressed with the magnificence of the tree beneath whose spreading branches we recline on a hot summer day; but who ever saw the life of the tree? We can see the millionth part of a grain of matter under the microscope; but what shape, what color is *life?* We look into the faces of our friends, our neighbors, our children; we see the sparkle of the eye and the flush of the cheek; they make an impression on us we never forget; we know them; but who ever saw a human soul? Who can tell us all about the peculiar form or complexion of the life within the body? Life, whether of nomad, worm, man, or angel, is invisible to mortal eye. "No man hath seen God at any time." In the great hereafter we may have a power of spiritual vision by which the invisible may appear and we shall see as we are seen. Whence came this life-force? Surely matter did not spring at one bound spontaneously into all such myriad and beautiful forms; for in all there is such order and through all such variety that the mind acting normally must see the finger-prints of a supreme Intelligence.

CHAPTER XI.

LIFE—A STUDY.

BUT life is not limited to the animal. Weigh the vegetation raised above the surface of the earth, in the air, ranging in height from a few inches to several hundreds of feet. How enormous the weight when we consider that a single good-sized tree would have a pressure of several tons! All this matter of the tree is from the earth and the air. What power lifted it out of the earth? Life. Life, then, is a force which began in the beginning and is constantly operating through all nature. When a man raises a weight from the ground he does it not by muscle, but by the life-force within him.

Life is persistent; one codfish by its natural increase without check in a half-dozen years would, to keep the figures within bounds, stock all the seas and oceans on the globe so completely that there would not be left a yard of space for any thing else. A single kernel of corn in ten or fifteen years would cover the entire surface of the planet. One grain of wheat, unchecked in twelve years, would furnish a food supply for the whole human family during a man's life-time. The small and delicate, almost invisible fern-seed, unchecked in its growth, would completely mat the entire earth in six years. If oysters were to increase in the same ratio they would pack the ocean solid in less than a decade or two.

There is one species of river-fish so very prolific that, according to the learned Mudie, in twenty-four years, it increases so enormously, it would outweigh all the planets of the solar system. I have spoken elsewhere of microscopic animals and of their enormous power of propagation; but here is the little plant-louse—the aphis so much dreaded by the gardener; one of these tiny creatures is estimated to produce in four of its generations of sixteen days more than five thousand millions of its kind; and in twenty generations aphides unchecked would cover every green thing on the earth. These minute insects may not be understood; they are called pests; but in the economy of nature they have their mission.

If we enter the mechanic's shop or factory, where there are many tools and complicated machinery, and look about us over all these implements, we perceive that they are all of some use, and each has a purpose peculiar to itself; all work together in harmony toward an end, however conflicting it may seem to us. We do not think for a moment that any one of these implements has been constructed without some special use, nor that any one thing has been made intentionally defective, much less for evil. Thus it is in nature, "all are but parts of one stupendous whole," in which there is unity of design, all working toward some ultimate end beyond our sight and comprehension.

Wonderful as are the animal and plant worlds, none impress us more than the insect world. We are told that the wasps drove armies from the battle-fields of Palestine: "I sent the hornet before you which drove them out before you, even the two kings of the Amorites; but not with thy sword nor thy bow." A king besieging a city in the East with his army of elephants and men was driven from his siege by gnats so small as scarcely to be visible to the naked eye, and yet they were more powerful than elephants and men. In the war of the great rebellion armies met and contended in awful conflict. There were wasps and hornets enough in the "Wilderness" of Virginia to have driven both Grant and Lee out if they had been concentrated. Vast countries have been swept by locusts as by a "maddened holocaust of fiery vengeance." The sun has sometimes been obscured by them. From authoritative reports we are informed that one season in the Rocky Mountains locusts numbering, it was supposed, more than two hundred and fifty thousand millions passed over a given area in six hours. Of course they were not counted, but estimated. Imagine such a current sweeping on for several days! What wonder that in the olden times "the grasshopper was a burden."

The insect world is a great study. We span our streams with our suspension-bridges, and call the world's attention to these giant works which we have wrought; and they are very great. But does it ever occur to us that we are really surpassed by the little spider in both calculation and perfection. The body of every spider contains four little masses pierced with a multitude of imperceptible holes, each hole permitting the passage of a single thread. All the threads to the amount of a thousand to each mass join together when they come out and make the single thread with which the spider spins its web; so that what we call a spider's thread consists of more than four thousand strands united. Leuwenhoek, by means of the microscope, observed spiders, no larger than a grain of sand, which spun threads so fine that it took four thousand of them to equal the size of a single hair.

This world of ours is full of wonders; the microscope reveals them as fully as the telescope. We have been studying for ages how to fly through the air by means of air-ships or balloons, and yet the insect we crush with contempt has spun its diving-bell and descended to the bottom of the stream, or made its little balloon and sailed away through the air with safety and delight, gathering up its parachute and descending at its own will. Wonders, did I say? Nature is full of them. There are four thousand and forty-one muscles in a common caterpillar. Hooke discovered fourteen thousand mirrors in the eye of a drone; and to effect the respiration of a carp thirteen thousand three hundred arteries, veins, and bones are necessary.

We have our schools of art and science, from which our children are graduated with honor after years of pupilage. But not one of these can be called scholarly who has not attended the school of nature and learned from insects and animals, often despised, the highest wisdom.

Long ago the patriarch of Uz counseled his friends to learn of the beasts, the earth, and the fishes. We often close our eyes against light of the greatest brilliancy by neglecting this great field of instruction.

There is a little insect known as the *Teredo navales*, of the family *Pholadidæ*, which is sometimes also called the "ship-worm," because it perforates and lives in timber. Its ravages are often terrible. It swarms in the seas in some regions of the globe, and but for the copper sheathing on vessels their destruction would be speedy and certain. In 1731 it was discovered that these little shell-fish had so riddled the timbers composing the dykes which protect Holland from the sea that the whole country was threatened with inundation.

Man has learned much even from insects; to a hint from one of them—the teredo—was due the invention of a machine by which was accomplished one of the most wonderful works of modern times—the excavation of the great tunnel under the Thames in England. Brunel, the celebrated engineer, was standing one day, nearly a century ago, in a ship-yard, it is said, watching incidentally the movements of this destructive insect, the *Teredo navales*, when a brilliant thought occurred to him. He saw that this creature bored its way into the wood by means of a very extraordinary mechanical contrivance. Studying it thoughtfully, he found that it was covered in front by a pair of valvular shells; that with its foot as a purchase it communicated a rotary motion and a forward impulse to the valves, which, acting upon the wood like a gimlet, penetrated its substance, and that as the particles of wood were loosened they passed through a fissure in the foot and thence through the body of the borer to its mouth, where they were expelled. The famous boring-shield of Brunel was thus but an imitation, with some variations, of an insect almost microscopic.

We are forced sometimes to seek the destruction of insects precisely as we protect ourselves against storms and winds. But we should never wantonly kill any thing which the Infinite has seen fit to create. We cannot and ought not to annihilate any one family or species of insect unless we become wiser than the wisdom of nature. We should not invade their domain destructively without knowing what we are doing. We may kill friends supposing they are enemies. The religion of Buddha forbade killing the smallest insect, as to destroy it would be to invade the government of the Creator—a sublime and wise idea.

Insects are often enemies to each other—prey on each other, and so accomplish good even to man. It may be said to be the mission of the insect world to check the current of life and growth in nature. If it were not for their agency we can hardly tell what the fate of the world would be. And furthermore, they are ever-busy scavengers, and though they may annoy us by insinuating themselves into our dwellings, feeding on our crops and our clothing, sometimes destroying them in whole or in part, let us not forget that He who planned the world and all things included in that plan the beings we call "pests." Only when we are certain that they are doing us harm are we warranted in destroying them.

"When all the motions of the heavenly bodies have been reduced to the dominion of gravitation gravitation itself still remains an insolvable problem. Why it is that matter attracts matter we do not know; we perhaps never will know. Science can throw much light upon the laws that preside over the development of life; but what life is, and what is its ultimate cause, we are utterly unable to say. The mind of man, which can track the course of the comet and measure the velocity of light, has hitherto proved incapable of explaining the existence of the minutest insect or the growth of the most humble plant. In grouping phenomena, ascertaining their sequences and their analogies, its achievements have been marvelous; in discovering ultimate causes it has absolutely failed. An impenetrable mystery lies at the root of every existing thing. The first principle, the dynamic force, the vivifying power, the efficient causes of those successions which we term natural laws, elude the utmost efforts of our research. The scalpel of the anatomist and the analysis of the chemist are here at fault. The microscope, which reveals the traces of an all-pervading, all-ordaining intelligence in the minutest globule, and displays a world of organized and loving beings in a grain of dust, supplies no solution of the problem. We know nothing, or next to nothing, of the relations of mind to matter, either in our own persons or in the world that is around us; and to suppose that the progress of natural science eliminates the conception of a first cause from creation by supplying natural explanations is completely to ignore the sphere and limits to which it is confined." *

* W. E. H. Leckey, M. A.

CHAPTER XII.

DEATH.

HAVING spoken of that undefinable and mysterious something we call life, let us now consider that other equally undefinable and mysterious something we call death. In all the lower forms of living beings death is simply the antithesis of life; for there is no pledge or sign of any existence to a mere animal beyond the moment of its dissolution. The Bible says that the "Spirit of the beast . . . goeth downward toward the earth." This can only refer to its physical death. With man also death is the antithesis of life so far as the body is concerned. But in his creation a higher gift was bestowed, a principle was "breathed into him" which differentiates him almost infinitely from all other terrestrial beings. "The spirit of a man . . . goeth upward." In the one case it is extinction; in the other it is the "change that cometh."

For ages mankind believed that human sin was the cause of universal death, that of animals as well as of men; for had it not been written, "Death came by sin?" This idea obtained its first hold, like some others, in an unscientific age, an age of too severe an interpretation of Scripture.

The curse pronounced in Eden was taken in a literal rendering: "And the Lord said unto the serpent, Because thou hast done this, thou art cursed above all cattle, and above every beast of the field; upon thy belly shalt thou go, and dust shalt thou eat all the days of thy life." To Adam he said: "Cursed is the ground for thy sake; in sorrow shalt thou eat of it all the days of thy life; thorns also and thistles shall it bring forth to thee; and thou shalt eat the herb of the field: in the sweat of thy face shalt thou eat bread, till thou return unto the ground; for out of it wast thou taken: for dust thou art, and unto dust shalt thou return." The serpent is here doomed, not as a serpent simply, but as the representative of Satan, the enemy of God and man.

If Satan entered into a single serpent and used it for a bad purpose why should punishment be sent upon the whole serpent race for the misfortune of one of the species? No, let us not misjudge God by reading an allegory as literal history. As elsewhere in this book shown, the serpent has always crawled on its belly. One writer on Darwinism tells us that "serpents were once four-legged animals that moved about like lizards; but through changes of habit they came to other and lower needs, so that their legs were no longer useful, and so shrunk away. They remain to show us how the species has been degraded from higher forms in the past." This theory rather supports the Bible account of Eve and the serpent. Possibly the intention was, if Darwinism be true, that these embryo legs were to "develop" in the long ages to come "by change of habit," and the serpent become a walking animal; but the curse of God doomed the whole race of serpents to their present mode of locomotion. Nay, the curse was not on the dumb animal, but on the evil one it personated. The lesson is that sin must be cast down and out and righteousness must reign on the earth.

Again we read : " Let the earth bring forth grass, the herb yielding seed, . . . whose seed is in itself, upon the earth : and it was so." The earth has brought forth herbs, thorns, weeds, thistles, from the beginning. It is according to God's plan in the creation that vegetable life should precede and sustain animal life. The plant, tree, shrub, grass, should grow out of the soil, assimilating to themselves earthy matter and thus become food for the animal. Besides, the plant not only does this, but it sucks the carbon from the atmosphere which enters into its own nature and life. What then has ever been the mission of weeds, thorns, thistles? To prepare the earth for animal life, to fit the atmosphere for animal lungs; and to-day the noxious weeds we so much despise and labor so hard to exterminate serve the greatest purpose by their office, drawing the carbon out of the atmosphere, where, if it becomes too abundant, it is injurious to animal life, and putting it into the soil to enrich it and thus add to the earth's fertility. But in what sense was this a curse? We answer, That which was no cause of vexation to the spirit of man in his purity becomes an aggravation to him after his alienation.

To forfeit the life of God in the soul by an act of transgression is to break relations with every thing. Is it not so to-day? The heart that is trustful and obedient to the commands of God will bear with far more sweetness of spirit the ills of life so common to all men. The change, therefore, was a relative one; the labor which was delightful before became irksome afterward.

Death is just as much a law of our being as life. All life implies death; it is only another birth. Every plant must die; every animal organism must dissolve; it is a law of the universe which holds good everywhere.

> "Life evermore is fed by death,
> In ocean, earth, and sky;
> And that a rose may breathe its breath
> Something must die."

Death is, then, a wise provision of God. But for death there could be no life. As has been shown before, the vegetable dies to support the life of the animal. Animals feed on one another in an endless chain of succession. The very soil of our garden was once pregnant with life. Organized beings have filled the earth, the air, the seas. Death's dominions crown those of life. Cycles and circles characterize all of the works of nature. Life and death, growth and decay, are in perfect harmony with the progressive works of that operative wisdom which governs the universe. All life and all growth would superinduce universal ruin. These are the fundamental laws of nature, and they are above the control of human power. Man comes under the same law. His days are "swifter than a weaver's shuttle." We call this a figure of speech to indicate the shortness of life compared with eternal ages.

But why should man die? There is no scientific reason for death; it rests on the plan, the purpose, and the power of God. Animals die because they are created to fill a mission in this world only. That man dies is because God wills it. Translation from this life to that which is to come without death was as possible to every man as it was to Enoch and Elijah. The sources of supply which perpetuate the bodily organs, renewing them once in seven years or less, do not become exhausted. There is just as much oxygen, lime, phosphorus, iron, etc., now as there ever was, out of which to build up tissues and preserve the physical human organization. The air is naturally as pure, the food as nutritive, the vital force in nature as abundant, and the supplies as ample as they were ages ago. Life is the same. The man of eighty years has the same consciousness, the same identity, he has always had. He can call up the thoughts and sayings and the forms and faces of his young childhood perfectly. Why may he not live on forever physically? There is only one answer—it is not God's will that he should do so. God does some things by what seems to us to be arbitrary will-power; he wills things for reasons which are only known to himself, but which may yet be revealed to us. It is well that he orders our lives and governs them by a wise providence. But other things are done by laws which he set in operation and which move on in the same line of action forever.

"Dust thou art, and unto dust shalt thou return," was said of man, but might have been said of every mere beast that walked the earth; for all of them are born to die, all turn to dust. Life unchecked would prove universal ruin. It carries an infinite power in its sway and requires the Infinite to arrest and control it, or turn it in a countervailing line in what we call death, which is but a conservative law or line of life itself. Every earthly being in its time must cease to live, and, as ways and means are essential to life and growth, so by the same devising wisdom ways and means of death and decay must be provided by agencies adapted to that end. In man's case there was a meaning in the decree of death that could not attach to mere animals, for hope of immortality stirred his heart, and so the word death meant more to him. But what is death? It is answered, Disorganization, disintegration, separation of soul and body, abatement of the life-force. The machine wears out. The time comes when the bones harden; the muscles become stiff; the cartilages turn to bone, and the soft membranes are converted into cartilage. The stomach ceases to digest food; the whole fabric refuses to obey the mandates of the will, and the "silver cord is loosed; the golden bowl is broken; the pitcher is broken at the fountain, the wheel broken at the cistern." We call it death.

There are some fictions in the world, but there are many more facts; and these are the things that are very certain. "It is appointed unto man once to die." Who doubts this? Sixty human beings cease to breathe every minute, and pass through the gates to the "undiscovered country;" three thousand six hundred every hour; eighty-seven thousand every revolution of the earth. Within the circle of a year possibly thirty-four or thirty-five millions return to dust.

Nothing is more certain than death. Furthermore, life, especially active, productive life, is very brief, though it may be prolonged "threescore and ten years," or even "fourscore years" or more.

The real work of life must be crowded into a very short period. From seventy years subtract seven for almost unconscious childhood; then take off ten more for the period of adolescence. Nature claims one third of our time for sleep; think of a well man lying in bed for a quarter of a century in a state of unconsciousness! And yet every man of seventy-five years has done this if he has not cheated Nature out of her dues. Now it results that our life-work must be done in about thirty-five years of daylight at most. There is certainly not much time for idleness in view of all these considerations.

We are under the control of a Supreme Power. Atheism says "No God"—only a "fortuitous concurrence of atoms"—only molecules which have combined in multitudinous and mysterious ways, and from these have come all things—trees, flowers, landscapes, cyclones, electricity, oceans, stars, planets, man. "Only atoms, that is all," shouts the atheist.

Well, if these molecules can combine and produce such wonderful and powerful entities as have been named they may possibly have formed some other things as well—a heaven for the righteous, a hell for the wicked. Which, let me ask, is preferable, God or molecules?

The death of the body is not the extinction of the man. That which is so universal as belief in the hereafter must have a real foundation in the "nature of things." No machine is made to destroy itself, though it may seem to wear out or rust out. Daniel Webster said: "It cannot be constitutional to destroy the constitution." Man's immortality is really not a question of dispute among intelligent people. In nature there is a change, but not destruction. Chicago burned, but not an atom of the matter in the vast acreages of its solid masonry was destroyed. Men die and turn to dust, but life flows on. This wonderful life-force of which we have been speaking seems to be destroyed by death; but is it? Vegetation decays, plants, trees, die; but by a law of nature they live in other plants and trees, that spring from the earth and air enriched by their decay. "Except a corn of wheat fall into the ground and die, it bideth alone; but if it die, it bringeth forth much fruit." Animals die; what becomes of their extinct life?

We do not wonder much that some have at least asked if there may not be some life-sphere which absorbs the vast aggregate of animal life. "There are more things in heaven and earth than are dreamed of in our philosophy." But man is conscious ever of his superiority; in him are intimations of the hereafter, while revelation assures him of a beyond where there will be no death.

We are informed by those who profess to know that the average length of human life is on the gain throughout the whole world, owing, it is presumable, to the "modern improvements" of civilized life. One cause of this lengthening doubtless lies in the more perfect understanding of the laws of life. Our city houses are better supplied with fresh air than formerly. Modern-built cities are not so compact as those of the olden times. Men have seen the advantages of parks and boulevards, where on foot or in vehicle the fresh, sweet air of heaven can be reached. There is nothing so health-giving as oxygen, by which is meant simply fresh air; and besides there is nothing so cheap. Our earth is surrounded with it to a depth of forty or fifty miles. We all live at the bottom of this air sea; and yet it is often excluded from our school-rooms, public halls, and churches. The latter have been constructed generally without any reference to ventilation. We have heard of an architect who, though he had planned thirty church edifices, admitted that he knew nothing about the laws of ventilation; he studied on space and lines of beauty.

We almost studiously shut out this life-giving and invigorating element, go to sleep, and then charge it over to the account of the "dull sermon." Is it any wonder that sermons are sometimes dull?

The devil and the architects have conspired together to destroy Christianity by depriving the worshipers of fresh air; and that they have not entirely succeeded is only another proof of its divinity. An ingenious writer, speaking of this element, oxygen, tells us that as there are fifteen pounds weight on every square inch of the earth's surface it follows that there are three pounds of oxygen to the same area, and by a mathematical calculation it therefore is seen that the amount of oxygen in the earth's atmosphere would be represented by these figures: 1,178,158,-000,000,000,000 tons. And yet with all this abundance of pure oxygen in the air we often arrange our houses so as to exclude it as much as possible and breathe a mixture of carbonic acid gas in its stead. Often, in summer-time even, the windows are kept closed, blinds are shut, heavy curtains are drawn, lest the pure sunlight should chance to fall on the velvet carpet and change its colors a little, or lest some dust should settle on the furniture, or a few insects should find their way to the walls, or the delicate articles of virtu should be marred; but in the exclusion of these the much-needed air is also shut out.

Our city parks are really ventilating apertures in the brick walls, and in this particular modern cities surpass those of former centuries. But even some of these modern improvements are only a re-appearance of ancient methods; some arts have been lost and found again. God has not only given us a good supply of oxygen, but he gave some directions about its use in ancient times. We are informed that in the divine allotment of the cities of Israel a provision was specifically made in the forty-eight cities of the Levites for a circle of open ground surrounding each city of a thousand cubits breadth, which was intended, probably, for gardens and fruits, and also an exterior circle of two thousand cubits more, called the "field of the suburbs," for pasture, and most likely for recreation, both forming a large space which was expressly forbidden to be encroached upon in any sale of dwellings or alienation of property.

"But the field of the suburbs of their cities may not be sold; for it is their perpetual possession."* Thus, for a people in that age, and a pastoral people at that, to have had such directions given them shows that the great Father had respect to the value of pure air and out-door recreation among his people.

One cause, we think, of a great amount of ill-health, among American women especially, lies in a custom which in some way ought to be abolished. Women attend church in very large numbers relatively, and they go there as a rule well protected from the severe cold of winter, the temperature, possibly,

* Lev. xxv, 34.

not infrequently, near or below zero. They take their seats robed in heavy outside garments—shawl or cloak, bonnet, etc. The service lasts an hour and a half, in a close atmosphere, where the temperature varies from seventy to eighty degrees. Then, when the service is over, they return home through this wintry atmosphere, and often a severe cold is the result. Is it any wonder? Men do the same thing, only that a man can lay aside his overcoat and hat during service and can put them on again when it is ended. If any woman in the world can inaugurate a reform in this she will deserve public thanks.

We do not expect to reach the patriarchal age, nor is it desirable to do so; but it is possible to increase somewhat the average length of human life beyond what it is at present.

It is our duty to live as long as we can; for we are responsible for our bodies and for their proper care. Every habit that abridges life, every neglect of our physical being, whether from overwork, underwork, food or drink, involves a measure of accountability. We should see to it that we do not sin against our bodies, which St. Paul declares are the "temples of the Holy Ghost." What that great apostle once said to the Philippian jailer who was about to kill himself —"Do thyself no harm"—should be the regular and daily rule of every one's life. To the present, not less than the future, the words of the great Teacher have a significant application: "I am come that ye might have life, and have it more abundantly."

General intelligence in a community operates in many ways in behalf of prolonging life. In the first place, while mere intellectual development does not redeem the heart from sin, yet intellectual pursuits do favor morality and virtue, the want of which by leading to fatal indulgences, sends many to untimely graves. Intelligence favors general longevity by making people better acquainted with the laws of life; and, furthermore, education furnishes the race with a knowledge of the various remedies which experience and skill have brought to light for the relief of human woe. Especially is this true in the department of surgery, where science can almost construct new organs.

The value of statistics lies in the fact that "figures do not lie." A celebrated Belgian philosopher some time ago gave the subject a very careful review. He compared England and the Mexican State, Guanajuato, as representing the two extremes in the scale of civilization. In England he reckons one death in fifty-eight inhabitants; in the Mexican State one in nineteen inhabitants, being three times as numerous in one as in the other in proportion. Life insurance tables tell the same story; mortality among the poor and uneducated is greater than among the opposite grade, where the average age of the well-to-do is forty-two years, that of the poor being only thirty years. A recent German writer has made some curious explorations in the great field of human longevity, and has given special attention to life as influenced by the learned professions, and comes to the conclusion that of all the various pursuits of mankind that of the clerical profession is most conducive to a "green old age." According to this writer, of one hundred clergymen forty-two lived to be seventy years old and upward; in one hundred lawyers only twenty-nine reached that age; and in one hundred artists only twenty-eight reached threescore and ten years; while in the same number of physicians only twenty-four reached that point.

With the advancing civilization of this age the rate of mortality proportionately decreases. In the seventeenth century the annual death record in London rose to twenty-one thousand. One hundred years later, though there was a great increase in the population, the number was but seventeen thousand. In the middle of the last century the yearly mortality was one in twenty; now it is only one in forty, having diminished fifty per cent. Similar interesting results are reached if we contemplate men in their different social positions.

Of ten thousand persons in agricultural districts in England, where education was more universal, three thousand three hundred and fifty-three attained the age of forty years; while of an equal number in manufacturing sections only nineteen hundred lived to that age. A comparison in France between sixteen hundred persons in high stations in life with two thousand in a section of Paris containing rag-men, street-sweepers, and day laborers showed a mortality twice as great among the latter as among the former.

The tables of mortality show us some curious facts, as, for instance, that out of every one thousand men twenty die annually; that the inhabitants of a city are renewed once in about thirty-five years; that the number of old men who die in cold weather is to the number of those who die in warm weather as seven to five.

Only one in one hundred reaches the age of sixty; only one in five hundred lives to be eighty years old.

The men able to bear arms form twenty-five per cent. of the inhabitants of a country. The proportion of the deaths of women and those of men is as one hundred to one hundred and eight. The probable duration or expectancy of a woman's life is sixty years; but after that period the calculation is more favorable to women than to men. One quarter of all who are born die under seven years. Not more than one in nine thousand reaches one hundred years. Tall people live longer than short ones, and men live longer in elevated regions of the globe than they do in low, flat countries. Married people live longer than single ones.

Under all the circumstances incident to even an attempted enumeration of populations among civilized nations, we cannot imagine how figures even approximating exactness could be obtained; and yet it is stated by the statisticians, with seeming authority, that the annual deaths amount to 35,693,350, and that the births are many millions in excess of these, one writer placing the excess at over 300,000,000, which is only a vague estimate. The population of the earth is increasing, notwithstanding pestilences, famines, wars, and other limitations of life. We can easily see that at no vastly remote period the earth will be filled; and if by any sanitary means the average age can be increased the sooner will the whole earth be inhabited. Had all men attained to the age of Methuselah there would not to-day be standing-room for any of us, and life would be a curse rather than a blessing.

CHAPTER XIII.

LONGEVITY—THE PATRIARCHS.

THE Bible gives an account of a class of men who are said to have attained to a very great age, varying, indeed, from three hundred and sixty-five years to nine hundred and sixty-nine years. When we speak of our "oldest inhabitant" we mean some one who has lived ninety or a hundred years; but when the antediluvian talked about his "oldest inhabitant" he referred to somebody whose life had spanned nearly a thousand years. As a matter of course, such a startling record could not pass unchallenged, for the people of modern times have no experience in such an enormous length of life.

It would not seem unreasonable, however, to suppose that when the human race was in its infancy and the earth was to be peopled that a longer average life among men would be providentially provided for, precisely as some other things were intelligently arranged. Science tells us that there was a time when carbonic acid, in the form of an invisible gas, was so abundant in the atmosphere of the earth that an air-breathing animal could not have lived, but that in the course of time this superabundance of the poisonous element was removed and put into other forms, such as coal and limestone, etc., which to-day are used by mankind in their various industries, and without which the world would suffer. That there was plan in all this who can doubt? This is but one of a thousand instances of design manifested in the affairs of this world. Could not the "All Father" regulate the life of man as easily as the conditions of matter? There was plan in the one, why not in the other? We must not rule God out of his own dominions as some people are trying to do.

It is true that life was more simple, less artificial, then than now; and some have thought this to be the reason of the longer lives of the patriarchs; but this will not account for it. If they lived as long as our English Bible declares it was because of a divine arrangement for a purpose in the order of things. But the time came when it was better for the world that the term of human life should be reduced; what secondary causes were employed to effect the change we do not know—only the fact. Between Adam and Moses there are three distinct periods in the length of human life; first, that from Adam to Noah, in which the shortest in the Bible record is that of Enoch, who died young, having only attained the age of three hundred and sixty-five years, and Methuselah, whose earthly existence extended through almost a millennium. The second period was that immediately following the flood—from Shem to Terah—in which the life-time dropped down on the average to three hundred and fifty years below that of the antediluvians. Shem lived six hundred years, Arphaxad four hundred and thirty-eight years, Serug only two hundred and thirty years. In the third period, beginning with Abraham, the length of human life was yet further diminished. Abraham lived to be one hundred and seventy-five years old, his son Isaac one hundred and eighty years old, Moses one hundred and twenty years.

Over this question of patriarchal longevity there has been a great amount of discussion, not only among theologians, but by men of the highest scientific attainment. Two notable English names may be mentioned, Professor Owen and E. Harrold Brown, D.D., Bishop of Ely. The former enters his protest against the belief in the extreme longevity of the antediluvians contained in the book of Genesis, while the latter takes the ground that it is not only within reason, but that some very eminent physiologists have thought it not at all impossible. Professor Owen proceeds in his way to demonstrate the utter impossibility of any individual of the human species ever having lived to such a fabulous age. He calls the belief a superstition, and scorns the idea that these men lived beyond the average of "threescore years and ten," or, at most, a decade or two beyond. Then there came to the front Professor Erasmus Rask, of Copenhagen, who claims to have solved the whole theory by a new construction of the word rendered in our Englsh Bible *year*. The root of the Hebrew word really means repetition, or iteration, and may signify any recurring period, day, week, month, or year; hence, instead of solar we are to understand lunar years—that is, months.

His argument attempts to show that these ancient men were not sufficiently versed in astronomical science to be able to compute accurately the year of three hundred and sixty-five days, and thus inaugurate that period as the unit for measuring time, while he claims they could more easily determine the period of the moon's orbital rotation. And so the professor thinks we may, without fear of maltreating the text, consider these so-called years as months.

It is not necessary to deal with the whole line of these long-lived men; let us take Methuselah, the oldest one of the group, as an illustration. So we read, "And Methuselah lived a hundred eighty and seven years, and begat Lamech: and Methuselah lived after he begat Lamech seven hundred eighty and two years, and begat sons and daughters: and all the days of Methuselah were nine hundred sixty and nine years: and he died."*

The word *year*, we are told, does not mean a solar year of three hundred and sixty-five days, but a lunar year—a *month*, or two or more months, for some of the ancient people did reckon time in this way. When we consider the age at which this patriarch died this may seem reasonable. Methuselah lived nine hundred and sixty-nine months, or about eighty years and nine months, and died. He was just about the age of Homer, not quite so old as Dr. Franklin, who lived to be eighty-four years old. By this method of reckoning Adam died at seventy-seven years and six months, Noah at seventy-nine years and two months. Enoch only lived thirty years and five months, when "God took him." This mode of calculation makes the average life-term of the ten patriarchs from Adam to Noah just seventy-three years less one month. But there is another side to it: if by "years" was meant *months* when men died, it must have meant the same when they were born. Then Methuselah lived one hundred and eighty-seven months—fifteen years and seven months—"and be-

* Gen. v, 25-27.

gat Lamech." This only plunges us into deeper and muddier waters. In the case of Enoch, the youngest of these antediluvian patriarchs, the waters are still deeper and muddier, for he was only sixty-five months —five years and five months—old when he begat Methuselah. Various devices have been employed to escape these difficulties. One is by subtracting (on the ground of some errors having crept in through transcribers or translators) from the ages years or months after the birth of the first son and adding the same to the period before such birth, all the while preserving the total number of years which the patriarchs lived. Another is to make the year consist of two, three, four, or even six months, according to the exigencies of the case. It may be that the ancient Egyptians did reckon by months and not by our years, as we are informed by Eudoxus, a disciple of Plato, and also by Diodorus and Plutarch; but to apply this to the scriptural account of the antediluvians involves us in more and more confusion. There are some arguments along this line which have considerable force, we admit. Professor Rask has displayed much ingenuity, to say the least; but the difficulties, on the other hand, are great, and so we prefer to accept the statements as they appear in the sacred writings. It involves less confusion and was not impossible.

In the human species brevity of life is contemplated with feelings of regret; and yet its limitation, within a certain degree, is one of the most powerful factors in the world's progress.

The human mind has its law of growth; the philosophy and opinions which govern the conduct of men continue to be modified and molded until about mid-life, when the character becomes practically unchangeable; opinions grow into prejudices, and the whole mind is in a sense petrified. Then further progress would be impossible but for the fact that another generation, with minds still plastic, comes forward, takes up and carries on the work, and it in turn becomes petrified in the same way. There are certainly some noble exceptions to this rule, instances of minds which with their maturity retain the plasticity of youth, but the very rarity of the exception proves the rule. There is a class in almost every community who are opposed to progress in all directions—half a dozen funerals often lift a whole community out of its ruts.

The account of the patriarchal longevity is disbelieved by many because it does not come within the range of modern experience. But this is not a proper ground of objection. Perhaps the critics are right; but are there not some other things that fall outside of our experience? We shall see as we proceed.

It is a law of nature that all organized bodies shall be dissolved sooner or later. It is said of the patriarch Methuselah, "and he died also." It matters not whether it be a tree, insect, animal, or man, life may be protracted to never so great a length, but dissolution will come. The term longevity is used to express the organized life—duration of any thing. Any *ephemera*, for instance—an insect which comes slowly to its maturity and survives but a day or possibly an hour—has its longevity as surely as the eagle, the swan, or even man. The difference between the age of an animalcule whose life spans a day only and that of the patriarch Methuselah would not be greater than the difference of size between the animalcule and the long-lived patriarch, so that the one is as possible as the other. Length of life is variable, as it depends on conditions which may change: and, besides, what is very long to one being would be very short to another. At longest human life is brief: "As a flower of the field, so he flourisheth."

When we remember that so large a percentage of the human family die in childhood there does seem to be something at fault in our manner of life. God may permit this, but is it his plan?

None are to be envied whose lives are prolonged to an age when all the faculties are eclipsed, nor should they be considered " favorites of nature." The average man does not reach the full maturity of his mental powers until about mid-life; give him then thirty or thirty-five years at most and his work is done. With a few exceptions those who survive much beyond this do not *live;* they merely exist; the intellectual enjoyments and exertions which constitute the chief dignity and happiness of life are gone.

It is very remarkable to what great ages living organisms, both vegetable and animal, do attain sometimes. An ivy has been known to reach the age of four hundred and fifty years, palms and olives seven hundred years, cedars eight hundred years, the oak from one thousand to fifteen hundred years.

Trees have been found in Africa which were computed to be four or five thousand years old. The oldest tree, if not the oldest living thing upon the earth, is the famous cypress of Santa Maria del Tule in the Mexican State of Oajaca. The life of this venerable tree has spanned the whole of written history. It was seen by Humboldt in 1851, when it measured 42 feet in diameter, 126 feet in circumference, and 382 feet between the extremities of two branches. At last account it was still growing, though feebly. The animalcule runs through its whole life-period in about forty-eight hours at most; were it to live a week, which, for aught we know, it may sometimes have done, it would be the Methuselah of its species.

A sea-anemone has been known to attain the age of seventy years. Fishes are proverbially long-lived. In ancient Rome gentlemen's fish-ponds were often known to contain lampreys that were half a century old. Count Buffon, the great naturalist, informs us that he had seen carp whose ages were one hundred and fifty years, perfectly well attested; he even mentions one which he supposed to be two hundred years old.

Two methods have been devised for ascertaining the age of fishes, namely, by circles of the scales and by a transverse section of the backbone. When the scale of a fish is examined under a microscope it is found to consist of a number of circles, one within another, resembling in some measure the rings that appear on the transverse section of trees, by which their ages are computed. In the same manner the age of a fish may be ascertained by the number of circles on its scales, reckoning for each ring a year in its life.

Crows are said to have lived a century; the elephant from one to two centuries, camels half a century. In proportion to their size, birds are much longer lived than either men or quadrupeds. Among birds the swan is one of the longest lived; it has been known to live for half a century, and sometimes longer. A goose has been known to live fourscore years. In France, the raven, known to be a long-lived bird, is said to have attained the age of nearly a century. A pelican that was kept at Mechlin, in Brabant, during the reign of the Emperor Maximilian, attained the age of eighty years.

While habits of life and other conditions affect the averages in the matter of longevity, the individual life is not always influenced by these. Among civilized and savage, rich and poor, masters and slaves, there have been some individuals who have lived to extreme old age. Luxury and intemperance in the use of alcoholic drinks are known to be the greatest enemies of the race, and do most to shorten the life of mankind. The mountains of Scotland, Wales, Switzerland, and America have furnished more examples of extreme old age than the plains of Holland, Germany, or Poland.

In all ages and in all lands there have been instances of great longevity. Pliny, in his natural history, tells us that "the year A. D. 76, falling into the time of Vespasian, is memorable, in which we shall find as it were a calendar of long-lived men; for that year there was a taxing (now a taxing is the most authentical and truest informer touching the ages of men), and in that part of Italy which lieth between the Apennine Mountains and the river Po there were found one hundred and twenty-four persons that either equaled or exceeded one hundred years of age." He then goes on to give the list: "Of the one hundred and twenty-four persons, fifty-four had attained the age of 100 years; fifty-seven, 110 years; two, 125 years; four, 130 years; four, 135 years; two, 140 years; and one, Marcus Aponius, was 150 years." Pliny wrote of a warm latitude, but in cold climates the conditions are as favorable for long life as in the milder. England has always been noted for its old people.

Colonel Thomas Winslow, a native of Ireland, died on the 22d day of August, 1766, at the age of one hundred and forty-six years. The Countess Desmond, of that same country, reached the age of one hundred and forty-five years. There are many other cases on record, but perhaps the best authenticated of the kind is that of the famous Thomas Parr, of Shropshire. At one hundred and twenty years he married his second wife; when one hundred and thirty he performed his usual work; at one hundred and fifty-two by invitation he visited the king as a living curiosity; nine months afterward he died, and a post-mortem examination made by Dr. Harvey, the discoverer of the circulation of the blood, showed that all the organs of this old man's body were sound. Instances in our own country of very long-lived people, owing to the restlessness of the American character, have not been so numerous; nevertheless, there have been many cases in all the States of individuals who have lived from one hundred to one hundred and fifty years. That of "Old Gabriel," so-called, who died in 1890, at the advanced age of one hundred and fifty years, in California, is in proof of the fact that we as a people are not without our Methuselahs. If we ask, On what does long life depend? the answer must be that in the case of the antediluvian world it was the will of God, exercised for a purpose. It was not a miracle, only as life in itself may be regarded as such. It was simply in accordance with the laws of life at that time, while its abridgment to the present length was also according to the same will.

All life is from God, whether it be that of man, beast, or tree, and is the gift of God. Centenarians have been found among American Indians and Negroes, as well as among the whites.

Manner of life, nature of occupation, and heredity are causes which may be taken into the account; but the man who said that he "owed his long life to the persistency of his vitality" came about as near stating the case as it is possible to do. "It is not according to our experience," say some, "to believe in this Bible story of the patriarchal ages;" but I ask, Is it consistent to accept the statements of scientists and historians implicitly when they tell us of such wonderful things in the natural world, even the great ages of trees, fishes, elephants, ravens, etc., and yet deny that God had power to protract the lives of men so greatly? Human experience cannot be the criterion always.

God's ways are not our ways. He does not intend that we shall destroy ourselves by extravagance in living or by crimes; but he has planned for us so that we may live and enjoy life, whether it be long or short, and faithfully serve him by serving our kind. It is his purpose that we shall put life to the best possible use in our development, and that of others, regarding it as the supreme gift of the Author of all good.

The intimate relation between religion and the care of the body is perceptible in the history of every nation. The higher the civilization and the purer the faith the higher the estimate placed on life. The value which the Bible attaches to the days of a human being is very great. From the beginning to the close of the Scriptures we find a constantly increasing estimate placed upon the very hours of one's stay on earth. With all the importance which Christ attaches to the life to come he does not fail to set forth the present in its true magnitude. When the great Teacher said, "Take no thought for your life, what ye shall eat; neither for the body, what ye shall put on," it is very clear that he refers to undue thought on the necessities which enter into the daily sustenance, as we see from the words which follow: "The life is more than meat, and the body than raiment."

CHAPTER XIV.

NOAH AND THE FLOOD.

TO take up *seriatum* all the statements of facts which lie beyond the reach of our intellections or our experiences and observations would cover more ground than I have at my disposal in this book. I have therefore selected a few of the more prominent, which must be taken as types of all others, on the principle that the greater always includes the less. There are some topics of greater moment and dignity than others, even in the Bible. The account of the creation is greater than the story of Samson; the advent of Christ and the establishment of the Christian religion involve more than the narrative of Jonah. Nothing is unimportant in this book, as in our daily life small things, words, actions are often great in their results, if not in themselves. The point toward which the author has been drifting is to present and explain the wonders of the Bible as far as they can be explained, and to draw the parallel between some of the marvelous things therein contained and the marvelous things outside of it in nature and in human life. We must bear in mind that a miracle is not necessarily a contradiction of any law. It may be above our experience. God's laws are only partially revealed in the natural world; and that which we understand is but trifling in the comparison with what we do not understand.

Let us consider in this chapter the story of the overthrow of the world of mankind by the deluge, an event said to have taken place several thousand years ago. It is not spoken of simply as a great calamity that befell a portion of the earth, but as a visitation of God on the human race. The reason assigned for it was the continued wickedness of mankind. "God saw that the wickedness of man was great in the earth, and that every imagination of the thought of his heart was only evil continually." Nor was it simply a punishment, it was an extermination of all men, save the few persons named who were preserved in an ark. We shall not recount in this place the history as given in the book of Genesis. The reader can easily refresh his memory on the subject, if he desires to do so, by reading the story for himself.

To discredit this history, as some do along with some other events, is to take the ground either that much of the Bible is not to be believed or that God does not in fact exercise any direct personal government over the world, which is equivalent to the espousal of the philosophy of materialism. Every thing in the narration of the flood-story comes within the scope of reason. We are told that in the midst of a race of distinctly evil men there was one family composed of persons who were righteous. "Noah was a just man and perfect in his generation," a man who "walked with God."

That was a reasonable statement. Wicked communities have abounded in all times, and there have generally been some people of uprightness in the most wicked communities. That there was such a flood of waters on the earth, lasting, from the first outpouring of the clouds until the final subsidence, about a year, is related circumstantially. That the waters were abundant for such an inundation we shall see as we progress.

The skeptic takes the position that this whole account is mythical, legendary; that the flood never did occur. He furthermore says that if God is as good as Christians believe and teach he would not resort to so dire an extremity as this; for in sending on the earth such a calamity innocent children, along with wicked men, must have been drowned in the engulfing waters. All of this is true; but is it not equally true that in earthquakes, cyclones, pestilence, etc., the lives of innocent children are often destroyed. And yet it would hardly be in accordance with Christian belief to teach that God sustains no relation to such terrestrial events. God rules in the heavens and earth.

We may plead ignorance, but ignorance is no argument against a fact or the possibility of a fact. How very numerous are the laws in nature which we but poorly understand, and how many the events which startle us, causing us to ask why? There was such a flood of waters, no doubt, and Noah did build an ark "to the saving of his house." On this the Bible is explicit.

It may, however, be remarked right here that a belief in this matter is not of a saving character. A man may honestly think that there is some other explanation and yet be possessed of true spiritual life. But as an historical portion of the Bible, unless it can be shown to be mythical, it should be accepted as a part of Holy Writ.

As a fact, it is one which may well cause reflection.

What an event! The destruction, not of the globe itself, but the overflowing of the earth, in part, and the consequent extermination of the inhabitants of the world. There is no argument to show that it was a universal deluge of the entire globe. The language takes on a form, however, which conveys that idea; but let us study it.

These ancient people knew but very little of the earth as to its size and form. The world to them was just what it seemed to be, what they knew of it. For example, it is said, " The fear of Israel was upon every nation under heaven "—that is, it was upon the inhabitants of Arabia and Mesopotamia, who were afraid of them. The reader will call to mind the expression in the book of the Acts: " Jews were at Jerusalem out of every nation under heaven." Job tells us, " The lightnings flashed over the whole heavens "— that is, they illuminated the whole horizon. In the same way, when we read, " And the waters prevailed exceedingly upon the earth, and all the high hills that were under the whole heavens were covered," it must be understood as telling us that the flow extended over the region occupied by the human family, namely, Assyria, Mesopotamia, Palestine, Arabia, etc., which is all that is required in our belief. A partial deluge, destroying the whole race of man, or even, perhaps, only that race to which the survivors belonged, would meet every requirement. That such a flood was possible, even from natural causes, in those parts of Asia where Noah probably lived, is shown by the fact that the whole of one enormous tract of land is far below the level of the sea, and part of this region of the Caspian Sea exhibits comparatively recent evidences of the action of water. This conclusion has not been reached without much controversy; and it is well said in the new *Speaker's Commentary:*

"The peculiar unfairness of the objections urged is to be found, not so much in the objections themselves as in the insisting at the same time on an interpretation of the scripture narrative on principles which would not be applied to any other history. Not only are we required to expound ancient and Eastern phraseology with the cold exactness applicable only to the tongues of northern Europe, but moreover to adhere to all the interpretations of past uncritical ages, to believe that there was but a single window in the ark, that the ark stranded on the top of a mountain, within sight of which it very probably never sailed, that the waters of the flood rose three, or even five, miles above the sea-level, and other prodigies which the sacred text, even in its most natural significance, nowhere either asserts or implies."

We may not be able to explain how the beasts in pairs belonging to the region came into the ark, nor how they were preserved for so long a time. Neither can any man tell how a chick comes to life in the shell, or how a rose gets its aroma, or how the heart beats, or how a thousand other things that might be named come to pass. But we do know that animal instincts are very wonderful. Their lives are preserved by migrations from one region to another when some danger threatens. They flock in herds and droves in a particular direction from causes which no human wisdom can explain. Wolves and deer have been often known to rush into the villages in mountainous regions to escape forest fires. Who shall say that they did not by instinct seek escape from the coming danger—that the God who formed them and endowed them with their instincts did not guide them?

If it be asked, How could four men build such an ark? it may be answered that other men have done some wonderful things in the way of building.

How were the great pyramids of Egypt built? By what power were the huge rocks reared to such heights? The world to-day cannot answer the question. By what appliances were the great stones, some of which weighed from eight hundred to twelve hundred tons, put in place in Baalbec? Some go even so far as to say that we could not to-day, with what we know of mechanical arts, do this work. With this I do not agree. How did the druids of Celtic times erect the massive blocks at Stonehenge? What powers were employed in the building of the Cyclopean walls in Greece, Italy, and Asia Minor?

What could four men of primitive gigantic strength do in the time allotted for the building of the ark, aided as they may have been in the work? Let us not judge too hastily.

The author visited once the great pyramid of Cholula, in central Mexico; and that it was at one time regular in form can hardly be doubted, though some have thought it to be only a natural hillock faced in places with adobe—a hill converted into a pyramid. It covers at its base almost forty-five acres and originally had an elevation of over two hundred feet. We climbed about its ragged slopes, made ragged by the chafing of the elements during some hundreds of years, and we could there trace the lines of the bricks with the most perfect distinctness. It stands out boldly on a broad plain, in full view of the great mountain Popocatepetl, as if man had tried to imitate God. But what a work it was to erect a structure so vast! And yet no matter which theory is adopted, that it was a natural hill faced with adobe or that it was built wholly of adobe, the work was vast, beside which the building of the ark was a minor task.

It is nowhere said that the four men built the ark alone and unaided. What a man causes to be done he does. Napoleon, we are told, constructed a roadway over the Alps in 1803–10 at an expense of $1,500,000, but he did not do the work himself; it was done by his orders. The ark was not a ship, but a great quadrangular box—a mere float which was about four hundred and fifty feet in length, seventy-five feet wide, and forty-five feet deep, of three stories, made water-tight by pitch or bitumen, in which the country abounded and abounds yet.

This great float, for such it was, had enormous capacity, as any one can see by a little calculation. Allowing nothing for machinery and merchandise, it had a tonnage equal to almost forty thousand tons; it had a greater tonnage capacity than the *Great Eastern*, the largest steam-ship of modern times, which has had a singular history, but for which it is doubtful if the Atlantic cable could have been successfully laid when it was. This monstrous vessel, the *Great Eastern*, was built with facilities to accommodate eight hundred saloon passengers, two thousand second-class passengers, and twelve hundred of the third class; its crew was composed of four hundred officers and men; but these constitute a small part of a ship's freight; the ten boilers, filled, weighed one hundred tons each; the coal-bunkers of the monster craft were made to carry fourteen thousand tons of coal; it also had a capacity for transporting five thousand soldiers, for which it was used. The ark was greater in carrying capacity than the *Great Eastern;* it certainly was equal to all that was required of it. The objection made that the ark was not large enough to accommodate all that was said to have been preserved in it falls to the ground when its size is taken into the account in connection with the limited area over which the flood extended. If it had prevailed over the whole earth literally, and risen above the highest mountains on the globe, the depth in some sections would have been inconceivable. The account says, "And the waters prevailed exceedingly upon the earth, and all the high hills that were under the whole heaven were covered. Fifteen cubits"—that is, twenty-five feet—"upward did the waters prevail; and the mountains were covered,"* which would be an equivalent to a water envelope of about five miles over the whole earth. "With God all things are possible."

Water! what a boon when it bubbles from the mountain spring or rises from the rocks at the well's bottom! What a blessing as it descends in gentle showers on field and garden! What a curse when in awful torrents it sweeps down some valley from bursting dam, laying waste a city! How varied its appearance, now in vapor in the skies and then in great ice-fields solid as the granite rocks, here a thundering Niagara, there a pearly dewdrop in the cup of the flower! What abysses of the deep there are that

* Gen. vii, 18, 19.

almost defy the measuring-line! There is a spot in the Southern Atlantic between Rio de Janeiro and the Cape of Good Hope where the line has been known to run out for nine hours! The bottom was reached at seven thousand seven hundred fathoms, or seven geographical miles.

About nine thousand eight hundred cubic miles of water—nearly one half of the fresh water on the globe—is in the upper lakes. Eighteen millions of cubic feet of water plunge over Niagara Falls every minute of time. But it would require one hundred and fifty-two years for all the waters of these inland seas to make the circuit of the lakes, the falls, the St. Lawrence River, and back from the ocean through vapor and rain into the lakes again.

How much water is there on the earth and in the air that surrounds it? There was a time in the history of our globe when all the waters now on the surface in rivers, lakes, oceans, etc., existed in the form of elemental gases, oxygen, and hydrogen. The atmosphere has a depth of about fifty miles, and contains vast quantities of water in the form of vapor. An ocean is above us continually. "And God made the firmament, and divided the waters which were under the firmament from the waters which were above the firmament."

We know but little of the amount of water in the earth—in the seas, oceans, lakes, rivers, soil, and atmosphere. Three fourths of the earth's surface is water.

"When we watch a gentle summer rain does it ever occur to us that this familiar sight involves the previous expenditure of almost incredible quantities of energy, or do we think of a drizzly day as perhaps calling for a greater exertion of nature's powers than an earthquake? Probably not; but these suppositions are both reasonable. Take Manhattan Island, for instance, which contains twenty square miles, and on which, one year with another, over thirty inches of rain falls. (To be within the mark we call the area twenty miles, and the annual rain-fall thirty inches.) One square mile contains 640 acres, and each acre 43,560 square feet. Multiplying by 640 and dividing by 12, we have 2,323,200 as the number of cubic feet of water on one mile in a rain-fall of one inch; and as a cubic foot of water weighs about 997 ounces avoirdupois, and there are 35,840 ounces to the ton, this weighs 2,323,200 multiplied by 997 divided by 35,840, or, in round numbers, 64,636 tons (to one mile and one inch of rain). As there are twenty miles and thirty inches, the annual rain-fall on this little island is 1,393,290,000 cubic feet, or 38,781,600 tons. The amount of this may be better appreciated by comparison. Thus, the pyramid of Cheops contains less than one hundred million cubic feet, and weighs less than seven million tons, and this water then, in the form of ice, would many times replace the largest pyramids of Egypt. If we had to cart it away it would require 3,231,800 cars carrying twelve tons each to remove it, and these at an average length of thirty feet to the car would make six trains, each reaching in one continuous line of cars across the continent, so that the leading locomotive of each train would be at San Francisco before the rear had left New York—a result which appears at first so incredible that it seems best to give the figures on which we rest the statement." *

* Professor S. P. Langley.

But not only did the clouds pour out their floods from above; "the foundations of the great deep were broken up;" the earth sank most likely in all the regions.

One of the most remarkable facts in the discussion of the deluge is that almost every people on earth have some tradition concerning it. This might be expected in countries visited by missionaries. But it has been found in regions most remote, and where civilization has never set up its banners.

The Polynesians have the following story of the deluge: "Two men had gone out to sea to fish with the line, Roo and Teahoroa by name. They threw their hooks into the sea, which caught in the hair of the god Ruahatu. They exclaimed, 'A fish!' They drew up the line and saw that it was a man they had caught. At sight of the god they bounded to the other end of their bark, and were half dead with fear. Ruahatu asked them, 'What is this?' The two fishermen replied, 'We came to fish, and we did not know that our hooks would catch thee.' The god then said, 'Unfasten my hair;' and they did so. Then Ruahatu asked, 'What are your names?' They replied, 'Roo and Teahoroa.' Ruahatu next said, 'Return to the shore, and tell men that the earth will be covered with water, and all the world will perish. To-morrow morning repair to the isle called Toamarams; it will be a place of safety for you and your children.' Ruahatu caused the sea to cover the lands, and all men perished except Roo, Teahoroa, and their families."

Connected with the great flood of water there is a Mexican tradition, presenting some analogies to the story of Noah and the ark. In most of the printed manuscripts supposed to relate to this event a kind of boat is represented floating over the waste of waters and containing a man and a woman. Even the Tlascaltecs, the Zapotecs, the Miztecs, and the people of Michoacan are said to have had such pictures. The man is variously called Coxcox, Teocipactli, Tezpi, and Nata; the woman, Xochiquetzal and Nena.

The following has been usually accepted as the ordinary Mexican version of this myth: "In Atonatiuh, the Age of Water, a great flood covered all the face of the earth, and the inhabitants thereof were turned into fishes. Only one man and one woman escaped, saving themselves in the hollow trunk of an ahahuete, or bald cypress; the name of the man being Coxcox, and that of his wife Xochiquetzal. On the waters abating a little they grounded their ark on the peak of Colhuacan, the Ararat of Mexico. Here they increased and multiplied, and children began to gather about them—children who were all born dumb. And a dove came and gave them tongues, innumerable languages. Only fifteen of the descendants of Coxcox, who afterward became heads of families, spake the same language, or could at all understand each other; and from these fifteen are descended the Toltecs, the Aztecs, and the Acolhuas." This dove is not the only bird mentioned in these diluvial traditions, and must by no means be confounded with the birds of another palpably Christianized story. For in Michoacan a tradition was preserved, in which the name of the Mexican Noah was Tezpi. "With better fortune than that ascribed to Coxcox he was able to save in a spacious vessel, not only himself and his wife, but also his children, several animals, and a quantity of grain for the common use. When the waters began to subside he sent out a vulture, that it might go to and fro on the earth and bring him word again when the dry land began to appear. But the vulture fed upon the carcasses that were strewn in every part, and never returned. Then Tezpi sent out other birds, and among these was a humming-bird. And when the sun began to cover the earth with a new verdure the humming-bird returned to its old refuge, bearing green leaves. And Tezpi saw that his vessel was aground near the mountain of Colhuacan, and he landed there." *

The old mythologies are filled with the shadowy traditions of a flood, which caused the destruction of well-nigh the whole human race; it has been discovered in the most distant countries and among the most barbarous tribes. Humboldt found in the wilderness that surrounds the Orinoco, among a people whose names were unknown to the civilized world, traditions of a great flood.

"We find," writes the great naturalist, "in all simplicity among nations now in a savage state a tradition which the Greeks embellished with all the charms of imagination." The ancient Brazilians had, too, some notion of a general deluge. The Peruvians reported that many years before there were any Incas all the people were drowned by a flood save six, who were the progenitors of the existing races, who were saved in a float. The original inhabitants of Cuba related that "an old man, knowing that a deluge was to come, built a great ship and went into it with all his family and abundance of animals."

* Bancroft's *Native Races.*

One of the ancient books of the Persians records that "the world having been corrupted by Ahriman, the Evil One, it was thought necessary to bring on a flood of waters, that all impurity might be washed out." And so I might go on through Scandinavia, whose wild fables repeat the same story in some form. The Chinese and Hindus had their tradition of a deluge that "flowed abundantly, and then subsided; but covered for a time the whole earth." But why bring forward any others? The fact that such a tradition should be found in every land is at least strong evidence, not only that mankind have sprung from a common center, and that therefore the race is a unit in its origin, but that such a deluge did occur, stamping the survivors with an impression that time cannot efface. We do not see how such an impression could ever have been made if there was no such flood upon the earth. All must admit that a deluge such as is here described was a possibility. The earth could sink anywhere sufficiently to allow of the submerging of any extent of territory. Many islands are known to be but the abraded summits of mountains that may once have lifted their heads far above the waters. Every part of the earth has been under water at some period or another. If there never was a deluge such as the Bible tells of, yet there have been floods, deluges; water-washed bowlders are seen on the highest regions of the earth. Sea-shells are found far up on the mountains, showing that the seas have prevailed over the earth. Land and water have interchanged many times, and may do so again.

There was a time when the temperature of the earth was equal in all parts, when Greenland and

Siberia were as warm as Florida or Cuba. Remains of tropical animals are found incrusted with ice where they have been held for ages. Upon Mount Katahdin, in the Moosehead region of Maine, bowlders can be seen lying over four thousand feet above the sea-level which contain fossils of the sea. There is one bowlder in Vermont known as the "Green Mountain Giant," which is estimated to weigh thirty-four hundred tons. What was the power which transported from north to south such masses? It was ice, but ice borne forward by a mighty flood of water in some age.

The story of Atlantis may, after all, be more than wild romance. When we look at a terrestrial globe or map it requires no great stretch of imagination to see how the eastern hemisphere may have been torn from the western. The Atlantic Ocean occupies the basin made by the awful cataclysm.

The American continent is the oldest of any geologically, and was peopled in the earliest ages of the world. In the breaking up of which we speak it is easy to see how in some previous age the people of Assyria could find their way to regions in the West, or how the West could have peopled the East. However this all may be, it is evident that some hundreds of years ago there was a great population in the West. Remains exist to-day, and are becoming more and more apparent as the years go by. The mounds all over the South-west, the ruins of more than half a hundred stone-built cities in Yucatan, the wonderful old highways in South America, all point to a great people who once had empire in the Western world.

It is not claimed that the flood of Noah caused this

overthrow; but I wish simply to show that floods have been as great as that described in the Bible; and so to avow one's self a believer in the story of the flood is not a sign of weak credulity.

In view of such startling events as those which have transpired in the history of our world, recorded in the Book of Books, rooted in the traditions of nearly or quite all nations, civilized and barbarous, with evidences of great upheavals and other changes of which signs are in the earth every-where, it seems like presumption for any one to lift his feeble voice and say, "I do not believe." A misty veil may cover the past, but an apocalyptic day will come—"At even it shall be light."

CHAPTER XV.

BOOK WONDERS—SAMSON THE MIGHTY.

THE Bible contains some things which seem to almost any one as belonging in the realm of the impossible—that is, judged of by the present, taking our experience as the test. But let us not forget that our knowledge, even in this scientific age, is quite circumscribed, while our experience reaches through a very short segment of time; so that, after all, statements which seem to be at variance with the truth—such, for instance, as that relating to the strength of Samson—may, after all, be entirely reasonable. This account of the great Israelitish champion is related circumstantially in the book of Judges, and is one at which skeptics sneer, and they are free to call people very credulous who can put faith in such "legendary" and impossible things. Samson was not only a real person, but he was an odd sort of character in history; he was above the average man of his times in some respects, and below him in others. He was one of the judges who ruled over Israel between the times of the death of Joshua and Saul's accession to the throne of Israel. These governors were usually chosen by the people; but Gideon and Samson were appointed by divine authority. The time of these judges was about four hundred and fifty years, and there were in all fifteen of them. At this time the Philistines were dominant over Israel, and Samson was selected to meet a particular emergency.

He was born in answer to prayer, and was a Nazarite of the strictest school. This judge was not a little eccentric; and one of the things he did which was not according to the laws of his people was to choose a wife from among his national enemies. Perhaps it was a species of state-craft or political maneuvering, for in modern times royal families in Europe blend in this way, regarding it as advantageous to the cause of peace, or strength in case of war. He was wise enough to consult his father and mother, however, and thus has set an example to all other young men. Any young man will be the gainer if he will allow his mother to advise him in the selection of a life-partner. On their way to Timnath, where the young lady resided, Samson and his parents in some way became separated for a little time, and during the separation the young man was attacked by a ferocious lion. He was unarmed, having neither spear nor javelin; but the "Spirit of the Lord moved upon him," and he rent the lion as if it had been a kid. Out of this affair was born a curious riddle that involved the hero and his wife in a family feud resulting in a separation for a time without divorce. There has been many another separation in human life between husband and wife with no greater cause. This was followed by the destruction of the corn-fields of his enemies, which was very ingenious, to say the least.

But it is not of these eccentricities and episodes in the life of Judge Samson of which we wish to speak, but rather of that part of his career which recounts his wonderful feats of muscular strength, such as the killing of thirty Philistines and plundering them, to enable him to obtain the wherewith to pay a forfeit; the bursting of the strong cords with which he was bound; the slaughter of a thousand of his enemies with the jaw-bone of an ass; the bearing away on his shoulders at midnight the gates of Gaza, with all their fixtures, and, finally, the overthrow of the temple of Dagon, which crumbled beneath the strength of his grasp. All these are wonderful things, so much so as to excite in some minds a suspicion of their truthfulness. But is not the whole universe full of the most wonderful things? Almost any thing may be a wonder to somebody; the first ship as it appeared to an Indian, the firing of guns and the braying of trumpets, all have excited the greatest wonder in some minds. When the Spaniards invaded Mexico the Aztecs, who had never seen horses, thought that horse and man were one being; they were wonders.

Samson was supernaturally strong, for the record says, "The Spirit of God came upon him;" and God, we know, is omnipotent. "God and one man are a majority." Of the size of this Israelitish wonder we know nothing; he may or may not have been of great physical stature. The Bible gives account in a number of places of a class of men called "giants;" and while the original may signify that they were violent men, rather than large men, it is more likely the latter idea was intended—that is, that they were men of unusual stature. It also says, "There were giants in those days," whose children "became mighty men, which were of old men of renown." From this there have gone out through all ages and nations accounts of giant men. The Anakim were a race of large-sized men, so great in stature as to be regarded as veritable giants. Goliath of Gath, the Philistine, whom the youthful David slew with his sling and a pebble from the brook, was a man of very great size. Taking the scriptural account, and reducing the cubit to modern measure, this champion was ten feet and six inches in height, and had an armor of great weight. His brazen helmet weighed fifteen pounds; his target, or collar, thirty pounds. His spear was twenty-six feet long, and the head of it weighed thirty-eight pounds; his sword weighed four pounds; the metal greaves for the covering of his legs, thirty pounds; his coat of mail, one hundred and thirty-six pounds. The whole weighed two hundred and fifty-three pounds! He must have been a giant to carry all this.

The spies who went out under the direction of Moses to reconnoiter the promised land, to see what it was like, as well as to judge of the strength of its inhabitants, brought back a very disheartening report. They said, "We saw giants, the sons of Anak, which come of the giants; and we were in our own sight as grasshoppers, and so we were in their sight." Most likely their foes were magnified by their fears; Caleb and Joshua were more courageous, and brought back a better account. Og, the king of Bashan, was a real giant; his bedstead was of iron, and according to scriptural measurements was about sixteen feet long and seven wide. If he was three quarters the length of his bed, or two thirds, even, he must have been of enormous stature. His bedstead was carried away after a battle by his enemies, as a curiosity, as well as a trophy of war.

The idea of a remote giant ancestry is somewhat peculiar to mankind; it runs through all nations and must somewhere have had a beginning. Berosus informs us that the ten antediluvian kings of Chaldea were giants. The same claim has been made for the early occupants of the British Isles. It is not at all improbable that in an earlier age of the world, when the habits of mankind were simple and conditions favorable, individuals in larger numbers were of greater strength and size, as well as longer lived than now. And yet from old records, from carvings, and from remains found in very old tombs we cannot think that the human race, as a whole, had averaged much above that of the present in any sense, so that giants were the exceptions. The races vary somewhat, we know. The Esquimaux average about four feet only in height; the Caucasians about five feet nine inches. The Patagonians were regarded in the last century as constituting a race of giants; but they are now known to be men of the ordinary stature. Science, in the sphere of comparative anatomy, has come in to abolish the idea of the human race ever having attained the size in any part of the earth which has been attributed to it by some writers. The giants the Chinese told about, who guarded the gates of their cities, and were said to be fifteen feet high, were evidently manufactured out of the fossil bones of mammoths or some other gigantic quadrupeds of a past age. But giants have existed. There was Gabara, who lived during the reign of Claudius Cæsar, and who was the equal of Goliath of Gath. A Scotchman, whose name was Funniman, and who lived in the times of Eugene II., was over ten feet high. The Emperor

Maximinus, A.D. 235, measured eight feet six inches. If there were giants in Bible times there have been since. The human race is a prolific study from whatever stand-point it is viewed. The giant of to-day is of little use; the world has not had very much use for men of extraordinarily large proportions; brains conquer the world, not muscle.

The average man has a height of about five feet nine, weighs about a hundred and fifty pounds, sleeps eight hours out of the twenty-four, works when he cannot help it, and prefers other men to do his thinking; and yet the average man is the best. So, too, the average intellect is better than precocity, as the average sunlight is better for vegetation than too much of burning heat.

"Some men are born great, some achieve greatness, and others have greatness thrust upon them." A giant in physical size may be feeble-minded and short-lived. A man may be a giant mentally, and yet be diminutive physically. Daniel Lambert, the Englishman, who died in July, 1809, weighed seven hundred and thirty-nine pounds. His coffin was built upon wheels, by which he was rolled into his grave. He was as well known, on account of his enormous size, as any man in England. On the other hand, Alexander Stephens, of Georgia, was so small in stature that it was playfully remarked that "he could cool himself in the shadow of a walking-stick;" but he was a man of magnificent mind.

A Frenchman* wrote a book in 1718 for the purpose of showing that the human race had greatly decreased in stature between the creation and the birth of

---

* M. Henrion, Academician.

Christ. He calculated that Adam was one hundred and twenty-three feet nine inches high; that Eve was only one hundred and eighteen feet. He also argued that the degeneration was very rapid; for Noah was only twenty-seven feet, while Abraham was down to twenty feet, and Moses was but thirteen feet tall. Alexander was misnamed "the Great," for he was but six feet. Julius Cæsar was five feet high. According to this erratic author the Christian dispensation arrested all further decrease. If it had not the human family would have dwindled down to almost microscopic objects by this time.

All the marvelous tales about finding the remains of men whose skulls would hold a bushel, and who were thirty feet high and upward, grew out of the fossil bones found in the earth before the science of geology or paleontology was born. They are now understood, and the enormous giants are no more.

Classical antiquity is peopled with giants, and sad havoc have they played. "Violent contortions of nature, huge spoutings of volcanoes, terrible storms, all of which modern science explains by physical laws, meteorological changes by climatic causes, the vivid imagination of poets and philosophers attributed to the enraged battlings of giants, or their mad revelings against a power more gigantic than their own. Hence, wind-storms were the breathings of some monster who must have possessed a huge mouth. Mount Etna rested on the body of a giant who breathed out fire and smoke at every uneasy toss he made from side to side, or at every dyspeptic belching or qualm his colossal stomach experienced.

"Though the ancients loved to magnify the records

of giants we sometimes are tempted to think that they were drawn in colors highly toned in order to show the great powers of such mortals or heroes as successfully vied with them. Ulysses, the Homeric hero, gets the solitary-eyed, man-eating Polyphemus blind drunk, runs a red-hot firebrand into his visionary organ, and crawls out of his reach beneath his stalwart legs. Nor has time in any way diminished humanity's admiration for giants. Poets have joked them, philosophers theorized, travelers discovered new ones, and a credulous and curiosity-loving public swelled the coffers of the Barnums and showmen who exhibited them. To be more specific, a poet thus describes one whose tastes were piscatorial:

> "'His angle-rod made of a sturdy oak,
> His line a cable that in storms ne'er broke,
> His hook he baited with a dragon's tail
> And sat on a rock as he bobbed for whale.'"

While the Bible makes frequent reference to men of giant size or giant tempers dwarfs have had a poor showing. In one place the law is laid down (Lev. xx, 21) that no dwarf shall offer sacrifices at the altar. In the New Testament Zaccheus was at least a man of small stature, for he climbed into a sycamore-tree that he might obtain a glimpse of the Lord as he passed by. In fabulous times they told of pygmies who were very diminutive. Both Stanley and Du Chaillu tell of very small people found in the equatorial regions of the Dark Continent.

The history of dwarfs, the other extreme, has been scarcely less remarkable than that of giants. The Romans, especially the ladies in high life, kept houses full of them. Julia, the daughter of the

Emperor Augustus, had one named Canopas, who was only two feet high, and another named Andromedia. Her father liked them if they were good-looking, so different from the Spanish court, where they only harbored them as they were hideous, deformed, hump-backed, and ugly. There are pictures by both Raphael and Velasquez, of court scenes, in which their hideous features form some part of the foreground. The wicked Catherine de' Medici, of St. Bartholomew notoriety, whose crimes by poison would fill a volume, and whose treacheries, plots, and schemes many more, had a penchant for little people. She conceived the brilliant idea of having a nation of them made to order; but her experiment was attended with no success. The first wife of Joachim Frederic, elector of Brandenburg, assembled a number of both sexes together for the same purpose; but she soon gave it up as a bad job. However, Peter the Great once made a great performance of a dwarf marriage, undoubtedly with a view of encouraging others to make the venture. It was in 1710. Peter proclaimed the bans many months before all over the kingdom, and peremptorily ordered all dwarfs within two hundred miles of the capital to be present. He even sent carriages after them and brought many by main force. An elegant banquet was spread for them, the tiniest little dishes, tables, and chairs, resembling more a modern dolls' tea-party than anything else. Those who came late were made to wait on the rest, and many were the bickerings they had among themselves as to who should sit first and where; but the grand time was when the ball came. The bride and groom led off, each being three feet two inches high.

Charles I. gave away the bride to the court dwarf, William Gibson, and the queen presented her with a diamond ring, on which occasion the long-forgotten Waller, the court poet, wrote some poor verses. In fact, Charles seemed fond of dwarfs, and had many at his court, with whom he played all sorts of pranks. On one occasion at a court banquet he had one served up in cold pie, out of which he jumped at the proper time, all armed, and accoutered with rapier and a tiny helmet. The king in a merry mood conferred the order of knighthood on him and suffered him to alternately make love and quarrel with the queen's monkey on grounds of equality.*

It is a fact well known that while giants are almost invariably characterized by mental and bodily weakness the opposite anomaly of humanity, the dwarfs, are generally active, intelligent, healthy, and long-lived persons.

In the seventeenth century, to gratify a whim of the Empress of Austria, all the giants and dwarfs in the German Empire were assembled at Vienna. As circumstances required that all should be housed in an extensive building it was feared that the imposing proportions of the giants would terrify the dwarfs, and means were taken to assure the latter of their perfect freedom and safety. But the result was very different to that contemplated. The dwarfs teased, insulted, and even robbed the giants to such an extent that the overgrown mortals, with tears in their eyes, complained of their stunted persecutors; and as a consequence sentinels had to be stationed in the building to protect the giants from the dwarfs.

* Article "Dwarfs," *Book of Days*.

It is not claimed that there have been any men in modern times equal in strength to Samson; but there have been Samsons in other ways, men in every respect his equal. Of these we shall speak in another chapter.

The prodigious muscular strength of the brothers Pospeschelli, of Vienna, was of a character sufficiently noteworthy to merit discussion at several meetings of the medical society of that city. Joseph Pospeschelli could hold a table suspended by his teeth while three persons stood upon it. He and his brother bore upon their shoulders a sort of bridge while a horse drawing a cart full of stones was driven over it. The feats of one Jorgnery, too, were simply Samsonian. The Frenchman would hang suspended by his legs from a swinging bar and by sheer muscular strength lift a heavy horse and its rider off the stage, suspending them several minutes and then letting them down gradually and evenly as he raised them. Stanley, the African explorer, describes a strong man who was six feet five inches tall, and rather disproportionately slender, who could toss an ordinary man into the air ten feet and catch him in his descent. In the wilds of northern Wisconsin there was a man by the name of Panquette, who was called the Samson of the region, who could perform feats of physical strength that were most astonishing.

Giovanni Battista Belzoni, born in the city of Padua, in 1778, where a statue is erected to his memory, traveled extensively as the "Patagonian giant"—for then the Patagonians were supposed to be of unusual size and strength—and astonished the world with his marvelous physical power. With a frame-work attached to his person he could walk with a dozen men on his back with as much grace as a soldier on dress parade.

Thomas Tapham, who was born in London in 1760, was possessed of a degree of strength which seemed supernatural. An authentic account of this man was given to the world by a gentleman well known in the literary world, William Hutton, who frequently witnessed his feats. He would carry a beam of a house as a soldier would his matchlock. Whatever he touched seemed to lose its gravitation. He could snap a rope which would sustain twenty hundred-weight, and do many other things which seemed far beyond the power of a mortal.

All of these are inferior to the Samson of the Bible; but they serve to show us that there are possibilities which lie in the domain of nature and nature's God beyond the experience of most men, in view of which we may well pause before saying, "I will not believe."

What physical giants there are in the insect world! Let us take the smallest speck of matter, a grain of sand, for instance, and place by its side a living insect, however small, and the difference between them is very great, because the one has life and the other is inanimate. God made the insect, we do not know for what purpose, but for some wise end, and for that end endowed it with the power which it possesses.

A common flea, of which it seems almost puerile to speak in this connection, can, without much apparent effort, leap, according to Fonville, more than two hundred times its own length; and several kinds of grasshoppers and locusts are said to be able to take leaps quite as wonderful. Now, in that proportion, with the same muscular endowments an ordinary man ought to be able to take his stand and at one bound spring twelve hundred feet into the air, which would be an equivalent exertion of muscular energy.

A man of average physical power can move without much difficulty a weight about one third to one half of his own. Subject a mole-cricket to the same test, and the result is quite different. This little creature, which weighs about sixty grains on the average, has been known to move a weight of three pounds, or three hundred and seventy-five times its own weight. So that if a man were proportionately strong he could carry a burden of about thirty tons!

In a volume published by Van Voorst, on the *Natural History of Animals*, several illustrations are given of the superherculean strength with which the commonest insects are endowed.

Again, for a man to run ten miles within the hour would be admitted to be a tolerably good display of pedestrianism; but what are we to say to the little insect observed by Mr. Delisle, " so minute as almost to be invisible," which ran nearly six inches in a second, and in that space was calculated to make one thousand and eighty steps? This, according to the calculation of Kirby and Spence, is as if a man whose steps measured only two feet should run at the incredible rate of twenty miles in a minute. Equally surprising are the instances of insect strength given by Mr. Newport.

The great stag-beetle, which tears off the bark from the roots and branches of trees, has been known to gnaw a hole an inch in diameter through the side of an iron canister in which it was confined, and on which the marks of its jaws were distinctly visible.

The common beetle can, without injury, support and even raise great weights and make its way beneath very great pressure. In order to put the strength of this insect-Atlas to the test, experiments have been made which prove that it is able to sustain and escape from beneath a load of from twenty to thirty ounces—a prodigious burden when it is remembered that the insect itself does not weigh as many grains.

There is a beetle known to entomologists called the Goliath—*Goliathus giganteus*—named after David's rival on account of its size and strength, which has wonderful power. In proportion to its bulk it is a hundred times stronger than the Samson of the Bible. There are many other wonders in the insect world. To one motion of your arm a common fly vibrates its wings three hundred and sixty times, and moves forward a distance of six feet. If a man were to equal it in the matter of locomotion, proportionately, he would travel sixty miles a minute, or sixty times faster than the fastest express train. Sir Walter Scott experimented on a garden snail, and came to the conclusion that no prison in Scotland could hold a single convict if he had the same relative strength; and if he were as strong in proportion to his size as a great many different insects he could go crashing through prison walls of granite and iron hundreds of feet in thickness.

There is surely no limit to the power of God; he who could give to these almost despised creatures such physical endowments can give to man any power or faculty which may be used for his glory.

CHAPTER XVI.

A GROUP OF SAMSONS.

SAMSON was a wonderful man in point of physical strength, the account of which has often been alluded to as a mere myth—an unbelievable tradition. It is my purpose to show that there are some world wonders as well as Bible wonders, and as great. If Samson was endowed with very marvelous physical strength by the Almighty could not he endow others with equal strength, muscular, or in some other way? The world is full of marvels. All strength is not merely physical.

Some people read the Bible, which contains so many things that are marvelous, and then throw it down and cry out, "Myth! fable! legend!" and possibly turn to nature, so full of the great things equally wonderful, mysterious, and inexplicable, and offer no objection. So in human life, in the life of the world, the mind is often startled by the most astounding revelations. If mere Nature, in her manifold workings, can exhibit such marvels, what may we expect when God puts forth his power in the life of man? How are we to explain the great characters which have appeared in all ages, great in so diverse a manner, only as we recognize the power of God in bestowing these gifts? Samson was great because God made him so. The same is true of all great characters.

The annals of precocity present no greater instance

than that of the brief career of Christian Heinecken, born at Lubeck, Germany, February 6, 1721. If the records of antiquity had told of him, or if it had been written in the Bible, the whole recital would have been regarded by some as purely mythical and dismissed as unworthy of any one's serious consideration. But the comparatively late period of his birth and the unimpeachable character of the numerous witnesses that testify to his extraordinary endowments leave no alternative from belief and wonder. This child, we are informed, spoke, and that quite sensibly, too, within a few hours after his birth. When ten months old he could converse on many subjects; when a year old he was quite well versed in the Old Testament Scriptures, and in another month was tolerably familiar with the New Testament. When two years and a half old he could answer almost any ordinary question in ancient history or geography. He next acquired the Latin and French languages, both of which he spoke with ease. The king of Denmark wishing to see this remarkable child, he was taken to Copenhagen in his fourth year, where he was examined and pronounced a great wonder. He was of feeble constitution, and died on the 27th of June, A. D. 1725, when only about four and a half years old. Both German and French savants wrote dissertations, in which they attempted to account for this psychological wonder. The ground taken by Martini, of Lubeck, was that it was precocity resulting from disease.

The origin of these marvelous gifts was deeper than that. Only the Creator himself could explain such a being.

The world has had a good many Samsons on one line or another, men whose endowments were startling. People talk about the Bible taxing their credulity; there are some things outside of the Bible which do the same thing, only that men believe the one and reject the other. Take the matter of memory. Lord Macaulay, when a student, it is said, committed to memory a copy of the *London Times* advertisements, and all between Saturday evening and Monday morning, on a wager. It was a mental feat more great than profitable. Themistocles, the old Greek, could call by name all the citizens of Athens to the number of twenty thousand. Cyrus knew by name, we are told, every soldier in his army.

Roman history tells of one Hortensius, who sat a whole day and listened to a sale, and then in the evening gave an account of every article sold, the price paid, and the name of the purchaser. There was a young Corsican at Padua who heard a roll-call of thirty-six thousand names, and then recited the list from memory, and could repeat the same backward. The first impulse on hearing or reading such statements is to cry out, "I don't believe it!"

There have been some wonderful mathematicians who were of Samsonian strength, but in a way different from that of the Israelitish giant. Dr. Wallace, of Oxford, could extract the square root in the dark to forty decimal places without making a figure on paper. And there was George Parker Bidder, who became a great civil engineer. When but a little boy he was examined in mental arithmetic by eminent persons, and greatly astonished them by answering mentally such questions as these: "What is the interest on £4,444 sterling for 4,444 days at 4 per cent.?" He gave a correct answer in two minutes. When eleven years old he was asked to divide 468,592,412,553 by 9,076, to which he gave a true answer in one minute. When twelve years old he was asked, "If a pendulum of a clock vibrates the distance of $9\frac{3}{4}$ inches in a second of time, how many inches will it vibrate in 7 years, 14 days, 2 hours, 1 minute, and 55 seconds?" He spoke the answer in less than a minute. He invented processes of his own, distinct from those given in the book in arithmetic, and could solve all the usual questions mentally more rapidly than others could with the aid of paper and pencil.

Jedediah Buxton, although his grandfather was a clergyman and his father a school-master, was so deficient in his education that he could not even write; his mental faculties were slow with the one wonderful exception of his power in mental arithmetic. After hearing a sermon he remembered and cared for nothing concerning it except the number of words which he had counted during its delivery. If a period of time or the size of an object were mentioned in his hearing he almost unconsciously began to count how many seconds or how many hair-breadths there were in it. He walked from Chesterfield to London on purpose to have the gratification of seeing George II.; and while in the metropolis he was taken much notice of by members of the Royal Society. If he went to the theater he occupied himself by counting the number of words uttered by each performer. If he walked across a field he could tell the number of square inches it contained. He would impose upon himself the severest tasks; one was to reckon how much a farthing would amount to if doubled one hundred and forty times; the result came out in such a stupendous number of pounds sterling as required thirty-nine places of figures to represent it. This problem was put to him: to find how many cubical eighths of an inch there are in a quadrangular mass measuring 23,145,789 yards long, 5,642,732 yards wide, and 54,965 yards thick. He answered this, as all others, mentally. He loved to calculate, and sometimes was fairly intoxicated, as he says, with reckoning. For instance, he determined how many grains, of eight different kinds of corn and pulse, and how many hairs an inch long, are contained in 200,000 cubic miles. One thing is certain, no one could very well dispute the correctness of his work. He began, of course, by calculating on a single cube. He could suspend any of his problems for any length of time, and at any point, and resume them at pleasure, and could even converse on other subjects while thus engaged. Of his methods he could give no explanation. All he knew was that he could do it.

There once lived in Paris a boy named Vito Mangiamele, a Sicilian, the son of a shepherd, who when eleven years old possessed powers of calculation that were truly astonishing. On the 3d of July, 1839, MM. Arago, Lacroix, and other eminent members of the Academy of Science, met to test the wonderful powers of this gifted child. They asked him several questions which they knew under ordinary circumstances to be tedious of solution, such as the cube root of 3,796,416, and the tenth root of 282,475,249; the first of these he answered in half a minute, the second in three minutes. One question was of the following complicated character: "What number has the following proportions, that if its cube is added to 5 times its square, and then 42 times the number, and the number 42 be subtracted from the result, the remainder is equal to 0 or zero?" M. Arago repeated the question a second time, but while he was finishing the last word the boy replied, "The number is 5."

Zera Colburn, of Vermont, was another instance of this sort of Samsonian strength. He began when he was six years old to answer arithmetical questions of most difficult character. When he was eight years of age he was in London, where he astonished the people. He could in a few moments raise 8 to the sixteenth power; extract the square root from such numbers as 106,929, give the cube root of 268,336,125, and tell, when asked, how many seconds are contained in 45, 37, 48, or almost any other number of years. The answers were all given in a few minutes, and sometimes in a few seconds. He was at this period ignorant of the ordinary rules of arithmetic, and did not know how or why particular modes of process came to his mind. At one time the Duke of Gloucester asked him to multiply 21,734 by 543. The answer was given at once. Something in the boy's manner induced the duke to ask how he did it, from which it appeared that the boy arrived at the result by multiplying 65,202 by 181, an equivalent process. But why he made this change in the factors neither he nor any one else could tell.

We have a most interesting personage in Charles Grandemange, a French boy, who was in all respects the most remarkable instance of natural genius in the department of mathematics the world has ever known. In the first place he was a physical wonder. The poor child was born without arms or legs, and could only be supported in an erect position by a sort of box in which he was compelled to live. His was a mere fragment of a human body, which in one age of the world and in some lands would have been cast away and left to die. But there are compensations in nature, and while this child was physically almost nothing his mental nature was marvelous. He wrote of himself as follows:

"I was born on the 10th of June, 1835, at Epinal, without arms or legs. At my birth I was concealed by order of the physicians for fifteen days from the sight of my mother, and it was not until she had been prepared for the misfortune which had befallen her and me that I was at length placed in her care. When she began to nurse me I weighed less than a pound and a half. It will readily be believed that my childhood was early surrounded with omens sufficiently gloomy. Born thus mutilated, what kind of a future could I expect in this world? I belonged to a family of laboring people, industrious and honest, but poor. My father, a carpenter by trade, had great difficulty even with what my mother, who was a weaver, could earn, to supply all the wants of four children. By means of constant care and watchfulness my mother succeeded in bringing me up to an age when I conceived in the constant inaction in which I lived some vague intuition of the peculiar talent with which Providence had endowed me in return for my privations and difficulties. M. Pelicot, surgeon of the town, and M. Haxo, surgeon-major of the regiment of cavalry in garrison at Epinal, who had assisted at my birth, and received my poor little body, weighing in all then a pound and a half, with the clothes, were not willing to forget the way to the humble roof that sheltered me. They came from time to time to see me, and, being witnesses of the first and sufficiently rare inclinations that I showed for mental calculations, they addressed to me some questions, very simple at first, and then those a little more difficult, and finally ventured upon some of the more abstruse questions of arithmetic. In this way and without any instruction I became able to solve almost instantly the little enigmas of calculation which they put to me. Indeed, I soon became sufficiently skillful to attempt likewise and with equal success some little problems in the province of geometry, of which, as to the practical part, my father had the rudiments sufficiently well to instruct me. By the advice of the physicians and some savants who had visited me my father resolved to introduce me to certain educational establishments most esteemed in our country of Vosges and the neighboring departments. The marked success that I obtained having emboldened me, I decided, after having lost my father, to visit Paris, the metropolis and center of science. I had the honor to appear there before a commission chosen to examine my intellectual faculties by the Academy of Science."

In the examination to which this boy was subjected a series of problems the most obscure and complex were put to him during three long hours, and he solved them with a rapidity which might be called electric. He was asked to multiply a quantity consisting of two hundred figures by one consisting of ten or twelve. After a brief pause he made known the product, which was found to be correct, and which would have required on paper perhaps half an hour of the most rapid calculation. One person among others asked him to give the remainder of the division by nine of an immense number in sextillions, quintillions, quadrillions, trillions, billions, millions, etc. The whole sum was scarcely stated when already the young calculator had answered like a flash, " Four is the remainder "—a reply the correctness and instantaneousness of which astonished the audience and the interrogator himself. This wonderful prodigy had a handsome and intellectual face, and, strange to say, though armless, could write beautifully, which he did by holding the pen between the cheek and the stump which supplied the place of the right arm. He could even execute pen-flourishes which possessed some considerable degree of grace and beauty. Was he not the equal of Samson? And did not his marvelous powers come from God?

How touching and beautiful the story of the blind! If "truth is stranger than fiction" anywhere, it is so in the history of the blind. They have filled almost every position in life, and when they have risen to distinction, as they have in numerous instances, it has been of a character to win the applause of the world. From blind Homer to " Blind Tom " the world has had many marvels.

History tell us of Zisca, the Bohemian reformer, who, as a general, avenged the death of John Huss and Jerome of Prague by his consummate generalship on the field. Though blind he was a terror to the foes of Bohemia, driving before him the hosts of Sigismund. If the story of Zisca were in the Bible some would not believe it. Dr. Nicholas Saunderson lost his eye-sight when he was a mere babe a few months old; yet he whose vision was muffled deep and dark in the drapery of night became the successor of Sir Isaac Newton in a renowned university—a teacher of the laws of light who never saw the light excepting when a babe. Here was blind Huber, who knew more about the nature of the honey-bee than any man living. Blind men have acted as guides in some European cities. John Gough, though blind, became so expert as a botanist that he could give the name of almost any plant, however rare, merely by the touch. Some of the ablest divines, lawyers, and physicians of the world have been sightless. Mechanics skilled in the construction of edge-tools, watches, and clocks have groped their way in darkness.

One of the most remarkable instances on record was that of Joseph Strong, of Carlisle, England. At four years he lost his eye-sight. This blind boy early developed a genius for the construction of musical instruments, and at fifteen years was ambitious to build an organ, which he had learned to play. For the purpose of gaining a knowledge of the construction of the organ he concealed himself one afternoon in the cathedral when the congregation had retired, and proceeded to make the much-desired investigation. He occupied himself until midnight measuring and calculating, when he began to try the different stops and the proportions they bore to each other.

On hearing the organ at such an hour the neighbors were alarmed. What could it mean? Some one courageously entered the sacred edifice, and lo! Joseph Strong, the blind boy, was playing the instrument. The dean, as was his official duty, we suppose, reprimanded the innocent little fellow for his daring, but generously gave him permission to play whenever he desired to do so.

The boy now went to work and built his first organ, which is yet in existence. It is another illustration of the wonderful things which have occurred in the world's annals. If any one should say in reference to these things, "I don't believe them," he would call down on him the scorn of the intelligent world.

CHAPTER XVII.

WORLD WONDERS—CHORD AND CANVAS.

IN this chapter nothing new is claimed, unless it be in the application of the facts brought out to the general support of Bible prodigies—if it can be affirmed that the Bible contains the account of mere prodigies. I do not hold that the existence of such a character as Blind Tom or Cæsar Ducornet proves that Samson was what is claimed for him; but if there have been such marvels in modern times as these it shows at least that they have always been possible. Samson was more than an exceptional athlete, he was the creature of providence, and was endowed by his Maker with his great strength. But may not the same providence have given to others of God's children gifts of surpassing excellence, even greater and far more wonderful than muscular power?

There have been some most wonderful instances of musical genius, manifesting itself even in infancy. Two of these occurred in the Wesley family. Charles Wesley, son of the well-known hymn-writer of the same name, and nephew of John Wesley, was born at Bristol, England, December 11, 1757. Nearly from his birth his mother used to quiet and amuse the infant with her harpsichord. Even before he could speak his musical ear was so acute that he would not permit his mother to play with one hand only, but would take the other and place it on the keys. Soon attempting to play himself, his mother used to tie him in a chair at the harpsichord, where he would amuse himself for hours together. When only two years and nine months old he astonished his parents by playing a tune in correct time. Soon afterward he could play any air he chanced to hear with a true bass added, as if spontaneously, without study or hesitation. He then seemed to have little respect or reverence for any one not a musician. When called to play for a stranger he would inquire in his childish prattle, "Is he a musiker?" and if the answer were in the affirmative would run to the instrument with ready eagerness.

Samuel Wesley, his brother, was born in 1766, and evinced a talent for music almost as early as Charles. He could play a tune when two years and eleven months old, and could put a correct bass to airs long before he had acquired a knowledge of musical notation. He constantly attended his brother, playing or rather making believe to play, on a chair or table while Charles played the harpsichord. With the advantage of such an example he soon outstripped his brother. He learned to read from words of songs in music-books, and could compose music long before he could write. At the age of eight years he surprised the musical world by an oratorio entirely his own. In early life Charles was brought under the notice of George III., and often had the honor of entertaining the royal leisure by performances of Handel's music. But he never won any great distinction as a musician in after life. His brother Samuel achieved a greater success, but neither fulfilled the great promise of their precocious youth.

A very remarkable character appeared in the person of William Crotch, who was born at Norwich in July, 1775. The father of this boy was a carpenter by trade, and though he was not a skilled musician was fond of the art, and with great ingenuity succeeded in building an organ, on which he could play a few simple tunes. About 1776, at Christmas-time, when the infant William was not over eighteen months old, he discovered a great inclination for music by leaving even the table when the organ was being played; and six months afterward he would touch the key-notes of his favorite tunes to induce his father to play them. Soon after this, as he was unable to name the tunes, he would play the two or three first notes of them when he thought the key-note did not sufficiently express the air he wished played. Hearing a lady play one day whose excellence charmed him, he concluded to attempt to play himself. The same evening, when being carried through the room where the organ was, on his way to bed, the infant screamed and struggled violently to go to the instrument, and on his wish being complied with he eagerly beat down the keys with his little fist. The next day, being left with his brother, a youth of fourteen, in the same room, he persuaded the latter to blow the bellows, while he himself struck the keys of the organ. At first he played at random, but presently he produced with one hand so much of "God Save the King" as to awaken the curiosity of his father, then in the work-shop, who came into the room to know who it was that was playing. On being informed he was, of course, greatly surprised. At this time the young musician was two years and three weeks old.

Next day he made himself master of the treble of the second part, and the day after he attempted the bass, which he performed correctly in every particular, excepting the note immediately before the close; this, being an octave below the preceding sound, was beyond the reach of his little hand. In a few more months he mastered both treble and bass in certain selections, and erelong from this period he could extemporize the bass to any melody, whether performed by himself or others. Like the Wesleys, he never rose to any thing beyond local fame. Premature musical powers, like other precocious displays, seldom realize the anticipations to which they give rise.

Among the human wonders of the world there never was a greater than the so-called "Blind Tom," of musical fame. If he did not have the exquisite finish of a perfectly trained performer he had all the force and originality that heaven could inspire in a poor mortal. We often listened to him, and always with great astonishment. Was Samson strong—marvelously and miraculously so? We claim the same for Tom. Samson pulled down a house, a temple. Tom truly "brought down" many a house. In the great halls of Europe and America thousands cheered him to the echo. Only God could create the Samson of the Bible; only God could create the Samson of the piano.

There he sat before his piano, in the presence of some great audience—a lump of black flesh, a swarthy Negro of the Guinea type, with protruding heels and blubber lips, ape-jawed and open-mouthed, blind from his birth. On his countenance was stamped the vacant grin of idiocy, from which he was removed scarce a degree. But let us wait at this threshold and inquire somewhat about him. Just when he was born and where is not precisely known, for he turned up one day along with his mother on a Georgia plantation, the result of a purchase in the old slave times. But all of this is of such recent date there is no chance to relegate this story to the age of myths. This idiotic creature was more than he seemed to be. When bid off by the planter he was most likely thrown in as so much extra weight, which might in some way be used—but how? One thing we know, God anointed him with the "holy chrism" that should make of him the most remarkable musical genius of any age. The infant Mozart was wonderfully dowered, and when a mere child of five years astonished the world; but Tom was more wonderful, inasmuch as he had none of Mozart's intelligence, and was blind.

Blind Tom! his history is pathetic. He owned not even a name, and with all his marvelous gifts sustained to humanity in general about the same relation that a mushroom sustains to a rose-bush. "What a child of God!" we instinctively said the first time we saw and heard him, as with eyes closed in night, his head thrown far back on his shoulders, lying on the back, indeed, he took his seat before his favorite instrument and, sweeping the key-board, rained down on the audience a perfect shower of melody. Now it came in ripples and plashes, then in wild thunders—at one time soft as a lullaby, and anon with the crash of battle. He and the piano seemed to be one and inseparable. He would rise and turn his back to the instrument and finger the keys behind him; he played a tune with each hand and whistled a third at the same time. Wonderful!

There was no outgrowth of intellect or soul in Tom. His world was that of sound and melody. Indeed, sound of any kind always delighted him, even the crying of a child when he was himself a mere baby. If a piano was touched in his presence even before he could walk it would cause him to roll about on the floor in ecstasy. And it is said that he would even bite his little brothers and sisters to make them emit cries of pain that he might hear the sound.

It was somewhere in the fifties (1856 or 1857) when the phenomenal powers latent in this poor child were suddenly developed, and which stamped him the anomaly of the day. Tom, though a slave child, was not denied his master's house. Indeed, he was, through his very helplessness, an object of pity. Lying in the hot sun on the steps of the mansion, he received many a kind word from its occupants as they passed in and out over the broad verandas. One night in summer-time the family were awakened by the sound of music, which came from the drawing-room. The notes were produced by some one whose touch was timid, but singularly delicate; now a strain from some simple air, and then something more difficult. What could it mean? The mystery must be solved; and going down-stairs they found Tom, who had been left in the hall asleep, and possibly curled away under some table unnoticed, like a dog, now seated at the piano in the dark and in ecstasies of delight, breaking out at the end of each successful strain into shouts of laughter, delivering rollicking kicks with his heels and clapping his chubby hands. This was the first time he had ever touched a piano-key. Of course he at once became a wonder, as well as an after-dinner amusement. But no one realized then the depth of his nature. This all took place in the days when spiritualism was rife—that long-gone craze; and at once he was supposed to be under the "influence" of some musical ghost, that spoke through him in wild harmony and broken strains of startling beauty and pathos. No seal was put upon the piano, but Tom was allowed the freest possible access to the instrument, though he was not subjected to any musical training. He never received a lesson on any thing in all his life. When the poor child had once touched the keys he and the piano were friends ever afterward. If this little black figure had ever heard a tune in his life he knew it now and could produce it. Music of various grades, plantation ditties, sonnets, snatches of the masters which he had heard, seemed to be packed away in his soul, and he only needed to place his fat baby fingers on the ivory keys when they all flowed forth in soft murmurs, like water from a spring, or as violently as electric shocks from a charged battery. He literally made music, and these plantation people listened to strains that had never been heard before. They were born in the carcass of this little black nameless and unknown child. But as tradition has it, they were "sad minors, vexing the content of the hearer." What wonder that such a soul should fruit its lowly conditions of darkness and misery in sad refrains.

From this time Tom went forth to a wider field. Neighboring cities were permitted to hear and see the blind boy. Crowds hung entranced on the music which fairly leaped from the tips of his fingers. But musicians were skeptical, and said it could not be; he must be a pretender, a skilled performer in disguise. Tom was subjected to the severest and most critical tests, tests bordering on harshness. His powers could not pass along unchallenged. But Tom was victorious, and he went forth to the world an acknowledged prodigy. In the every-day apparent intellect, in reason or judgment, he was almost a nonentity. He may be said to have been incapable of comprehending the simplest conversation on ordinary topics. At thirty years he had the petulant disposition of a spoiled child of three. Once, it is said, when the agent attempted to make him stop playing a piano in a high-toned hotel at three o'clock in the morning, Tom seized him and threw him through the door; and in Washington he once threw a man down-stairs who came into his room. And yet he had an affection for a friend very much like a dog. He could detect the step of one he loved in a crowd. His memory was marvelous. He could repeat a discussion of fifteen minutes length from the remembrance of the word-sounds accurately and yet not understand the meaning of a single sentence. Songs in German and French after a single hearing he could reproduce, not only literally in words, but in notes, style, expression. When in London, soon after he began his career, a flute was procured for him of a very complicated pattern, having twenty-two keys. He would frequently rise up at night and play this instrument, imitating upon it all sorts of sounds which he might hear or had heard. He is thus described by one who saw him often: " When at home in Georgia he lives in a building about two hundred yards from the house, and there remains alone with his piano, playing all day and night, like one possessed with madness. Bad weather has an effect upon his music. In cloudy, rainy seasons he plays somber music in minor chords, and when the sun shines and the birds sing he indulges in waltzes and light music. Sometimes he will hammer away for hours, producing the most horrible discords imaginable. Suddenly a change comes over him and he indulges in magnificent bursts of harmony, taken from the best productions of the masters. Since his childhood he has been an idiot, and he played nearly as well at the age of seven as he does now; but now his *répertoire* is much larger, as he can play any thing he has ever heard. He now plays about seven thousand pieces, and picks up new ones every-where."

When twelve years of age this boy, blind and ignorant of every phase of musical science, could interpret severely classical compositions in music with a clearness of conception and a skill in mechanism truly remarkable. "His concerts," writes one, "usually include any themes selected by the audience from the higher grade of Italian or German opera. His comprehension of the meaning of music as a prophetic or historical voice, which few truly utter and fewer understand, is clear and vivid. . . . The peculiar power which Tom possesses, however, is one which requires no scientific knowledge of music in the audience to appreciate. Placed at the instrument with any musician, he plays a perfect bass accompaniment to the treble of music heard for the first time as he plays it. Then, taking the seat vacated by the performer, he instantly gives the entire piece, intact in brilliancy and symmetry, not a note lost or misplaced."

The selections of music by which this power of Tom's was tested were sometimes fourteen and sixteen pages in length. On one occasion at the White House, after a long concert, he was tried with two pieces, one thirteen and the other twenty pages long, and was successful.

There, too, was Cæsar Ducornet, the painter.* On the 6th of January, 1806, there was born in the humble dwelling of a poor shoe-maker in the Rue St. Jacques, at Lille, France, an infant so strangely helpless and deformed that the attendants at his birth hesitated to show it to its parents. They regarded it with a species of horror. Its utter feebleness foreboded its speedy death, and that they were ready to hail as a merciful dispensation both for mother and babe. But the mother took it to her bosom with all a mother's love, and the helpless little stranger did not die. Some days after, when the poor shoe-maker and his wife were left alone with their new-born son, they might have been seen stooping, with a mingled expression of terror, of pity, and parental compassion, over a cradle in which there rolled and twisted about a little *lusus naturæ*, sent into the world without arms, and whose lower extremities could be described as nothing better than a kind of bony stalks, with the barest indications of thighs and what might pass for rudiments of legs. On either little foot there were but four toes. It was happy for both these humble parents that the spectacle of their child's wretched condition, so far from exciting discontent and loathing, stirred up the deepest springs of affection in their bosoms, and they loved him all the more.

* Article in *National Magazine*.

Such was the entry upon life of the famous Cæsar Ducornet, historical painter, victor in the academic schools, winner of the gold medal in the exhibition of the Louvre, and corresponding member of the Imperial Society of Science, of Agriculture, and the Arts at Lille.

The early infancy of Ducornet is not perhaps to be regarded as unhappy; innocence is unconscious of its defects. Moreover, people found a charm in the vigorous and determined expression of his face; so much sprightly and precocious intelligence in his look; so much characteristic and curious dexterity in all his movements, that every one noticed him with sympathy and treated him with tenderness. Meanwhile the infant grew in years and stature, and the poor parents had to ponder the difficult problem of a profession for their boy. The shoe-maker gained a humble subsistence by the labor of his hands; but Providence had given the young Cæsar no hands to labor with, and they puzzled themselves in vain, since it was plain he could work at no known trade, as to what was to be done with him. Many poor parents in such a predicament would have made a beggar of the boy, and have found their account in it, or they would have hired him out for exhibition by some traveling showman; but the father of Ducornet was an honest and independent artisan who knew the true dignity of a workman, and was incapable of harboring any thought of this kind. Still the question arose, What was to be done? They had remarked that in his childish games the infant made use of his feet with most marvelous ability; he threw the ball to his comrades, cut things he wanted to cut with a knife, drew lines with chalk on the floor of the room, clipped out in paper figures and images with his mother's scissors; in a word, every thing which other children did with their hands he did with equal if not excelling adroitness with his four-toed feet. One day they surprised him in the act of drawing upon paper some masterly capital letters. An old writing-master named Dumoncel saw them with astonishment, and immediately proposed to the shoe-maker to take the boy under his gratuitous instruction. In less than a year the little Ducornet, we cannot say wrote the finest hand, but had become the first penman in the worthy Dumoncel's class. But the writing-master soon had fresh food for admiration. In addition to the boy's fine writing his copy-books began all at once to be illustrated by a crowd of designs remarkable for their originality and correctness of outline. These were so abundant and striking that Dumoncel, astonished, carried the productions of his pupil to the professor of design in the Academy at Lille. This second discovery had the same success as the first. The professor, in his turn, fell in love with the prodigious aptitude of the young Ducornet, and did not rest until he had gained his admittance as a student of design at the Lille Academy; only by a delicate attention the professor installed him in the class of the adults, to save him from the rude curiosity of the boys of his own age, who constituted the elementary chapel. At the Academy of Lille Cæsar Ducornet carried off successively the highest prize in each of the courses, and finished by having decreed to him the great medal in the living-model class. This last victory was regarded as an event in the good town of Lille.

From this period must be dated a friendship which proved the greatest happiness of Ducornet's life. It was now that he became intimate with a man who was destined to act as a guardian angel through the remainder of his career—a man of true nobility of mind, whose life had been one long devotion to the arts and artists of his native town, and who lavished upon Ducornet from his childhood to his death all the tenderness of a parent. M. Demailly, of Lille, adopted the poor boy, and undertook the charge of his future life. He took him into his house, fed him, clothed him, encouraged him in his efforts, in his trials, and at the same time, being himself an excellent judge and a distinguished amateur, aided him in his counsels. He went farther: he racked his ingenuity in the contrivance of seats, of easels, and of implements for painting adapted to the abnormal structure of his *protégé*. When we reflect that the benevolent hand which guided the first steps of the Lille artist was reserved to close the eyes that death glazed forty years afterward, are we not justified in believing that Providence prepares such loving hearts for the express solace of misfortune?

But another earnest of success was now at hand. About this time the Duke d'Angoulême, going to visit the museum at Lille, found our young artist there in the act of finishing a beautiful copy from a picture by Vandyke. Astonished at the sight of so strange a being executing a most difficult work of art, the prince took a lively interest in his fate; he conferred upon him a pension of twelve hundred francs and prevailed upon him to go to Paris, there to continue his studies at greater advantage. The town of Lille, less princely in its generosity, increased the artist's pension by three hundred francs more.

Upon this our artist sets out for Paris, whither, to complete his satisfaction, his friend, M. Demailly, is not slow to follow him. Now begins the grand struggle for reputation. He enters the Royal Academy of Painting, and at the same time his benefactor procures him admission into the studio of M. Lethière. Six months after his entrance at the Royal Academy, in 1826, he there obtains the third medal, and in the following year the second. In 1826 he presents himself as one of the candidates for the great prize to be awarded at Rome.

Here occurs a circumstance rather curious to record. The examination has commenced; the artist has fully succeeded in his preliminary trials, but the moment comes for competition, and now the professors, considering the diminutive figure and strange conformation of Ducornet, declare him practically incapable of managing a canvas prescribed by the regulation (about five feet by four), and close the arena against him. Thereupon Ducornet retires, and to vindicate himself in the face of their unqualifying decision he executes upon these same regulation dimensions his first picture, "The Parting of Hector and Andromache," which may be seen at this moment on the walls of the museum at Lille.

In 1829 the professors of the Royal Academy revoke their decision; Ducornet executes the proposed subject, "Jacob Refusing to Release the Young Benjamin to his Brethren." His picture, according to the opinion of the best judges, deserves at least a second prize; but the academy cannot condescend to grace with victory a man without arms. Thereupon M. Lethière, protesting against their injustice, has the picture exhibited along with the assembled prizes, during a visit of the Duchesse de Berry. The princess praises the work of the maimed painter, and the minister of the interior commands him to paint "St. Louis Administering Justice under an Oak," for the museum of his native town.

At this period Ducornet quits the studio of M. Lethière to follow his own independent course. The first-fruit of his emancipated labor is a picture representing the "Slave Market," now in the keeping of the museum of Arras. During the years which followed upon the revolution of 1830 Ducornet obtained from the government a commission for painting several of those portraits of Louis Philippe which, all precisely alike, were distributed by hundreds to the departments—an occupation sufficiently wearisome to the mind of a true artist, but to which poverty must resign itself. While Ducornet is thus laboring to gain a subsistence for himself and father, the state deprives him of his pension of twelve hundred francs; and the town of Lille, following the example of the state, withdraws its three hundred, thus admonishing him that misfortunes rarely come singly.

Nevertheless, poor Ducornet does not suffer himself to be cast down by this reverse of fortune; on the contrary, he redoubles the activity of his labors. In 1834 two of his works, "An Episode in the Siege of Antwerp," and "Magdalen at the Feet of the Saviour," are admitted to the exhibition of the Louvre. The last-mentioned of these two pictures is eleven feet high and eight feet wide. We cite these dimensions because they are very significant when we recollect the deformity of the painter and the exclusion of 1828.

We pass over a number of Ducornet's productions of less importance, which would occupy too much space were they mentioned in detail. Let us record, however, his successes at the several exhibitions at the Louvre. In 1840 he gained a medal of the third class, in 1841 a medal of the second class, in 1843 a medal of the first class, and at length, in 1844, the great gold medal was awarded him for his picture of "Christ at the Sepulcher"—a work of uncontestable excellence.

Ducornet was desirous of painting the portrait of General Négrier, who had been killed at the barricades of June, 1848. The painter had never seen the deceased general. The portrait was to be full-length, and for a guide he had only a tolerably well-executed bust and a few lithographs of the deceased soldier.

"No matter how long I live," writes one who visited him while at work at this portrait, "I shall never forget the wonderful impression I received upon entering his paint-room. There, extended upon an easel, stood a huge canvas, on which the image of General Négrier was beginning to assume the semblance of life; and across the whole extent of the canvas ran with incredible agility, like a fly upon a wall, the stunted trunk of a man, surmounted by a noble head, with expansive brow and eyes of fire; and wherever this apparition passed along the canvas he left the traces of color behind him. On approaching a few paces nearer we were aware of a lofty but slender scaffolding in front of the canvas, up and down and across the steps and stays of which climbed and crouched and twisted—it is impossible to describe how—the shapeless being we had come to see. We saw then that he was deprived of arms, that he had no thighs, that his short legs were closely united to the trunk, and that his feet were wanting of a toe each. By one of his feet he held a palette, by the other a pencil; in his mouth he also carried a large brush and a second pencil; and in all this harness he moved and rolled and writhed and painted in a manner more than marvelous! This portrait adorns the rooms of the artillery corps of Lille, and, what is really astonishing, it was painted by a man without arms and almost without legs, and is distinguished for wonderful resemblance to its subject."

CHAPTER XVIII.

WORLD WONDERS—TREES.

MUCH has been said about the "big stories" or the wonderful things related in the Bible. How could it be otherwise?

The moral world, as well as the physical, is great. Both have had their origin in the mind of God. We have seen in previous chapters how full nature is of marvels, whether it be star, animal, man, or worm; the microscope, no less than the telescope, opens to our vision a universe. Among the things that grow out of the ground every-where, seen every day, and consequently the less noticed and thought of, is a tree. What an object to look at and study as it towers far up into the air at times, as if to kiss the passing clouds, and spreads out its branches so gracefully! One tree in particular I shall not forget; it was of the species known as the American elm, and grew in my front door-yard. I remember how through the long hot summer this dear old tree would cast its cooling shadow over us. That single tree gave us more comfort each summer than can well be expressed—more than five hundred dollars would have purchased at a fashionable watering-place, where you pay for much and often get but little. Intimately connected with our lives for three years, as it was, I desire to erect to its memory this monument. When I was returning from an absence, and came in sight of the beautiful tree, I always felt like saluting it by taking off my hat and shaking hands with it.

Do you say that trees have no hands to shake? The Bible says, "All the trees of the field shall clap their hands;" but of course it is figurative.

We could describe its botanical characters as one can talk of a friend's eyes, hair, or complexion. My tree had come up as some people have come, through hardships. It had been used in its earlier life as a hitching-post until the horses had well-nigh destroyed it. I put a stop to that, however, by setting some hitching-posts so far removed from the tree as to save it from any further danger from that source.

With all its friendly acts at times it used to create some annoyance, especially in the winter, when the wind was strong, by reaching out its long slender branches and switching the side of the house when we were trying to sleep; but, remembering the delightful shade it cast in the summer, I readily forgave this misdemeanor. My tree used to make considerable litter when it went to bed. Some people throw off their clothes anywhere and every-where when they retire. So did my tree. Is not autumn the trees' bed-time? Is not winter their night of rest? Are not the leaves their cast-off garments? Again I thought of the sweet shade of the summer, and forgave all for the good the tree had done. I just quietly raked up these cast-off garments—a million or two of them—and wheeled them off to the barn for horse-bedding, knowing that my dear tree, like many of human kind, would come out with a brand-new suit in the early spring.

There it stood, and yet stands, quite probably, in its

living beauty a monument to human thoughtfulness; for it was dug up when a mere sapling and placed there by a young clergyman "once upon a time," which required only a couple of hours' work. "Blessed is the man who planteth a tree!" Up in the graceful curving branches of that tree the birds built their nests in the spring-time and reared their young. From these same branches they sang their matin songs and chanted their vespers. How often have we watched them from the window as they circulated among the branches, when it seemed a very paradise to them! So the man who planted the tree blessed his fellow mortals, and the birds too.

Trees are not alike in their appearance, to say nothing of other qualities, any more than men and women are alike. We never look at a grand tree waving its branches in the breezes but we think of the roots away down under the sod in the dampness and darkness working on busily, day and night, to keep the tree alive. The strong stem, the graceful branches, the leaves, flowers, and fruits, all depend on the roots hid away under-ground. They constitute the "working class" in the tree world. Edward Everett, when speaking once of the relations of labor, said: "I have now in my hands a gold watch which combines embellishment and utility in happy proportion, and is often considered a very valuable appendage to the person of a gentleman. Its hands and face, chain and case, are of chased and burnished gold. Its gold seals sparkle with the ruby, topaz, sapphire, and emerald. I open it and find that the works, without which this elegantly furnished case would be a mere shell, and those hands be motionless and those figures meaningless, are made of brass. Investigate still further, and ask, What is the spring by which all these are put in motion made of? I am told it is made of steel. I ask, What is steel? The reply is that it is iron which has undergone a certain process. So then I find the mainspring—without which this watch would always be motionless, and its hands, figures, and embellishments but toys—is not of gold, that is not sufficiently good; nor of brass, that would not do; but of iron. Iron, then, is the only precious metal. And this watch is an emblem of society; its hands and figures, which tell the hour of the day, resemble the master-spirits of the age, to whose movements every eye is directed. Its useless but sparkling appendages are the aristocracy. Its works of brass are the middle class, by the increasing intelligence and power of which the master-spirits of the age are moved. And its iron mainspring, shut up in a box, always at work, but never thought of, except when it is disorderly, broken, or wants winding up, symbolizes the laboring classes who are shut up in obscurity, and, though constantly at work and absolutely necessary to the movements of society, as the iron mainspring is to the gold watch, are never thought of except when they require their wages or are in some want or disorder of some kind or another."

Trees have their law of life. The bark grows toward the center, and the wood grows outward by concentric layers which are piled up one above the other. A ring is produced each year, so that the tree will show as many circles as it has endured years.

It is said by naturalists that the part which looks toward the north is narrower, and its rings are more close and dense than the others. So it happens that the trunks of trees are slightly flattened in a north and south direction, while they expand toward the east and west. Some trees grow more rapidly than others; the great size of certain species is well known. In the forests of Germany there have been trees of enormous proportions; one is described, from the trunk of which a canoe was made large enough to carry safely thirty persons. The Rev. J. Ray, an English botanist, tells of an oak existing in Germany which was large enough to be transformed into a citadel. The plane-trees on the banks of the Bosporus and Black Seas are of almost incredible size. Pliny, in his *Natural History*, states that in his time, which was nearly two thousand years ago, there was in Lycia a thriving plane-tree in the trunk of which was a grotto eighty-one feet in circumference, the whole extent of which nature had tapestried with green and velvet moss. This cavity was converted into a hall, where on one occasion a supper was given by Lucinius Mutiamus, governor of the province, to eighteen guests. De Candolle informs us that in the neighborhood of Constantinople a lime-tree existed once the trunk of which was one hundred and fifty feet in circumference. In Normandy an oak is still standing which has been converted into a chapel and is known as "The Chapel Oak of Allouville," in which is an altar dedicated to the Virgin Mary, where occasionally mass is held. Above the chapel is a sleeping-room which has been hollowed out, and to which steps lead from the outside. This oak is thirty feet in diameter near the ground. In the neighborhood of Smyrna there are some trees of such vast dimensions that openings have been made through the stems large enough to allow the passage of a soldier on horseback fully equipped. The famous cedars of Lebanon rose to a height of about one hundred and fifty feet. The wax-palm on the Andes " balances its waving crown " in the bosom of the clouds two hundred feet above the heights whereon it grows.

While the giant trees of the eastern world have been known for ages, those of the western world were unknown until 1853, when they were discovered by Mr. William Lobb, a scientific traveler and naturalist. They were first met with in a solitary district on the elevated slope of the Sierra Madre Mountains, in Calaveras County, Cal., about five hundred feet above the level of the sea, and all growing within the circuit of a mile or two. Their situation was at the head-waters of the San Antonio River.

There were only about one hundred of these veritable giants of the vegetable kingdom discovered by Mr. Lobb. The smallest of them was fifteen feet in diameter. Though large they were not unsightly. One writer, in describing them, says : " Long fringes and festoons of yellow moss and lichen hang around their proud trunks; a parasite growing from their roots shoots its graceful stems adorned with bracts and rose-colored flowers to a height of ten feet. The place has thus the double charm of beauty and magnificence."

These giants are a species of pine-tree known to the botanist as conifers, and, standing there for centuries wrestling with the storms, it is not strange that their tops are broken and ragged, while Indian camp-fires have injured others at the base. Excavations have been made in some of them by repeated burnings sufficiently large to enable a good-sized family to obtain shelter.

These trees are not all of the same age; there was one large one, known as the "Big Tree," which was particularly famous. It required the services of five men throughout the working-days of one whole month to fell this giant of the centuries. The work was not accomplished with axes in the ordinary way, but with huge boring instruments constructed for the purpose. When the monster lay upon the earth, the victim of human cupidity, it took three weeks to strip off its bark from the first fifty-two feet of its trunk. That the tree was cut down for the sake of the "almighty dollar" is certain, for one side was flattened for a bowling-alley, and at the end of it a saloon was built. A wagon and horses could travel easily along the overthrown stem; which, when flattened, formed a roadway twenty-four feet wide, without counting the bark, which would be about three feet more. The stump was turned into good financial account, as on its surface, smoothed off carefully, a pavilion was erected for the accommodation of visitors. By counting the number of annual rings in a transverse section it was ascertained that this monster of the forest must have been considerably over three thousand years old. It was a mere sapling when Samson was slaughtering the Philistines, or Æneas carrying off Anchises on his filial shoulders. It was in its prime when Hannibal was thundering at the gates of Rome.

These trees were named. There was the "Miner's Cabin," three hundred feet high and eighty-five feet in circumference; the "Old Bachelor," the "Hermit," standing off a little from the rest, and which was estimated to contain 725,000 feet of lumber; the "Husband and Wife," two hundred feet high, and leaning toward each other a little; the "Three Sisters," growing apparently from the same roots, ninety-two feet in girth and three hundred feet high; "Mother and Son," the one three hundred and twenty-five feet, the other three hundred feet high, the "Son" still growing; the "Siamese Twins" and their "Guardian," the "Old Maid," the "Bride of California," "Beauty of the Forest," "Uncle Tom's Cabin," etc. This latter has a hollow at the bottom of its trunk large enough to seat an audience of twenty-five persons. Another of these conifers hollowed out into a deep cavern has been named "The Riding-School," because a man on horseback can penetrate a distance of twenty yards into the dark cavern of its prostrate form. There is another cluster which is fancifully known as the "Family Group," comprising twenty-six trees, among which are seen the father and mother and twenty-four children. But the poor old "father" fell some years ago, his body measuring at the base one hundred and ten feet in circumference. When in his prime this venerable tree was supposed to be from four hundred and fifty to five hundred feet in height. The "mother" was three hundred feet high and ninety-one feet in circumference; the "children" were not so large.

Since Mr. Lobb's time other groups of these giants have been discovered in regions quite remote from the first named. They have been found on the top and sides of the Sierra Nevada Mountains at an elevation of 6,000 to 7,000 feet. In some clusters there are from 350 to 1,200 trees of all sizes. What their fate may be is scarcely problematical, for within the last few years a colony numbering six hundred members with the Bellamy idea as its leading attraction has located a large amount of land in this region and constructed a roadway to the timber belt. The intention is to turn into gold this most wonderful and perfect body of *sequoias gigantea* in the world.

But Australian forests have also their mammoth trees. Dr. Ferdinand Miller, government botanist of Victoria, Australia, discovered in that colony a forest of eucalypti, a species of gum-tree, some of which surpass somewhat in height the famous "big trees" of California.

After giving at some length the account of the journey and of the scenery of the district in which the giants were found the writer mentions a few particulars, by the aid of which some better idea may be formed of their height and size. They are taller than the trees of California, though not so large in girth, and have more slender and graceful stems. One of these trees, which had fallen, measured two hundred and ninety-five feet to the first branch, and seventy feet more to the point at which it had been broken off in its fall, and where its diameter was still one yard. One was found which had a circumference of eighty-one feet at its base, and towered upward to a height of five hundred feet. This extraordinary tree would have overshadowed Egypt's greatest pyramid. To afford a more vivid conception of its magnitude Dr. Miller made the estimate that one half of the wood wh'ch this forest mammoth would yield sawn into one-inch boards a foot wide would afford 426,720 running feet. If the same parts were cut into railroad-ties six feet long, and of the usual thickness, it would yield 17,780 of them, or sufficient numbers to lay a railway-track ten miles long; they would freight a vessel of a thousand tons burden. The oil obtained from its resinous leaves might be set down at thirty-one hogsheads, the charcoal from its wood at eighteen thousand bushels, the pyroligneous acid at two hundred and thirty thousand gallons, the tar at two hundred and thirty barrels, and the potash at three tons!

Trees of some species are short-lived, but others live four and five hundred years. A lime-tree was planted at Freyburg on the day of the celebrated battle, and stands yet. This event occurred in 1476. The venerated tree is encircled by a colonnade, to protect it from the curiosity-hunters. In 1884 the author stood under the shadow of an historic tree, the grand old cypress, hung with mosses and fire-scorched, well known to travelers in Mexico as the *Arbol de la Noche Triste*, or "Tree of the Sad Night," under which Cortez is said to have passed the night of July 1, 1520, where he wept over his misfortunes after the defeat of his forces by the army of Montezuma. That was three hundred and sixty years ago, and the tree must have been very old then. What is to be the fate of these forest mammoths? Doubtless before the march of civilization they will disappear in a few years; the cupidity of man can hardly resist the temptations they present; railroad-ties and lumber are valuable; the tree therefore means money. The famous pyramids of Egypt were stripped of their red granite casing ages ago to furnish material for other buildings. Stonehenge, the most remarkable antiquity of England, has almost been destroyed by the people that live near it, who have used its material for cowsheds and pig-sties. In like manner the giant conifers of California and the eucalypti of Australia will pass from human sight. Somebody may be wise enough to preserve a few specimens, either in California or Australia, for the sake of those who are to come after us, but the probabilities lie on the other side.*

Then let us project ourselves down over the ages a few thousand years, and if one should stumble upon an old book in some very ancient library telling the world of these enormous trees the story would be looked upon as a myth and entirely unbelievable; they would treat it precisely as some now treat the Bible. It does require faith to accept much that is written in the Bible; and does it not require faith to accept much that is written in the book of nature well as in the life of man?

The account given in the book of Numbers concerning the grapes of Eshcol have no doubt raised in many a mind a query; and yet there is nothing to justify a doubt. We are told that when the spies were sent forth to view the promised land most of them were terror-stricken at the giant race which they must meet in entering upon their inheritance; but, on the other hand, they were delighted with the fruits of the land. On their arrival at the valley of Eshcol

---

* The Secretary of the Interior has requested the Secretary of War to station a company of cavalry in the Sequoia National Park and another in the Yosemite Park to prevent depredations on the mammoth tree groves. It is said the so-called Bellamy colonists, who have in part a perfected title to the land on which these trees stand, have expressed a purpose to hold their claims in spite of opposition.

they cut down a branch with a cluster of grapes and bore it "between two on a staff." This, like some other things, has been regarded by some as an overdrawing of facts, as if they were so filled with thoughts of giants that even the clusters of grapes were gigantic also. Who ever heard of a cluster of grapes growing to such a size? The fact is, they bore it in this way in part because it was so large, and for convenience' sake in transporting it, in order that the fruit might not be bruised. In the far East, where the grape is indigenous, vines have often been known to attain a diameter of a foot and a half. Strabo, as quoted by Dr. Smith, states that it is on record "that there are vines in Margiana (Persia) whose stems are such as would require two men to span around, and whose clusters are two cubits long." Travelers in the Orient tell us to-day of single clusters which often weigh ten or twelve pounds.

I must be content with quoting the following extract from Dr. Kitto, which is strikingly illustrative of the manner in which the spies carried that remarkable cluster from Eshcol: "Even in our own country a bunch of grapes was produced at Welbeck and sent as a present from the Duke of Rutland to the Marquis of Rockingham which weighed nineteen pounds. It was conveyed to its destination, more than twenty miles distant, on a staff by four laborers, two of whom bore it in rotation. The greatest diameter of this cluster was nineteen and a half inches, its length twenty-three inches."

But let us go back into the records of past ages. There was the enormous vegetation of the coal period, which has left its impressions upon the rocks, as seen in our coal-mines. The vegetation of that age was peculiar; it grew for a purpose, and must have differed widely from any thing that grows upon the earth at present; it was a coal-producing vegetation, entirely unlike the vegetable growths of to-day.

The varieties were few, and are known to us now as tree-ferns, rushes, club-mosses, etc., whose size was very great. Ferns then reached the proportion of stately trees, fifty or sixty feet high, with trunks from one to two feet in diameter; the ferns surely had giant ancestors, whether we had or not. There was a species of vegetation which we call now by the name of *Calamite*, a jointed plant something like the rush; but instead of being a foot or two in height it rose to an altitude of twenty or thirty feet. Its fossil stems are found in the coal-seams. Then there was the *Sigillaria*, so-called from the seal-marks upon its vertical ribs. Its leaves wound spirally around its stem or trunk in the most graceful and beautiful order. Trunks of this species of tree frequently occur standing erect or lying prostrate in the coal-mines, and sometimes with their roots imbedded in the soil where they grew, beneath the coal of which they form a part, and when the miner cuts them off below their tapering form permits the whole mass to drop out, by which many a poor fellow has lost his life. Club-mosses then grew to a height of sixty feet. Cone-bearing trees of great size flourished in that age. It is truly wonderful that we should be able to trace these creations of an almost infinitely remote past; to be able to exhume their fossils from the earth, and to find even the leaf, stem, twigs, of trees and shrubs that flourished thousands upon thousands of years before man was created. The earth in those far-off ages must have presented a singular sight; the forests and jungles were so dense that the sunlight must have been in a great degree shut out. The air was heavy with carbonic acid gas, and such animals only as needed but little oxygen inhabited the waters of these primeval seas or roamed through the dense thickets which then covered the earth.

"The amount of vegetable matter in a single coal-seam six inches thick is greater than the most luxuriant vegetation of the present day could furnish in twelve hundred years. Boussingault calculates that luxuriant vegetation at the present day takes from the atmosphere about half a ton of carbon per acre annually, or fifty tons an acre per century. Fifty tons of stove-coal spread evenly over an acre of surface could make a layer of less than one third of an inch. But suppose it to be half an inch, then the time required for the accumulation of a seam of coal three feet thick—the thinnest that can be worked to advantage—would be 7,260 years. If the aggregate thickness of the seams of coal in any basin amounts to sixty feet the time required for its accumulation would be 144,000 years. In the coal-measures of Nova Scotia are seventy-six seams of coal, of which one is twenty-two feet thick and another thirty-seven feet thick." Imagine the time required for the deposit.

We speak of these great deposits and great epochs as if it meant only business. But there is beauty as well as utility. Dr. Buckland says of the interior lining of a coal-mine: 'The most elaborate imitations of living foliage upon the painted ceilings of

Italian palaces bear no comparison with the beauteous profusion with which the galleries of these instructive coal-mines are overhung. The roof is covered with a canopy of gorgeous tapestry enriched with festoons of most graceful foliage, flung in wild, irregular profusion over every portion of its surface. The effect is heightened by the contrast of the coal-black color of these vegetables with the light groundwork of rock to which they are attached. The spectator feels himself transported as if by enchantment into the forests of another world; he beholds trees of forms and characters now unknown upon the surface of the earth, presented to his senses almost in the beauty of their primeval life."

CHAPTER XIX.

WORLD WONDERS—ANIMALS.

WE have elsewhere in this book spoken of the fanciful idea of a French writer who in a learned volume attributed to the progenitor of our race such an enormous stature. It is really ludicrous to read the story of the "giants" as related by some of the savants of a century or two ago. By them we are told of that puissant lord, the Chevalier Rincon, whose remains were discovered at Rouen in 1509, whose skull was reported to "hold a bushel of wheat;" whose shin-bone was "four feet long," and others in proportion. The skeleton of a hero was also reported to have been found at Valence, France, in 1705, which was "twenty-two feet long;" and still others were calculated to have belonged to "giants thirty-six feet high;" and even greater wonders than these were the theme of pen and speech. Bones were dug up out of the earth unlike any belonging to the human species, and as men knew nothing of geology, paleontology, and comparative anatomy they were supposed to have been those of a race of human beings of enormous proportions, in whose veritable existence the world had generally believed. But how fanciful!

Sir Hans Sloane was one of the first to express an opinion that these so-called "bones of the giants" were not human remains at all, but animal. This announcement was at the time considered the rankest of heresy, and the philosopher was asked if he would dare to contradict the sacred Scriptures, in which it was said, "There were giants in those days." In time the celebrated Cuvier came to the front and fully proved that these bones were in reality the fossil remains of enormous animals which had become extinct. Great teeth had been discovered imbedded in the earth, some of which weighed from a dozen to nearly twenty pounds. These teeth were on exhibition in the museums, and were regarded as having belonged to these giant men of the past; but they, too, were shown by the learned naturalist to have been the molars of these same animals, or to have belonged to spermaceti whales.

If we uncover the earth under our feet in almost any section of the globe we come upon the remains of beings that formerly lived and sported on the land or in the seas. They were entirely unlike the present races of the animal kingdom, particularly in the matter of size and possible ferocity. Were they to reappear they would be regarded as a race of hideous monsters, the terror of every living being of to-day, whether man or beast; but in their own age they were as natural as are the animals of the earth at the present. And, furthermore, were it not for the fact that their remains are found in the strata of the older geological periods it would be difficult to believe that such monstrous beasts ever walked the earth or swam in the seas. But natural history has proven beyond any question that our earth was once the arena where these giant animals fought their battles, propagated their species, lived and died. The pre-adamite world was a fact as surely as the post-adamite. The former was one in which huge fantastic creatures of amazing magnitude and shape played their part.

The fossil remains and rocky impressions of these beings have been brought to light in so many places all over the world that their existence is no longer called in question. They have been found in complete form just as they lived ages ago, and often in natural positions when they were suddenly overtaken by some awful convulsion of nature, or in parts; a single bone has been found from which the whole animal has been reproduced in appearance, both as to size and shape. The skillful comparative anatomist is able even to decide upon the habits of these ancient denizens of sea and land.

It must be remembered that the laws of nature proceed with so much uniformity, and the types of the animal races have been so persistent, that the expert naturalist has not found it a very difficult task to reproduce these ancient organisms. In proof of this instances are on record quite numerous in which after the reproduction of some extinct animal from a bone or two, using artificial material, and following the well-known laws of animal life or existence, the geologist has discovered somewhere in the strata the entire fossil of such an animal, which has been found to correspond almost exactly with the reproduction of the anatomist.

A good illustration of this is seen in the well-known case of the great *Megalosaur* by Dr. B. Waterhouse Hawkins, who enriched the Crystal Palace at Sydenham, England, a few years ago, by filling one of the large sections of that building with reproductions in both form and size of the organic remains of the pre-adamite world which have been discovered by geologists. It was one of the most interesting as well as the most instructive sections at the exhibition. The dimensions of some of them may be seen in the fact that certain of these models contain thirty tons of clay, which had to be supported on four legs, as their natural history characteristics would not allow of recourse being had to any of the expedients for support allowed to sculptors in ordinary cases.

The best work in this field of science was done by Professor Hawkins, whose long acquaintance with recent forms of the animal kingdom enabled him to adapt to the extinct species which he has restored all of their natural habits. Perhaps the greatest one of these old-time monsters was the *Iguanodon*, a variety of the *Dinosaur*, which was not much less than the building of a house upon four columns. The quantity of material of which the standing iguanodon is composed consisted of four iron columns nine feet long and seven inches in diameter, six hundred bricks, six hundred and fifty five-inch, half-round drain tiles, nine hundred plain tiles, thirty-eight casks of cement, in all about six hundred and forty bushels of broken stone and other material. These, with a quantity of iron hooping and inch bar-iron, which constituted the bones, sinews, and muscles of this large model, the restored form stood before the world—a picture of an age which taxes the wildest imagination.

If this description does not give the reader an accurate idea of an old time "pet" it may be further stated that a party of twenty-one scientific gentlemen, at the invitation of Mr. Hawkins, on one occasion took dinner within the restored form of this animal. The iguanodon was herbivorous, living on the branches of the cypress-tree, which have been found fossil in its stomach.

But this is not all. There was the *Megalosaur*, a flesh-eating animal, whose teeth curved backward like pruning-knives, and with a double edge of enamel so as to cut like a sharp saber equally on each side. There was an animal which scientists have named the *Ichthyosaur*, a combination of fish and lizard, as the name imports. It was never seen by the eye of man, for it existed long before he came upon the scene. But how do we know that there ever were such beings on the earth? By the fossils that have been exhumed out of the earth's deep beds, and by the impressions they have made on the rocks. This last-named animal had the general shape of the dolphin, the snout of a porpoise, the head of a lizard, the jaws and teeth of a crocodile, the vertebræ of a fish, and the paddles of a whale. It lived in the waters, but breathed the air like the whale. Its neck was short and thick, its head was large, and its body at times attained a length of thirty to forty feet. Its jaws had an enormous opening, some having been found which contained one hundred and sixty teeth. The eyes were often two feet in diameter, and were so constructed that they could be used either as telescopes or microscopes, thus enabling the monster to see its prey near or far, and even in the darkness of the night. Verily there have been some things even in this world that lie out a good way beyond our ordinary experience. There was the so-called *Plesiosaur*, which had the head of a lizard, the teeth of a crocodile, a swan-shaped neck of enormous length and size, the trunk of a quadruped, the ribs of a chameleon. Each pair of ribs surrounded the body with a complete girdle formed of five pieces, thus affording great facility for the expansion and dilation of the lungs. The finding of one of these fossils is thus related by Professor J. Dorman Steele: "In 1811 Mary Anning, of Lyme Regis, England, a poor country girl who made her precarious living by picking up fossils, for which the neighborhood was famous, was pursuing her vocation, hammer in hand, when she perceived some bones projecting a little out of the cliff. Finding on examination that it was part of a large skeleton, she cleared away the rubbish and found the whole creature imbedded in the block of stone. She hired workmen to dig at the block of lias in which it was buried. In this manner was the first of these monsters brought to light—a monster thirty feet long, with jaws nearly a fathom in length, and huge saucer-shaped eyes, which have since been found so perfect that the petrified lenses have been split off and used as magnifiers."

The *Pterodactyl* was even more of a monster than the last named; it was, in fact, a huge bat, with hollow bones, and without feathers, and was armed with a mouth full of glittering teeth. When of full size this monster bat had wings which extended sometimes more than sixteen feet from tip to tip. It could walk upright with folded wings, perch upon the trees, or climb the ragged cliffs with its hooked claws, holding itself in readiness to descend upon its prey. This was a species of flying dragon, and may have given rise to that monster of the ancient belief which was pictured as having breath of fire, poisoning the air with its exhalations and disputing with man the possession of the earth itself.

Over the earth there roamed in great herds such monster beasts as we now know only by the names given to them by the naturalists. There was, for instance, the *Mammoth*, sometimes spoken of as a "fossil elephant," which was a third larger than the largest of that species of modern times whose well-preserved remains are found in the ice-banks of Siberia and other extreme northern regions, and whose teeth and tusks have formed much of the ivory used both in Europe and America.

The *Mastodon* was even larger and more massive than the mammoth, and existed on both continents. A single tooth of this beast has been known to weigh nearly twenty pounds. Ivory tusks have been found measuring fourteen feet in length and weighing several hundred pounds. A skeleton of one of these animals was accidentally found by a farmer in a bog in New Jersey a few years ago. In the place of his stomach there were seven bushels of vegetable matter which was ascertained to be cypress twigs, which doubtless constituted its last supper. It must have ventured into some marsh for a drink of water, where it became entangled, and on account of its great weight sank in the mire, where it had lain for ages.

But perhaps the greatest of all the distinctively land animals of ancient times was the *Megatherium* (the word means monstrous beast); this was one of the most clumsy and ill-shapen of all the extinct species yet exhumed. Its fore feet were each about one yard long and a foot broad, and were furnished with gigantic claws. The pelvis of this monster is one of the most massive bony structures that the world ever saw. And yet it is not so much the size as the strength of this Old World creature that is indicated by those colossal bones. It lived upon vegetables, and so great was its power that it could pull up large trees by their roots for the purpose of feeding upon the upper branches. Having with its vast claws broken the ground around the root of a tree, it would rise upon its haunches, and, using its tail, which was two or three feet in circumference, as a third leg or prop, it would take the tree in its powerful grasp, rocking it to and fro to loosen its roots, and would then gather up all its strength and lift it from the ground. Such, at least, is the supposition made by scientists from its peculiar form and solidity of the bony structure.

Since these creatures have passed away from the pampas of South America the world has seen nothing to equal them in pure physical power among animals. Then there was the *Glyptodon*, a mammal encased in a shell like a turtle, which was a dozen feet long, and must often have weighed half a ton. Were it living now and roaming about our fields and forests it would be rather a fearful object to meet either by day or night.

There is certainly no room for skepticism along these lines; that such huge quadrupeds, serpents, and saurians did live all intelligent readers of science know.

Directly under the waving prairie fields of Kansas, where all is now thrift and beauty, once swept the waters of an old cretaceous ocean. To-day are found in excavations made by man, or through the agency of great floods, animal remains of startling magnitude. Among them was discovered but recently the entire vertebral column, over thirty feet in length, of the *Ornithorhynchus*, and the bones of a paddle of a giant turtle or tortoise, which must have been at least eighteen feet long.

The richest find of all in Kansas, however, was made in a ravine which had been filled by a very heavy rain to overflowing. The water, passing off, washed away the loose earth and sediment of limestone on the sides, thus revealing almost an entire skeleton of a creature known as the *Liodon Dyspelor*, the longest of the antediluvian reptiles, and the head of the *Portheus Molossus*, a shark-like fish of formidable power. The dyspelor measured nearly sixty feet in length from the tip of his nose to the end of the long serpent-like tail, and the head of the molossus was some inches longer than that of a full-grown grizzly bear, and much broader and heavier.

To add to the interest of the discovery, it could be easily seen that the gigantic monsters had died in combat, for the great jaws of the molossus, with their terrible cylindric fangs, were closed in a death-grip on the hind leg of the dyspelor, crushing it between them, while from the position of the other giant it could plainly be seen that it had used its flexible though massive tail in beating to death its foe, which with bull-dog tenacity had still retained its hold. The capacious mouth of the dyspelor, with its glistening teeth, was wide open, the head thrown nearly back on the vertebræ, and the whole carcass was convulsed into a half coil. At that moment some great wave of power must have come suddenly upon them, covering them up in their tomb, to lie unseen and unknown until in after ages they should be brought to light to show man what had been on this earth in the ages of the past.

Those who have so much to say, when speaking of the Bible, about not believing things which do not accord with modern experience and observation would do well to examine the government collection of fossil remains recently found in the so-called "Bad Lands" of Wyoming, a region once densely populated with beasts, birds, and reptiles beside which our largest modern species would be mere pygmies. Who of Adam's race ever saw reptiles one hundred feet long and of corresponding bulk? flying dragons with twenty-five feet spread of wings? great birds with rows of glittering teeth? mammals three times the size of our largest elephants? sharks as enormous as whales? fish clad in mighty plates of armor? Who ever saw saurians such as have been exhumed in these regions, sixty feet long, and that stood fifteen feet high, and must have weighed twenty tons? Imagine—for that is all we can do—that wonderful reptilian monster named by paleontologists the *Triceratop*, whose neck measured six feet across the back, intended for the attachment of great muscles for holding up the huge head—an animal covered with plates of armor, and from whose head projected great horns, or that other species called the *Atlantosaur*, the bulkiest animal possibly that ever walked the earth. It attained a length of one hundred feet at times. Its thigh-bones have been found measuring eight feet in length and two feet in diameter. If man had lived in the age when these beasts were on the earth his experience would have differed from ours surely. Then he would also have seen great swimming lizards eighty feet long, turtles twenty feet long and seven or eight feet high, and many other living forms in which it taxes one's credulity to believe. But believe in them we do, for there are the remains, dug out of the earth like coal or limestone, and placed in museums for the inspection of mankind.

It is well known that the great cities of London and Paris both occupy positions directly above what were once great centers of animal life; both cities are built over the tombs of extinct species. What life, activity, business, pleasure, there are in these marts! what death below them! The buildings of Paris, that gay, beautiful, wealthy city, are constructed of stone made up largely of animal forms. There was a species of whale which once existed in the seas known to us as the *Zeuglodon*, so called from the yoke-shape of its fossil teeth. The seas in which it swam have passed away; the animals are gone; but they have left their bones in the earth which formed the old sea-bottom. In places in our own South their vertebræ are so numerous that the farmers have plowed them out and laid them up in fences or burned them for their lime. A single vertebra is so heavy as to tax the strength of a man to lift it. These animals existed before man came upon the stage. Indeed, they were agents sent of God to do their part in fitting up this world-residence for man. Like the coral and thousands of other microscopic creatures, they played their part. To them even we are indebted for many things we enjoy. The great Father sent them as our forerunners, and we are in our way only completing the work they began. Let us suppose now that some slab or series of slabs had been discovered in one of the deserted temples of Central America, on which in strange hieroglyphics had been recorded this story of these Old World monsters, or that some dusty volume in some old library had been found somewhere in the world describing these giant creatures; how ready some of us would be to cry out, "Impossible!" How many would call the story mythical, and say that no such beings ever walked the earth, for it is not according to our experience and observation!

CHAPTER XX.

STRUGGLES WITH UNBELIEF.

IT seems to be a law of the universe that every thing which lives must in some sense battle for its existence. Life itself is a series of contests, which begin in our infancy and only terminate when the heart ceases to beat. The tendency in all things is toward change and decay; out of these come all true progress. The mental and moral world are as full of struggles as the physical. The highest life we may live is the life of faith, which means that there are some things that lie beyond our comprehension, and so must be taken on trust.

> "The steps of faith fall on the seeming void,
> But find a rock beneath."

Nothing is gained in this world without a struggle. The law holds good every-where, in every department of life; even our faith must be tried, "that the trial of your faith might be much more precious than gold." He who never doubts never inquires, and he who never asks questions never learns. An active mental life is a chain of interrogation-points. Let it be our motto to reverently approach the gate of the temple of knowledge and ask admittance. "Her ways are ways of pleasantness."

We have kept steadily in mind all along the fact of the two books which God has written for our instruction—Nature and Scripture. The rocky tables of the one and the flexible pages of the other have been traced all over with the finger-marks of divinity. In both are wonderful chronicles, in both are some mysterious records too profound for our thought. Who understands fully the earth? Who can possibly find out God or know the infinite? If the Bible is not an inspired book, then it has deceived the world, and out of this deception have come the best society, the best books, the best schools, and the best of every thing. The claim is frequently made that the light of nature is all-sufficient, and some men boastfully declare that they need nothing more. But Nature is not able to teach us spiritual truths. Nature is sometimes misunderstood, or at least we do not fully take in her meaning. The mirage is a natural phenomenon that has lured many a traveler to his death amid the burning sands of an African desert. The earth seems to be a plane, but it is not. To the sense of sight the heavens are a dome over us, in which the stars are set as "jewels in the crown of night." The horizon is a circle which bounds our vision, and where the sky seems to drop down upon the land or the sea, actually inclosing a given area of the earth's plane. The sun and moon seem to be flying in a westward course over our heads, whereas we are only moving eastward. We "walk by faith and not by sight;" so, too, we read by faith and not by sight always. For any one in this materialistic age to affirm his belief in the whole Bible is to run the risk of being called very credulous by some people, to say the least, if not to incur the positive ridicule of many; while to declare one's entire belief in the teachings of science, with all its marvels, is to win the respect of the world.

"Faith in the supernatural supplies the grandest inspiration, alike in respect to action and endurance, that the human mind can receive. It gives hope to the soul and scatters clouds that would otherwise darken its sky. Can that be essentially false which is productive of the best results? Is it to be supposed that a pure illusion is practically better than the truth? Let those answer these questions who treat the supernatural as a falsehood and a sham."

Science has in it some things as incomprehensible and as mysterious as anything contained in the Scriptures; indeed, the teachings of the Bible do not make as much of a draft on our credence as many things that are known to be true in the natural world about us. The story of Jonah, and especially that part of it which relates to his experience in the belly of a "great fish," more than anything in the Bible, seems too mythical. Even some very eminent Bible scholars have not agreed concerning it. Some have called it a fiction, others an allegory, still others a legend or fable, and have accepted it as merely a method employed to teach certain things. The account is before us and constitutes a portion of the Scriptures, and so has a claim upon our consideration. Let it be remembered that Jonah is not a modern discovery. The incomprehensibility of the miracle by which he was arrested and brought to duty has provoked mockery and jest from the very earliest times, and there is a sense in which the narrative has been a stumbling-block to many for ages.

It is allowable in biblical as well as in all other

studies to let reason guide us as far as it can; but every one must admit that there are some things which lie beyond the boundary of human reason. This is true in the material world; why not in the wider, deeper, spiritual realm? The Bible instructs us in moral duties by plain speech, by metaphor, allegory, parable, poem, and history. When we read it let us not forget that here as elsewhere in secular literature words are but "signs of ideas;" and so these statements, whether in one form of speech or another, have a meaning. The question should be, What do they mean? Furthermore, in God's dealings with mankind he has invariably employed natural agencies and processes as far as possible. It is not, therefore, to be supposed that when he said to Noah, "I do set my bow in the cloud, and it shall be for a token of a covenant between me and the earth," * that the rainbow was then and there created, and for that purpose alone. The beautiful bow that spans the dark cloud is caused by the sun-ray falling on descending drops of water, and by refraction and reflection presents to the eye of the beholder this charming celestial phenomenon. But now for the first time it was made use of for a "sign." When we have gone to the extent of reason faith comes to our aid and we are able to reach out further and know more.

Jonah was one of the oldest of the prophets. He lived when Nineveh was in the very zenith of its power, the greatest city in the world. This prophet was commanded to go to Nineveh and warn all the people, from the king down, to turn from their iniqui-

* Gen. ix, 13.

ties, either political sins or individual sins, possibly both. He seems to have had a dread of being considered a false prophet in case mercy should be shown to the city. But he finally reached the place, delivered his message, a fast was appointed, the people repented, and the city was not overthrown.

Here is a field for the doubter and the unbeliever. He declares that he cannot accept all this as true. Well, is it not a fact that until quite recent times even the story of Nineveh and Babylon were considered by many to be mythical? But the confirmations of the historical accuracy are increasing every year. It is within the memory of men still living that skeptics have asked, "Where is Nineveh? Where is Babylon? These places never existed." People laughed at the story of these cities as they did at that of ancient Troy.

Sennacherib, Shalmaneser, Tiglath-pileser, were as mythical as Agamemnon, Hector, and Achilles; but Rawlinson, Layard, and Schliemann have unearthed these buried cities, and lo! the Scriptures are confirmed minutely. All men who have given this question careful and impartial thought have come to regard the Scriptures as containing authentic history of Nineveh and Babylon. But what is it that the skeptic disbelieves in this account of Jonah? The story of the fish. Let us examine it, therefore.

After the command of God the prophet failed to "obey marching orders." He went to Joppa to escape duty, and took passage in a ship for Tarshish, thus refusing to work in the field to which he had been appointed. Then a great storm arose. The sailors called upon their gods, but no deliverance came. They remembered the poor traveler in the ship's hold asleep. They roused him from his stupor with the question, "What meanest thou, O sleeper? arise, call upon thy God, if so be that God will think upon us, that we perish not."* Then, as was customary in such extremities, they cast lots for the purpose of discovering who was the provoking cause of this storm. The renegade prophet confessed his nationality and his flight, and bade them cast him into the sea. Let it be said to the credit of these heathen sailors that they did all in their power to save the life of this passenger who had paid his fare and committed himself to their keeping. But the storm continued to rage and the ship was in peril with every one on it, and, as a last resort, Jonah was heaved overboard into the angry waters, and immediately the waves ceased their furious raging, and these sailors acknowledged the sovereignty of God.

Now the narrative informs us that a "great fish" swallowed the prophet Jonah. So far as that may be concerned there was nothing in the least degree miraculous, for many a man has fallen into the sea and been devoured by some ferocious sea-monster. If we were to read in the newspaper any day that a man had fallen overboard into the sea or had been thrown overboard by the crew and a huge shark had devoured him, it is not at all likely that any one would throw down the paper and refuse to believe it. But it is written: "Now the Lord had prepared a great fish to swallow up Jonah. And Jonah was in the belly of the fish three days and three nights,"† and Jonah was ejected from the fish's stomach. The

* Jonah i, 6. † Jonah i, 17.

story of the overthrow is easily credited, but the preservation of life under such anomalous circumstances, together with the ejectment, are the points at which some people demur. This whole account comes under the head of miracles, and if these have been wrought under any circumstances, then this narration is certainly not difficult to believe. There have been so many strange occurrences in the history of the world that it behooves one to be cautious in rejecting statements which involve the marvelous, the mysterious, the miraculous. But all strange things are not miracles, let us remember. It may be interesting to note a few occurrences that reveal to us the inexplicable.

Many years ago a gentleman accidentally dropped his gold watch into the Atlantic Ocean when the vessel was off the banks of Newfoundland. It was a valuable watch, engraved with his name and residence. As it fell into the ocean it was lost forever, seemingly. But in the course of a year it was sent to him, no longer a valuable time-keeper, to be sure, but as a mere curiosity. As the watch descended through the waters of the sea it was caught and swallowed by a cod-fish; the fish was also caught afterward, as myriads are every year, and in its maw was found the watch. There was nothing miraculous in all this; it was simply a curious circumstance, and any one can see that it was entirely within the realm of the possible. Such a thing, however, would not take place once in millions of times under similar circumstances. An instance somewhat like this occurred in England a few years ago when a gentleman dropped a finger-ring into the river Tyne while leaning over a bridge, gazing into the water. In a few days his servant brought the ring to him and laid it on his table. On being asked by her master where she had obtained it she replied, "Indeed, was it not in the stomach of the fish which yourself bought in the market to-day?"

A remarkable instance was that of the book discovered in the stomach of a fish in England. On the 23d of June, 1626, a cod-fish was brought to Cambridge market which upon being opened was found to contain a book in its maw or stomach. The book was much soiled and covered with slime, though it had been wrapped in a piece of sail-cloth. It was a duodecimo work, written by one John Frith, comprising several treatises on religious subjects. In a letter now in the British Museum, written by Mr. Mead, of Christ Church College, to Sir M. Stuteville, the writer says that he had "seen with his own eyes the fish, the maw, the piece of sail-cloth, and the book." The treatises contained in the book were written by Mr. Frith when in prison. Strange to say, he had been long confined in a fish-cellar at Oxford, where many of his fellow-prisoners died from the impure exhalation of unsound fish. He was removed from thence to the Tower, and in 1533 was burned at the stake for his adherence to the reformed religion. The authorities at Cambridge reprinted the work, which had been completely forgotten till it turned up in this strange manner. The reprint is entitled *Vox Piscis*, and was adorned with a woodcut representing the stall at Cambridge market, with the fish, book, and knife.

One of the most singular circumstances of modern times was that in which a newly married couple were journeying eastward from Chicago, over one of the leading railroad lines half a dozen years ago, and in the toilet-room in the morning the lady let slip from her finger into the basin a valuable diamond ring, given to her on the occasion of her betrothal. The train swept on, and the lady mourned her lost ring. But a year or two afterward a fish-monger in Toledo, Ohio, found this ring in the stomach of a fish. It must have been that the ring fell off as the train was passing over a bridge which spanned some stream flowing into Lake Erie. The fish had wandered about until it was caught in Lake Erie and opened in the market, and thus gave up its treasure. The jewel having been engraved with the lady's name and residence, it was sent to the chief of police of Chicago and through him returned to its owner. A one-hundred-dollar check from the husband was sent as a mark of appreciation to the honest fish-monger.

These were not miracles, they were only marvels. But when Jesus sent his disciples to the water to catch a fish, in whose mouth they would find money wherewith to pay their taxes, that was a miracle; and when "God prepared" a "great fish" to swallow up Jonah, that too was a miracle.

That this prophet was a real person is shown by the fact that he is spoken of as the son of Amittai. He was a prophet of God whose history can no more be reasonably doubted than we can doubt that such a man as Cyrus lived. That Nineveh was a great city is equally true. These are simple historic statements; both are authentic. Some years ago the French consul at Mosul gave an account of a three-days' feast observed by the inhabitants of that Moslem city in commemoration of the penance imposed on the people of the region of Nineveh by Jonah.

He says that the fast has been kept up from time immemorial in that country, and observed not only by the few Christians there, but by the whole Moslem population. Mosul itself is within sight of the ruins of Nineveh, and close by is a tomb traditionally assigned to Jonah. It is a striking confirmation of the ancient Hebrew writings thus to find a fast in commemoration of an important event recorded in them still observed almost on the very spot where it first began. Nineveh has been desolate for centuries; the surrounding plains have become a desert. The Hebrew people themselves have been scattered over the earth for twenty centuries, yet still the three-days' penance enforced on the population of that corrupt capital of the ancient world is kept by the miserable descendants of the old Assyrians and by the strangers who have intermarried with them, whether Nestorian or Moslem in their faith. Whoever has read Layard's volumes, however, needs not to be reminded that Mesopotamia is still full of traditions recalling the scenes and customs described in the Old Testament. The cucumber gardens overhang the river exactly as they did in the days of Isaiah. The boats formed of skins, of which the Bible speaks, navigate to this hour the waters of the Tigris. But, more than all, the sculptures on the disinterred palaces and the cuneiform writing, so far as they have been deciphered, recall the chariots of war, the bearded kings, the royal insignia, the manners, the dress, nay, even the names, of the monarchs mentioned in the Hebrew Scriptures. No profane history of ages far less remote is confirmed in this respect by antiquarian discoveries more complete than the Bible. It is said that even the name of Jonah has been found in some of these old ruins.

The Bible speaks of the great fish, which in our English translation is called a "whale;" it should be rendered rather by the word "sea-monster." There are some great fish known to naturalists which, according to Gregory Nazianzen, swallow their young when danger threatens, and vomit them forth again at will. We are told by Pliny and Athenæus that an entire man clad in armor has been found in the stomach of a great sea-monster. Keil tells us on the authority of Oken that a great fish was caught in the waters of Sardinia which had in its stomach an entire horse. Sharks have been seen and captured on the west coast of France with throats sufficiently capacious to admit the passage of a full-grown man.

In the year 1758, when an English fleet was cruising in the Mediterranean waters during a violent storm, a sailor fell overboard from one of the frigates and was immediately seized by a monster fish, which partially disappeared. The captain of the vessel caused a cannon, which was standing on deck, to be discharged at the fish, which, being struck by the ball, ejected the man, but slightly injured, who was then taken up alive into the sloop, which had come to his assistance, and thus was rescued. This was stated in the report of the admiral of the fleet to his home government. There are some things, as we have before stated, in human life that astonish us on account of their seeming impossibility. That God could send a sea-monster of some species to carry out his plans we certainly must admit to be a possibility. This whole account is circumstantial; the details are all given specifically, and even the great Teacher himself refers to it in the following language: "For as Jonah was three days and three nights in the whale's belly; so shall the Son of man be three days and three nights in the heart of the earth." *

* Matt. xii, 40.

CHAPTER XXI.

WHAT IS TRUTH?

TO doubt is not necessarily to commit a great sin; if it were, then most people have sinned, for few have lived without doubting at some period of their lives; if not, it is proof that they did not think. All doubt is partial belief, and is sometimes only equivalent to asking for more evidence. When a man is seeking proof of a proposition, with his mind "open to conviction," he is an honest doubter. But when he cherishes the spirit of doubt until it becomes a mental habit with him there is danger of his reaching a point where he will be proof against reason and may run into the veriest atheism; in that case doubt is not only dangerous, it is a sin. There is such a thing as dishonest doubt—a condition that is described as "an evil heart of unbelief."

Distrust is born of evil experience. We are liable to lose our faith in good people by too close a contact or association with the bad. An innocent child is trustful as well as credulous; it does not reason, it simply believes and confides; it has not come in contact with the evil side of life. But it does not remain a child: the body develops, the brain expands, the experience ripens, and the credulous and trustful child becomes the incredulous and distrustful boy, and, alas! often the unbelieving and infidel man.

One of the most dangerous forms of infidelity is

materialism; for it dishonors our noblest nature. Its aim is to dethrone a king, to discrown a royal monarch. It does not discern, because it does not admit, the soul-life of the world. Let materialism prevail, and the highest and grandest qualities of human nature would be starved to death. Its whole theory of the human origin and human nature is degrading. Infidelity, in whatever form, in all ages and in all lands, has neglected the human soul and spent its force upon the lower nature of man. What would he be without a belief in the unseen, the spiritual? No man is ever great in any department of life who does not reach out after the things that are invisible; in other words, who does not act upon the belief in things which lie beyond the sight of his eyes. The statesman in the hall of the senate has to do with the material of the State, but he does more, he grasps the great principles which govern things and deals with them as they affect the life of the nation. It is this that gives him breadth, depth, and power.

The scientist is ever searching for the invisible— the atom, molecule, germ, or occult law in nature. The poet thus inspired beholds clearly what others do not see. The fact is outward and tangible, but the philosophy is inward, subtle, and invisible. Newton saw the apple fall to the ground, but he did not see gravitation with the same eyes; and yet he surely looked upon the invisible. What a grasp this insight, or, better, the spiritual sight, gives to philosophy! It makes the master every-where. The greatest power in us is the faith-power, which has made possible "the evidence of things not seen." Here we can strike hands with St. Paul across the spanning centuries and say, "While we look not at the things which are seen, but at the things which are not seen: for the things which are seen are temporal; but the things which are not seen are eternal." No man can lay any claim to greatness who does not believe in the things which lie beyond the range of mortal sight.

Skepticism is often a covert for sin; the skeptic says, "I do not accept your creed. I do not believe in your Bible; it is as full of myths and fables as Homer or any other of the old Greek classics;" and so he plunges too often into sin. Infidel eras in all ages and in all lands have been connected with selfishness, luxury, and license. A recent writer thus puts the case strongly: "The miser has no faith in kindness, the seducer no faith in woman's virtue, the trader in souls no faith in the rights of the weak, the traitor, no faith in loyalty; and such men as Nabal, Judas Iscariot, and Benedict Arnold carry about them inherent damnation."

There is a close relation between skepticism and crime.

The question is ever being asked, "Why are there so many suicides?" We answer, Because men live abnormally. Suicide is held by the courts to be an insane act. He who deliberately sends the bullet crashing through his brain, or takes his life by any other method, gives proof to the world that he is either mentally wrecked or that he has wrong views of God and human accountability. Look at it more broadly, and nothing is truer than that want of faith in a community or nation is followed by a corresponding deterioration of the moral spirit. The Germany of to-day is reaping the harvest of "advanced thought," or skepticism. Crime is said to have increased in some parts of the empire during the last few years two or three hundred per cent. The number of imprisonments, from recent statistical reports, in several German States has advanced enormously. The prisons are full, and patriotic men are urging the government to found a penal colony on some island of the Pacific Ocean or in western Africa, not for nihilists and socialists, but for common criminals. The court chaplain (Rev. Dr. Baur) preached a sermon before the late Emperor William in which he said: "Affection, faith, and obedience to the word of God are unknown in this country—in this our great German fatherland, which formerly was justly called 'the home of the faith.' On the contrary, it really seems as if it were the father of all lies who is now worshiped in Prussia. What formerly was considered generous and noble is now looked upon with contempt, and theft and swindling are called by the euphonic name 'business.' Marriages are concluded without the blessing of the Church, concluded 'on trial,' to be broken if not found to answer. We still have a Sunday, but it is only a Sunday in name, as the people work during church hours and spend the afternoon and evening in rioting in the public-houses and music-halls; while the upper classes rush to the races, preferring to hear the panting of the tortured horses to hearing the word of God, which is ridiculed in the press and turned into blasphemy in the popular assemblies; the servants of God are insulted daily."

The value of truth lies not in any mere theory, but in its practical application. We need the Christian belief, and we need the Christian practice, for where there is no criterion of the true there can be no standard of the good; and in the chaos of universal doubt and unbelief virtue must also founder and perish. The world—and twenty centuries ago imperial Rome meant the world—had reached the very acme of sensualism. Wealth was unbounded; individual fortunes were enormous among the great. Luxury, idleness, amusements, brought their curses on society. Men read philosophy—believed in the gods and oracles; but alas! virtue was almost banished from the earth. There was then just such a condition morally as some dreamers court at this hour, and whose teachings, if believed and practiced, would reproduce in modern America the foul stench of ancient Rome. There were, however, a few dim lights that almost flickered to their death; if they did no more they served to reveal the surrounding darkness. It was time that heaven should send a Teacher, if truth and virtue were to be preserved upon the earth; and the wisest of the heathen looked for the advent of One whom the ancient oracles had dimly announced as the Revealer of truth to men. In the fullness of time he came, and his word authoritatively ascertains to us both the *reality* and the *certainty* of truth. "To this end was I born, and for this cause came I into the world, that I should bear witness unto the truth." Notwithstanding the failure of human speculations, truth still has a substantive existence; and it is sufficiently dear to the heart of the honest searcher.

Many besides Pontius Pilate have asked the question, "What is truth?" And so despaired they of answer that they paused not long enough to hear the echo of their own question. This was the mistake of Pilate. Had he bowed his head and waited it would have flashed upon him, for Truth stood before him. Truth does exist, and the great Teacher told his disciples the "truth should make *them* free."

Truth is defined as "conformity to reality." It is the exact statement of things as they are; not falsehood nor illusion, nor even appearance, but simply reality. It runs through every thing. Falsehood may supplant it in the individual life, in society, and even in national life; but nothing can live and prosper long that is not buttressed on the Rock of Ages. Jesus said, "I am the Truth." The individual who attempts to make black white, or white black, will fail sooner or later. There is a golden line of truth which starts with God and runs through the universe. And wherever mankind have found this golden way, and walked in it, they have gone forward to great destinies. All truth is essentially moral—may it not be said religious?—whether it be called historic, scientific, or political, and this because it is born of God and affects the life of the humblest intelligent being. There is such a condition as righteousness, to promote which the Bible exists; it has its foundation in right thinking.

Let us take up history and traverse its development through the ages, from the day which was honored by man's appearance on the earth to this hour, and what do we find? The answer is plain: there have been conflicts in these historic epochs; age has seemingly been arrayed against age; force has contended against force, and law has been in conflict with law.

But these conflicts of history have been less real than apparent. To show this let us turn from any and all single epochs to the great cycle of historic development, and in doing so we see that these unfoldings of history have been due to great natural laws regulated, counterbalanced, overruled by the Author of nature, for he has not withdrawn his presence from the world and retired off into the serene heavens, to be eternally lost in self-contemplation. "My father worketh hitherto, and I work." God is in the material world its Origin and its Governor; no less is he in human life, ever present, ever active; and they must indeed be blind who cannot see the footprints of Jehovah in the sands of time. Take a single illustration among many that might be selected from ancient and modern history.

The power of Napoleon Bonaparte culminated at the peace of Tilsit. All Europe, England excepted, was at his feet. To perpetuate his power he then conceived the project of a close alliance with Alexander of Russia, who, though beaten in the field, was fascinated by the dazzling splendor of his adversary's peerless genius. United by close ties to that mighty autocrat, what power could disturb the security of his throne? Thus reasoned Napoleon's selfish judgment. To gain this end he made a promise—to let Alexander in due time wrest Constantinople from the Turks. This promise he did not intend to keep. While flattering he consciously deceived his ally, who, believing him sincere, swallowed the bait and avowed himself the friend, the admirer, and the ally of the dreaded conqueror.

That deceptive promise, begotten of his intense

selfishness, ruined Napoleon. When his insincerity became apparent Alexander became his irreconcilable enemy and tempted him to hurl his magnificent army of six hundred thousand men upon the capital of his dominions. Then Napoleon's selfishness gave birth to that proud self-confidence which originated his insane march on Moscow. The failure of that fearful campaign, by destroying the bulk and flower of his army, sapped the foundations of his throne. It is impossible to see how he could have been overthrown but for those irreparable losses, which were succeeded by combinations among his enemies that terminated his empire and his life at St. Helena.

Thus was Napoleon self-punished. There is no evidence that God interfered by any immediate personal act to effect his overthrow. Every step in the process can be traced to the natural action of his own self-disordered mind. With equal truth it may be affirmed that God overthrew him, inasmuch as it is by his arrangement that a selfish rejection of divine claims becomes the cause of such disordered mental and moral action in the ruin of the selfish man. Thus does sin punish itself, and history finds its equilibrium in the long periods.

If we turn to science, or to nature, of which science is but the dictionary, we shall see the marks of great contests. Volcanic fires have upheaved the rocky crust of the globe, as if to beat back the ocean, while the ocean has swelled and heaved like an omnipotent giant in defense, seemingly, of its own dominions. In nature all about us there are in daily operation forces and counter-forces. Vital force uplifts vegetation, from the moss that festoons the rock to the oak in the forest, creating leaves, flowers, fruits, and then the frosts, winds, and snows turn them back into their primal elements again. Decay follows growth, and growth succeeds decay in an endless series. Fire and water are natural antagonists. The sun's ray lifts the vapor toward the skies, while the earth's attractive power draws it back in refreshing showers or sometimes in devastating storms. These are opposing forces, each considered by itself; but that very opposition implies a unity in fact, resulting from the law which gives us seed-time and harvest, summer and winter, flowers and fruits in their season.

In the physical world, as well as in the world's moral history, conflicts are only in the short periods, and hence are only apparent. One age in the world's progress is found to have been in conflict with other ages; but if we keep in view all the ages it is clear that they harmonize into one beautiful age. All point to a completed period, a great and symmetrical whole composed of many parts, unlike, possibly, but each contributing to the sum. For illustration, suppose we lay a car-load of crude iron at the door of the machine-shop and leave an order for a locomotive. These men of clear brains and strong arms will go to work; they will take up this metal and subject it to the heat of the furnace and the strokes of the trip-hammer. It will pass into all shapes by the action of fire and forge and lathe; and, scattered through all the departments, it will soon be lost to the unpracticed eye. There is no locomotive in those single pieces of iron lying about the building or revolving in the lathes. But wait until the chief mechanic shall bring all together, these arms, cylinders, and pistons and wheels, and put each to its place. Then you have the most magnificent piece of mechanism the eye of man ever beheld. It would ill become one not skilled in such industries to go in there and condemn the work he does not understand. Let us apply this to the world about us. To the finite mind there is seeming disorder and confusion; but let us wait for the coming together of all the parts—the epochs, the eras, the time of completion when the great builder shall make the true adjustments; then it will be seen, if not before, that in all there was a ruling mind, a Being into whose face we reverently look and say, "Father!" In the light of these reflections we can see how every thing has had its work to do, whether the invisible animalcule or the mastodon. Whether fires that have melted the granites, or ice-fields that have covered half the globe in cold and darkness—"all things have worked together for good;" "fire, and hail; snow, and vapor; stormy wind fulfilling his word."

And all this applies equally to the moral world—the world of religious and speculative thought. Here, too, we have system in conflict with system: on the one hand materialism, on the other spiritualism; now unitarianism, and then trinitarianism. In philosophy we have idealism, sensationalism, rationalism, etc. There are many systems, and each has its adherents. These moral and intellectual conflicts answer to the physical, where sea has contended with land, and water has waged war with flame. If it be asked which shall conquer, this form of religion or that, this philosophy or that, we answer, "Stand still and see the salvation of God."

In the progress of society some things will perish entirely because not begotten in the truth; but the right will win.

> "For truth shall conquer at last,
>   As round and round we run;
> For ever the right comes uppermost,
>   And ever is justice done."

It is well for us to know the truth in all things, in science, in history, in politics; but the highest truth we have is that which concerns us as spiritual beings. For us to know whether the planets are inhabited or not is of small consequence, though the subject is not devoid of interest. But to know how to grow Godward, how to increase in spiritual life and joy, is important in view of the immortal state. What is truth? To know God. It is to this the Bible points. It deals with the loftiest truth, because it teaches the way of life. But the doubter asks, What about this immortality? Arguments are not needed. Sir Lytton Bulwer, the great English novelist, has this beautiful passage on "Our Destiny," or a future life: "It cannot be that earth is man's only abiding-place. It cannot be that our life is a bubble, cast up by the ocean of eternity, to float a moment upon its waves and then sink into nothingness. Else why is it that the high and glorious. aspirations which leap like angels from the temples of our hearts are forever wandering about unsatisfied? Why is it that the stars which hold their festival around the midnight throne are set above the grasp of our limited faculties, forever mocking us with their unapproachable glory? And, finally, why is it that bright forms of beauty are represented to our view and then taken from us, leaving the ten thousand streams of our affections to flow back in one Alpine torrent upon our hearts? *Surely we are born for a higher destiny than that of earth.* There is a realm where the rainbow never fades, where the stars will spread out before us like islands that slumber on the ocean, and where the beautiful beings which here pass before us like shadows will stay in our presence forever." Surely no one disbelieves the statement that nature is a great book of truth, and can be read as any other book is read.

We can talk with each other without words, with signs and symbols; even the eye or countenance may express the desires of the heart or the thoughts of the mind. Language may be a divine gift in the sense of a power or faculty created in us to enable us to communicate our ideas and understand each other; but mere speech is conventional, and a new language is possible at any time or in any place.

God has spoken to mankind in words, but he has also spoken in signs. The sun, the moon, the mountains, the birds and lilies of the field are signs of his ideas. Here we are told of his power, as when the earth rocks or the mountains are lifted toward the skies. The daisy that smiles at us in the green fields and the rose which blooms in the garden tell us of God's idea of beauty. Every law of God in nature reveals his infinite wisdom. "The heavens declare the glory of God." All nature proclaims its Author. Who can doubt the existence of God? What lessons of power, wisdom, and love are every-where presented to us in the universe? Ten thousand voices are ever speaking to us out of the deep where he dwells. But the doubter says, "It is not this book of nature I disbelieve, but the written volume, the Bible." And so he rejects the latter because of its few mysteries, but accepts the former with all its ten thousand mysteries, alas! for man.

We were rambling one day several years ago through that beautiful region, the Connecticut valley, a locality famous for wonderful—so-called—"bird-tracks" that appear in the red sandstone which crops out in that region. And as we gazed upon some of the slabs which retain the impressions of these ancient footprints of bird or batrachian—some think the latter—we were deeply moved, not so much at the tracks themselves as at their wonderful—shall we say miraculous?—preservation. Think of it a moment! Thousands, possibly tens of thousands, of years ago a mammoth bird belonging to an extinct species walked along the sea-beach one day in quest of food, followed in her search, as we see now among our fowls, by her brood of birdlings. Right, left, right, left, the mother-bird and the baby-birds put their feet into the soft sand of the old sea-beach, left by the retiring tide. The birds went away, no one knows whither; but by and by the tides came again upon the tracked beach; the new sand filled them up and covered them over. The days, the years, the ages sped away; other tides ebbed and flowed; the planet swept round in its orbit, the globe's great face changed, and the very sea on whose sandy beach the birds walked was no more. The continents were reconstructed, the seas re-formed, and the beach rose to a higher level; the waters flowed to other depths. Centuries by tens and hundreds rolled into eternity; other geological eras succeeded that of the "Red Sandstone." Man comes, the lord of this lower world; he seeks the brown-stone to build his great palace in the city. Yonder, by screw and derrick, he lifts out of their old beds the rocky pages on which are inscribed these records of a former world. The huge block is cut out, raised up, and turned upon its edge; the wedge of iron is driven in, and lo! it parts right where the birds walked, and the casts of their foot-prints are perfect, showing even the rings of the toes and the joints and the claw-nails as if they had been made but yesterday. We say it is marvelous. Truly it is; and so is it marvelous that the words we speak, the deeds we perform, are recorded in God's great book of memory. Ages will pass away, and some day the steps we have taken will re-appear. For in God's mind nothing shall ever be forgotten. Not only are we ourselves immortal, but our very thoughts, our words, are immortal. When we are gone no one can tell whither some careless word or deed may come up to darken our life record and confront us in the judgment; or some good word or deed will yield its hallowed fruit. Yes, and the affection of the old bird for her young is even chronicled in the stone of the ages. Love lives on when seas have departed and the globe has changed its face. Surely the greatest of principles is love.

CHAPTER XXII.

THE AGE OF SCIENCE.

IT is well to speak of "science *and* religion," for, while they mutually support each other, when properly understood, they are as distinct from each other as the earth and the heavens. Science is not a religion; at least it should not be so considered, though some men worship only at this shrine. Nor is religion science; they walk the earth hand in hand, and, like the sun and moon, both shine upon the pathway of man, but with as much difference of light as the sun and moon. Science has served the world well in that it has dispelled many a cloud of superstition and abolished many a myth and dreamy speculation. The drift of all the religions in the past has been toward mere superstition; and even Christianity has not always been free from the charge. But do we not know that the tendency of cold science is to blot out much that is characteristic of religion? Poetry, imagination, and emotion fare hardly at the hands of science when her votaries misemploy her teachings.

We have elsewhere stated that the Bible is not a text-book on science; and yet the sacred writers are not untrue to its claims. That Moses should have described the great scheme of creation so correctly proves something. The account of the world's beginning as given in Genesis, in our English version, is marred somewhat by its form; it is broken up into arbitrary verses, and is then split right across the middle into two chapters, which renders it, as somebody has said, "like a shattered mirror."

The division into verses of the whole book is very helpful; but it often detracts from the real meaning unless the reader is well versed in the sacred word. Some writers have treated this portion of the Bible as a poem. Klopstock in his time spoke of it as "an ode to creation." Dr. Whedon styled it "a grand symbolic hymn to creation." He says: "The rhythmical character of the passage, its stately grandeur, its parallelisms, its refrains, its unity within itself, all combine to show that it is a poem." The late Dr. B. F. Cocker writes:* "But to him that can look with a clear eye on this sublime composition and grasp its real unity it is unquestionably a real hymn, composed, in all probability, by Adam, and chanted in the tents of the patriarchs in their evening and morning worship for more than two thousand years, to commemorate the fact and keep alive the faith that this is the work of the Triune God." The same author goes on to say, "It has first an *exordium*, the proemial part; then it is articulated into six *strophes;* then there is an *epode*, or peroration. The six strophes part spontaneously into two groups, in which there is a balance and correlation of parts celebrating the first three, and the last three concordant steps of the creative act, the strophe and the antistrophe."

While admitting that great truths may be taught by poems, psalms, or hymns, with these sentiments just quoted we cannot, with all deference, coincide. The condensed history of creation as given by Moses is

* *University Lectures.*

far more than a mere poem, however rhythmic it may be or formal. The theory of Hugh Miller and others seems to be more in harmony with the teachings of Moses than that which has just been advanced. Mr. Miller, following in the footsteps of continental writers, adopted the theory of a series of sublime visions that passed before the eye of Moses, in which, as it were, he "read prophecy backward." Both Kurtz and Eichhorn see in Genesis rather a "creative picture than a creative history," a series of prophetic tableaux, each containing a leading phase in the drama of creation. "Before the eye of the seer," remarks Dr. Kurtz, "scene after scene is unfolded, until at length in the seven of them the course of creation in its main momenta has been fully represented;" to which Hugh Miller adds: "The revelation has every characteristic of prophecy by vision, prophecy by eye-witnessing; and may perhaps be best understood by regarding it simply as an exhibition of the actual phenomena of creation presented to the mental eye of the prophet under the ordinary laws of perspective, and truthfully described by him in the simple language of his time." On the other hand, Professor McCaul, of Kings College, London,* tells us that a comparison of the actual statement of Moses with the discoveries and conclusions of modern science is so far from shaking that it confirms our faith in the accuracy of the sacred narrative. We are astonished to see how the Hebrew prophet in his brief and rapid outline, sketched three thousand years ago, has anticipated some of the most wonderful of recent discoveries, and we can ascribe the accuracy of his state-

* *Aids to Faith.*

ments and language to nothing but inspiration. Moses relates how God created the heavens and the earth at an indefinitely remote period, before the earth was inhabited by man. Geology has lately discovered the existence of a long prehuman period. A comparison with other Scriptures shows that the "heavens" of Moses include the abode of angels and the place of the fixed stars which existed before the earth. Astronomy points out remote worlds, whose light began its journey long before the existence of man. Moses declares that the earth was or became covered with water and was desolate and empty. Geology has found by investigation that the primitive globe was covered with a uniform ocean, and that there was a long azoic period during which neither plant nor animal could live. Moses states that there was a time when the earth was not dependent upon the sun for light or heat, when, therefore, there could be no climatic differences. Geology has lately verified this statement by finding the remains of tropical plants and animals scattered over all parts of the frozen North. Moses affirms that the sun as well as the moon is only a "light-holder." Astronomy teaches that the sun itself is a non-illuminating body, dependent for its light on the luminous atmosphere. Moses asserts that the earth existed before the sun was given as a luminary. Modern science proposes a theory which explains how this was possible. Moses asserts that there is an expanse extending from earth to distant heights, in which the heavenly bodies are placed. Recent discoveries lead to the supposition of some subtile fluid medium through which they move. Moses describes the process of creation as gradual, and mentions the order in which living things appear—plants, fishes, fowls, land animals, man. By the study of nature, geology has arrived independently at the same conclusion. Where did Moses obtain all this knowledge? How was it that he worded his rapid sketch with such scientific accuracy? If he in his day possessed the knowledge which genius and science have attained only recently, that knowledge was superhuman. If he did not possess the knowledge, then his pen must have been guided by superhuman wisdom.

Dr. Samuel Kinns, in a recent lecture given in the late Earl of Shaftesbury's drawing-room, describes fifteen creative events which Moses had placed in the direct order of sequence, according to the latest discoveries in science. The bearing of this fact upon the inspiration of Moses may be seen from the following summary of Dr. Kinns' remarks.

The lecturer proved that the number of changes that can be made in the order of fifteen things is more than a billion, namely, 1,307,674,368,000. Therefore, if Moses placed fifteen important creative events in their proper order, without the possibility of traditional help, as most of them happened millions of years before man was created, it is a strong proof of his inspiration. For, group them as one may, and take off a further percentage for any scientific knowledge possessed by him, still the chances must be reckoned by hundreds of millions against his giving the order correctly without a special revelation from God.

To lead his auditors to appreciate this, Dr. Kinns mentioned that a clock beating seconds would take over thirty thousand years to tick a billion times.

If any fifteen different events could be written down once in every ten minutes it would take twenty-four millions of years to write all the variations that could be made in their order, writing them day and night without intermission.

To further illustrate it he distributed slips of paper for each to write down the first fifteen letters of the alphabet in an order known only to himself, something in this way:

g m h d a j b k c f e n i o l,

and not one corresponded with his. He told them that if all the people in the world were to try to imitate his unknown order there would be still a thousand chances to one that the whole 1,200,000,000 attempts would be incorrect. Or, in other words, if all the people in a thousand worlds, each having a population equal to our own, were to try there would still be a probability that not one list would agree in sequence with the unknown list.

After this he asks, How will the skeptic explain the marvelous, nay, miraculous, accuracy in sequence of the Mosaic cosmogony? Faith, therefore, has nothing to fear from science. So far the records of nature, fairly studied and rightly interpreted, have proved the most valuable and satisfying of all commentaries upon the statements of Scripture. The first chapter of this oldest book, to say nothing of any other part, is proof of the whole theory of inspiration. Moses lived in an age long antedating scientific discovery. Geology, chemistry, and astronomy were then unknown, and for ages afterward mankind had no conception either of the extent of the universe or of the laws regulating it. Of its extent we yet know but little, while its laws are only partially known. A good many thousand years have passed since Moses wrote. Great progress has been made, and to-day we must conclude that Moses was either versed in science or that he was divinely aided. No one claims the former.

While not aiming to teach science, it is a simple fact that not only Moses, but Solomon, Job, and some others of the sacred penmen wrote what is now admitted to be scientific truth. Professor M. F. Maury* presents some very striking illustrations of this subject, showing that the facts of both science and Scripture remain unchanged. He points out many traces in the Old Testament of scientific knowledge.

In that oldest book in the Bible—the book of Job—written sometime between the days of Moses and Abraham, the question is asked, "Canst thou bind the sweet influences of Pleiades, or loose the bands of Orion?" † The word "Pleiades" is derived from the Greek, and means to *sail*. The name has been applied to the beautiful cluster of the Seven Stars known as the "Little Dipper," because Greek navigation began at their rise and closed at their setting. The star Alcyon is the principal star in this cluster, and has been thought to be the center of the stellar universe to which our system more immediately belongs. "It is a curious fact," writes Professor Maury, "that the revelations of science have led astronomers in our own day to the discovery that the sun is not the dead center of motion around which comets sweep and planets whirl, but that it, with its splendid retinue

* *Physical Geography of the Sea.* † Job xxxviii, 31.

of worlds and satellites, is revolving through the realms of space at the rate of millions of miles in a year, and in obedience to some influence situated precisely in the direction of the star Alcyon, one of the Pleiades. We do not know how far off in the immensities of space that center of revolving cycles and epicycles may be; nor have our oldest observers or nicest instruments been able to tell how far off in the skies that beautiful cluster of stars is hung whose 'influences' man can never bind. In this question and the answer to it are involved both the recognition and exposition of the whole theory of gravitation."

In that same book it is written, "He maketh the weight for the winds." * Galileo in prison knew that the atmospheric pressure was equal to fifteen pounds to the square inch, and that the reason why a certain pump of that day did not lift water higher than thirty-two feet was because of this law in nature. But Galileo did not have courage to tell the world all he knew. Job, thousands of years before, had enunciated the fact in the brief text above quoted. What did this old Arabian philosopher mean when he said, "He stretcheth out the north over the empty place, and hangeth the earth upon nothing?" † How could the idea of gravitation have been more beautifully set forth?

"Here is another proof," says Maury, "that Job was familiar with the laws of gravitation, for he knew how the world was held in its place; and as for the 'empty place' in the sky, Sir John Herschel has been sounding the heavens with his powerful telescope and gauging the stars, and where do you think he finds

* Job xxviii, 25. † Job xxvi, 7.

the most barren part—the empty place—of the sky? In the north, precisely as Job told Bildad the Shuhite, the empty place was stretched out. It is there where comets most incline to roam and hide themselves in emptiness."

Elsewhere the patriarch of Uz uses an expression which contains the idea of the magnetic telegraph. He asks the question, "Canst thou send lightnings, that they may go, and say unto thee, Here we are?"* We answer, "Yes, Job, we are sending the 'lightnings' on errands now all over the world." David in like manner says: "Their line is gone out through all the earth, and their words to the end of the world." † This is quite a good description of the modern telegraph system, whether the royal singer meant it to be so or not. But this we know, the forces of nature employed in human life to-day existed in the times of Solomon and Job and Moses, and could have been utilized then just as well as now if mankind had known how. But we must conclude that the time had not yet come for such things. "The mills of God grind slow." The world has been a long while in reaching its present perfection.

Solomon, too, was a man of science. In a simple verse he describes the circulation of the atmosphere as actual observation is now showing it to be. "The wind goeth toward the south, and turneth about unto the north; it whirleth about continually, and the wind returneth again according to his circuits." ‡ This describes correctly certain aerial currents known to the meteorologist. So that, without professing to be so, Solomon was scientific.

* Job xxxviii, 35.   † Psa. xix, 4.   ‡ Eccl. i, 6.

Not only has the atmosphere its laws, but the ocean is obedient to order as the heavenly host in their movement, we infer from the fact announced by him, and which contains the essence of volumes by other men: "All the rivers run into the sea; yet the sea is not full: unto the place from whence the rivers come, thither they return again."*—a passage that somewhat obscurely refers to the evaporation from large bodies of water, particularly in the temperate and torrid belts, then rising to form clouds which fall again in the rain, and also to the flow of streams, caused thereby, to the sea again for other and continuous evaporations and circulations. "To investigate the laws which govern the winds, the rain, the sun, is one of the most profitable and beautiful occupations that a man, an improving, progressive man, can have. The field of astronomy affords no subjects of contemplation more ennobling than those which we may find in the air and the sea." Wayward and fickle as seem their movements, they are orderly and subject to laws. "When the morning stars," says Professor Maury, "sang together, the waves also lifted up their voice, and the winds, too, joined in the almighty anthem. As discovery advances we find the marks of order in the sea and in the air that is in tune with the music of the spheres, and the conviction is forced upon us that the laws of all are nothing else but perfect harmony."

We often hear the wonders of modern science spoken of, and yet how few of us realize their extent! We are constantly making use of them in our daily life without scarce thinking of them. The late Horace

* Eccl. i, 7.

Greeley once gave utterance to the following high-colored and very popular remark when delivering a speech at an agricultural fair:

"The farmer of the coming age—master and manager of steam and other forces—shall not need painfully to heave the ponderous rock from its base, but will rather, by some little chemical solvent, pulverize it to fertile dust where it lies. To his informed, observant mind the changes of temperature, the succession of calm and storm, shall bring no surprise, no disaster, being unerringly foreseen and profited by, like the rotation of the seasons. For his behoof the plow shall pursue its unguided, resistless course across the spacious landscape, and the following seed shall fall regularly into its appointed place without need of special oversight and guidance. The inequalities of surface and of soil shall disappear before the steady, inexpensive action of natural forces thereon. Steam agents shall loosen and deepen the soil to any extent desirable, sweeping down forests as a fire does the dry grass of the prairies, and extracting roots like a tornado. There is no practical limit to the powers at all times presenting themselves to do the bidding of man had he but the talent and genius to adapt and apply them. Nature wills that the plow, the scythe, the ax, the harvest-wain, shall move forward on their proper errands as irresistibly, inexpensively as the saw, the throttle, the shuttle, and with equally beneficent results."

In this paragraph the orator pictured things somewhat. There can be no doubt but it was a trifle overdrawn. Others besides Mr. Greeley have indulged in that same vein, intimating, if not expressly stating, that in the nature of things, if time endures, science will so perfect machinery, eventually, as vastly to decrease, if not altogether displace, human labor, and effectually disarm the very elements of their power to inflict disaster on the human race. That the increase and multiplication of machinery will vastly decrease a certain kind of labor is certain—that we have realized; and at the same time science will help us to guard against disasters arising from the " war of the elements."

We have thermometers and barometers, which serve their beneficent purpose. The rising or the falling barometer tell unerringly of approaching meteoric changes. The thermometer does not forewarn us of any future change, but simply records the present. We have heard of a church sexton who declared that he " didn't take any stock in them there thermometers, for he couldn't see as they made nary a bit of difference in warming up the meetin'-house."

With all of Mr. Greeley's vivid portrayal of the perfected age of science we have not yet reached the period of hailstorm-ometers, which farmers would like, nor cyclone-ometers and earthquake-ometers, to enable us to escape the dreadful consequences which follow in their wake. We may yet, however, reach such a state of scientific perfection that the tiller of the soil will be warned with so much accuracy as to make the safe gathering of his crops a certainty, and the sailor be enabled to reach port with his craft with equal safety. The world is on the march, and if we have not yet found the " simple chemical solvent " by which the granite bowlder may be instantaneously " pulverized into fertile dust," we have discovered dynamite, which comes very near fulfilling the prediction of the Sage of Chappaqua.

There are two things lacking to make that perfect age : the "philosopher's stone," which transmutes whatever it touches into gold, and the long-sought "perpetual motion," to discover which much time and money have been spent. If we had these, say some, we might rest and be rich. But suppose we had them, then what ? Gold and diamonds, like praise, owe their value to their scarcity. Things become cheap when they become plenty. If gold were as plenty as sand it would have the same value as sand. As to rest, perfect rest from toil in this life would be fatal. "There remaineth, therefore, a rest to the people of God." That it "remains" is well for us and the world. Even the dream of the "philosopher's stone" included the idea of toil, for the stone had to be rubbed against the object to be transmuted, and that would require effort. To obtain money without honestly earning it has been the study of too many men, as our state-prisons testify. Philosophy teaches us that there is no motion without some resistance or friction. Physical power implies a producing agent. There can be no effect without an adequate cause, no result without original, continued effort. A state of perfect rest, were such possible, would be the death of efficiency, usefulness, and progress, because the result of a loss of actual power. The progress of every nation in modern times in substantial wealth, comfort, and civilization has always been in exact proportion to its increase in the amount and respectability of its labor, which is a nation's power. It is labor which puts value on every thing. A pine-tree standing in a forest is valueless; cut into lumber by human labor it is the equivalent of a certain amount of gold. The coal and iron have no value buried away in the mines of the earth until man touches them. Man is the true philosopher's stone that transmutes things into gold.

Mr. Greeley's prophecy was very taking, but it does not annul the declaration of Holy Writ: "In the sweat of thy face shalt thou eat bread until thou return unto the ground."

The bright and hopeful signs of the times is that a given amount of human labor under the improved science of this age produces much greater result than formerly. The increase is constant and will continue. History tells us of the "Jacks" in feudal times, and of the serfs of Russia and the slaves of our own country. When these systems prevailed labor was degraded. But feudalism, serfdom, and slavery are gone, and labor where those systems prevailed has become and is becoming more and more dignified and honorable in the estimation of mankind. The increased wants of the present age could hardly be supplied by the old methods. The unassisted labor of the ruder times was sufficient then, but would be very inadequate for these times; and if labor still remained as debased and odious as it was two or three hundred years ago we should be unable to supply our wants if we had any wants.

To labor is man's destiny, and its fulfillment ought not to make him unhappy, but it often does. We may ameliorate toil by our machinery, but not free ourselves from it. No development of physical power will ever be permitted by divine Providence to transcend the purposes of manual toil and defeat the laws which regulate it. Human perfection does not imply an age of indolence. The highest glory of mankind is that of labor, and such an entire acquiescence in the destiny of toil as to cheerfully discharge all duties and resignedly bear all the vicissitudes of life.

Labor is every thing—it gives to all things their true value. Take a mass of iron which in its rough state is worth four or five dollars, let it be made into horseshoes, and its value has increased two or three times that amount. Why? Because labor has been expended upon it. And its usefulness has increased also; it protects the horses' feet. But convert that bar of iron into needles for sewing, and it is now worth, by virtue of the labor which has been expended upon it, three or four hundred dollars. But make of that iron knife-blades, and it has gone up in value to twenty-five hundred dollars. Turn it into balance-wheels for watches, and it is worth more than twenty-five thousand dollars. The iron remains the same all the while, but the labor has been increasing.

Fifteen hundred acres of land, a part of the territory on which the city of Pittsburg, that great and busy mart, now stands, was once given in exchange for a little lot of wood worth almost nothing to any one merely as wood. It would not have weighed half a dozen pounds; but it was wood on which labor of the most skilled and delicate kind had been bestowed —a rare violin, a " Stainer." These rare old instruments have been known to bring fabulous prices; but this was surely the greatest price ever paid for a handful of wood and a trifle of paint and varnish. But the price was not given for the wood with its paint and varnish, but for the inspiration of a matchless workman; for the concentrated experience of not one life, but many, put into a curve or fluting; for a few thin plates of wood fixed together with an instinct that is dead, but which before it died made those slips of wood almost a living organism. Well, here it is again—labor, skilled labor, is what adds to the value and usefulness of all things.

The almost perfect accuracy with which scientists are able to deduce the most minute particulars in their several departments appears quite miraculous; and if in the early ages of the world such revelations had been made they would have been considered supernatural. Take the wonderful phonograph, which records sounds, songs, speeches, etc., and preserves them to be heard in other lands and distant ages. But perhaps the most wonderful of all modern discoveries is that which puts to a daily use the electric force. Between the Old World and the New, below the waters of the Atlantic lies a cable, nearly three thousand miles long, over which this force passes in some mysterious way and is made to convey our messages of love, business, or politics. No words are carried through the dull wire, but an impression is made which conventionally means something. But somewhere in the ocean, a mile or a thousand or more miles away, under some strain or molecular action, the cable parts and the instrument fails to do its work. Now the wonderful part is that the break can be so accurately located. How? Science knows. A ship starts from shore and follows the direction of the cable in the deep sea. The miles are counted as the ship goes on her way. The sun, millions of miles distant in the heavens, is invoked to help ascertain the latitude and longitude; the earth's magnetism is made to play its part. By and by the spot is reached, the irons are sent down, the cable brought up from its bed, the break repaired, and the ship returns to her dock—all by the power of science.

The electrical engineer sits in his office at the nation's capitol and by means of this force can foretell what the weather will be in Florida, Ohio, or Massachusetts on the morrow. Nature is stable and has well-established laws; these mastered, science easily forms her conclusions. So well is the earth understood that, a few fossils sent to any part of the world, the expert geologist is easily able to determine the rocky formation from which they were taken. The chemist has analyzed the light that has come from sun and star, and determined their physical characteristics as accurately as if he lived on them. The "infinitude of space" is nothing. From the dimmest light which shoots out of the sky-vault, from a star so distant that its light, darting through space at the rate of twelve million miles a minute, would not reach us in a score of years, he tells the elements which it contains. What wonders there are in the universe of which we form a part!

And so while the Bible teaches us the duties and obligations we owe to our fellow-man, a knowledge of nature explains to us the things with which we have to do in our relations to the world about us. Man has invented the telescope, by means of which he is enabled to sound the depths of space, and he has invented the microscope, which reveals to his senses the wonders of the invisible world. The human mind instinctively seeks for knowledge of that which lies beyond our natural sight. Nature implies the supernatural; we partake of both. It is with this relation that religion deals, and instruction in the supernatural is of far more importance to us than in the natural. The Bible regulates the life of the individual and of society. Science interests the mind and enhances human power, but it cannot satisfy our spiritual cravings, for it is not a religion. It cannot furnish a safe and permanent basis of ethics. Mankind will have a religion, and that which is now accepted as the best cannot be displaced unless it be by a better religion, if that were possible; but it must contain supernatural elements, and, therefore, equally transcending the sphere within which physical science moves. Away with this clamor about Christianity being opposed to science! A recent writer says on this subject, what needs to be kept in view by all:

"Who or what has raised science to its present commanding position? What influence is it that has trained the investigator, educated the people, and made it possible for the scientific man to exist and the people to comprehend him? Who built Harvard College? What motives form the foundation-stones of Yale? To whom and to what are the great institutions of learning, scattered all over this country, indebted for their existence? There is hardly one of these that did not have its birth in and has not had its growth from Christianity. The founders of all these institutions, more particularly of greatest influence and largest facilities, were Christian men who worked simply in the interest of their Master. The special scientific schools that have been grafted upon these institutions are children of the same parents, reared and endowed for the same work. Christianity is the undoubted and indisputable mother of the scientific colleges of the country. But for her our colleges would never have been built, our common schools would never have been instituted. Wherever a free Christianity has gone it has carried with it education and culture.

"The public, or a portion of it, seems to forget this, or has come to regard Christianity as opposed to science in its nature and aims. It is almost regarded by many minds as the friend of darkness, as the opponent of free inquiry and the enslaver of thought. The very men who have been reared by her in some instances turn against her, disowning their mother and denying the sources of their attainments, and to-day she has herself almost forgotten that it is her hand that has reared all the temples of learning, framed the educational policy of the nation, and, with wide sacrifice of treasure, reared the very men who are now defaming her."

We hold it to be the province of science to emancipate the mind from the dreadful superstitions which have bound the race in all the past. In all ages of the world the processes of nature have been viewed from the stand-point of the supernatural. When Captain Cook, in his voyage around the world, was threatened with starvation by the withholding of food by the inhabitants of Santa Gloria, knowing that an eclipse of the moon was about to take place, he told the simple-minded people when it began that it was the indignation of the Deity at their evil conduct, and food came with the eclipse in abundance. Had they understood science this trick would not have succeeded. It was, of course, a prevarication, but then, in the mind of the sturdy navigator, "the end justified the means."

But that is not all. Science emancipates the race from a large degree of vassalage to labor. Much that has always been done by the hand can be done better, quicker, and cheaper by machinery. The spinning-jenny, the sewing-machine, and kindred inventions are real emancipators. The laws and forces of nature thus come to man's relief. He does not cease to labor, but there is a change in the direction of his energy. There is less hand-work, more brain-work. Man is more of a power the moment he begins to use levers, wheels, screws, steam, electricity, etc. And the time will come when every tree will be cut down and every furrow plowed and every ditch be dug by the employment of the forces inherent in matter as they may be under the control of the human mind. Here we see an explanation of the Scriptures which places man at the head of affairs in this world—the lord of this lower world—"Thou shalt have dominion." Dominion he has over fish and fowl and beast, over water, fire, and air. All things are put under his feet.

Professor Silliman, the elder, at the age of eighty-two years, spoke thus to the young men: "Still, by God's forbearance and blessing, possessing my mental powers unimpaired, and looking over the barrier beyond which I soon must pass, I can truly declare that in the study and exhibition of science to my pupils and fellow-men I have never forgotten to give all honor and glory to the infinite Creator, happy if I might be the honored interpreter of a portion of his works, and of the beautiful structure and beneficent laws discovered therein by the labors of my illustrious predecessors. It is the result to which right reasoning and sound philosophy, as well as religion, would naturally lead. While I have never concealed my convictions on these subjects, nor hesitated to declare them on all proper occasions, I have also proclaimed my belief that while natural religion stands on the basis of revelation, consisting as it does of the facts and laws which form the domain of science, science has never revealed a system of mercy commensurate with the moral wants of man. In nature—in God's creation—we discover only laws, laws of undeviating strictness and sore penalties attached to their violation. There is associated with natural laws no system of mercy. That dispensation is not revealed in nature, it is contained in the Scriptures alone. With the double view just presented I feel that science and religion may walk hand in hand. They form two distinct volumes of revelation, and both being records of the will of the Creator both may be received as constituting a unity declaring the mind of God, and therefore the study of both becomes a duty and is perfectly in accord with our highest moral obligations.

"I feel that as this subject respects my fellow-men I have done no more than my duty, and I reflect upon my course with subdued satisfaction, being persuaded that nothing which I have said or omitted to say in my published lectures or before the college classes or before popular audiences can have favored the erroneous impression that science is hostile to religion. My own conviction is so decidedly in the opposite direction that I could wish that students of theology should also be students of natural science, certainly of astronomy, geology, natural philosophy, chemistry, and the outlines of natural history."

> "O Science, reaching backward through the distance,
>   Most earnest child of God;
> Exposing all the secrets of existence
>   With thy divining-rod!
> I bid thee speed up to the heights supernal,
>   Clear thinker ne'er sufficed;
> Go seek and find the laws and truth eternal,
>   But leave me Christ.
>
> "Upon the vanity of pious sages
>   Let in the light of day,
> Break down the superstition of all ages,
>   Thrust bigotry away.
> Stride on, and bid all stubborn foes defiance,
>   Let truth and reason reign;
> But I beseech thee, O, immortal Science,
>   Let Christ remain!
>
> "What canst thou give to help me bear my crosses
>   In place of him my Lord?
> And what to compensate for all my losses,
>   And bring me sweet reward?
> With thy clear, cold eye of reason
>   Thou couldst not comfort me
> Like One who passed through that dark valley
>   In sad Gethsemane.
>
> "Through all the many hours of sorrow
>   What word that thou hast said
> Would make me strong to wait for that to-morrow
>   Where I should find my dead?
> When I am weak and desolate and lonely,
>   And prone to follow wrong,
> Not thou, O Science, Christ, my Saviour, only
>   Can make me strong!

"Thou art so cold, so lofty, and so distant,
  Though great my need should be,
No prayer, however constant and persistent,
  Could bring thee down to me.
Christ stands so near to help me through each hour,
  To guide me day by day,
O Science, sweeping all before thy power,
  Leave Christ, I pray!"

CHAPTER XXIII.

RESPONSIBILITY FOR OUR BELIEF.

WHEN we come to analyze the human constitution we find that the faculties which constitute our responsible agency are intelligence, conscience, affection, and will. If we could conceive of a human being without knowledge to give direction to his energies, then human action would be merely mechanical. If we could conceive of a man without moral perceptive faculties we should have simply a monster. If man were to exist destitute of sympathies there could be no play of emotion. If that godlike power of choice were stricken out of his being, then his life would be only dead inertia.

The existence in the human organization of these wonderful powers and faculties, which in their entirety make man, is the groundwork of his accountability. Each faculty of the soul is under law, so that truth is the law of the intellect, uprightness of moral life the law of the conscience, affection the law of the heart and the spring of its impulses, while obedience is the law of the will. It is a fearful responsibility to possess a soul thus endowed with the power of intelligence and to find ourselves in a world which is a vast whispering-gallery circling all around with the voices of God's truth—"voices that speak from the sparkling star above us; voices heard in the hoarse surge of the sea and in the murmuring wind that dallies with the leaves and the flowers; voices which come up from the sea, earth, and air, and awake the echoes of this vast temple of nature in which man should worship God." How gentle is the tone that would win us with its love! How full of pathos when his pity speaks of sin and his grace of the pardon which his mercy has procured! And yet how severe when offended! Heaven proclaims judgment on the wickedness of mankind: "Repent, or else I will come unto you quickly, and will fight against you with the sword of my Spirit."

Who doubts the fact that we are physically accountable? Who but an insane man would leap from a precipice and not expect injury? God is love, but still fire will burn, gravitation act on matter, and poison kill. Who doubts intellectual accountability? Has not many a brilliant mind been overtaxed and ruined? Why, therefore, should any one doubt the fact of moral accountability? How much has every rational being to do with his own destiny? What means this wonderful will-power resident in us? If it is neglected we drift with the current and are mastered by circumstances; if it is used we become masters of ourselves and to a great degree of our surroundings. In other words, are we rational, godlike beings, or are we mere machines? Are we the victims of mere circumstances, or have we power to master them? The answers to these questions are the solution of the problem of human life. Here all philosophy has its beginning, and here is the starting-point of all human accountability. If human life is finally and inevitably shaped by its environment, then we are the victims of some sort of blind power, call it by what name you will, and there responsibility ceases. But if, on the other hand, we are masters within certain limits of our surroundings, then we are more than machines, and accountability is one of the great facts of human life.

There are conditions we do not understand in nature; but to speak of chance is atheistic. We are closely related to the outward world through our senses—touch, taste, sight, etc.—but we are not "of the world." The ideas we get from without ourselves are taken into the mind, where they are assimilated and assorted and worked over very much as food is taken into the stomach, digested and assimilated and converted over into muscle, nerve, brain, and bone. As this wonderful body is built up out of the matter which is in the earth, and carried to these bodily organs in our food and drink and become a part of our physical being, so the thoughts we cherish, the beliefs we put in practice, the moral principles we adopt, enter into our soul-nature and become part of our real selves; they "grow with our growth and strengthen with our strength" until they constitute our very life. "For as a man thinketh in his heart, so is he."

There are two words in common use which mean very nearly the same thing, namely, belief and faith. We use the first of these, generally, when we are speaking of the ordinary affairs of life; the latter is used in a religious or theological sense. In the heading of this chapter I have used the term *belief* because it includes more fully the topic I am considering. The question is a pertinent one, Are we responsible for our belief in religious things? The subject is one of very great importance, for it enters into the relations of life daily. Our belief makes or it unmakes us. An individual who believes in himself, in his own powers and faculties, is far more likely to win the prizes of the world than he who has no confidence in himself. There is, of course, a difference between undue self-consciousness, which may run into offensive egotism, and a proper estimate which one may put upon his natural powers. Humility is esteemed a virtue, but even that does not warrant us in unreasonably underrating the talents which the good Father has bestowed upon his child. Every man should recognize in himself a moral and intellectual force sent into the world for the world's good, and consequently not to be despised nor wasted in riotous living.

Let us hold in mind the parallel between our physical and moral environments. We are forced by the very conditions of the lives we are living to contend with many warring elements in making any headway in the physical world. Difficulties are to be overcome, innumerable obstacles to be removed, natural enemies to be subdued, before we can hope to wear the crown of the victor. Success means patient thought and patient toil; all mastery is born out of endurance. And what is true in the physical is equally true in all of the moral relations of life. We are continually confronted with difficulties; the mind must reach out after the truth. Many things must be taken on trust; they must simply be accepted and believed, even if not understood. Doubt must be overcome by the vigorous putting forth of reason and by opening the heart to experience. If any young man reads this, let me say to him, "Be considerate." If he were sitting by my side this minute, with a sensitive soul resting under the shadow of an honest doubt, I would like to take him by the hand and say, "My brother, come, now, and let us reason together." The spiritual warfare of a human soul is represented in the Bible as depending on certain truths which have been made known to mankind, while at the same time disbelief, or unbelief, is assigned as the cause of spiritual death. Belief is something positive; unbelief is negative. We can find many illustrations of this in the physical world. This great atmospheric sea which completely envelops our earth, and is fifty or sixty miles deep, is a mixture of two principal substances, oxygen and nitrogen. Oxygen is the positive element; it supports life and gives vigor, while nitrogen is a mere diluent, and is negative, non-life-giving. Immersed in it death would soon follow. Again, the plant deprived of the sunlight and shut up in the dark lacks the element necessary for its growth, and soon becomes sickly and dies. Now, precisely so are we helped or hindered by belief and unbelief, faith and unfaith. In speaking of unbelief as something negative it is not to be thought of as innocent, and therefore to be trifled with. A noted divine says: *

"Unbelief is a *principle* as well as an *act*, always operative with a continuous force, which is not fictitious, but most dreadfully real. The principle abides, even when it is not developed in outward acts. It lies behind in the secret disposition, which is the spring of all action and gives it complexion. For the existence of this we are responsible, and must plead guilty before God. In this view we are chargeable

* M. B. Palmer, D.D.

with unbelief at all times, so long as the disposition exists which would prompt the act. In the deepest sleep, or when the thoughts are absorbed in worldly care, it is the sleep or the preoccupation of an unbeliever. A tiger is as much a tiger when he sleeps, or when he is gorged with his prey, as when the ferocity of his nature is fully aroused. The generic disposition which forms his characteristic is there—a constant quantity; whether it be dormant or in full activity is more an accident than otherwise. So the sinner's attitude toward God is one of abiding hostility, whether it break forth in insurrection or not; and the believing temper which could reject the Saviour at any given time will reject him at all times, and with this continuous repetition we accordingly stand accused at the bar of final judgment."

The plea that a man is not responsible for his belief in religious things, and that belief is involuntary, has no foundation in the psychological nature. We know that by experience. What is belief? What is its relation to the natural progress of society? How does it enter into our moral and religious life? These are questions which come naturally. Belief is the assent which the mind gives to a fact or proposition on the testimony of the senses or on the ground of certain evidence aside from personal knowledge. For example, a story is told by some person in whose veracity we place the utmost confidence; it relates to something of which we have no personal knowledge. Every human being of intelligence can call to mind instances of this kind. We are constantly believing things on the strength of testimony given by other persons. We are ever saying, "I believe." That confidence we place in those about us forms the basis of innumerable relationships in business, friendship, and love. But belief is something different from knowledge or science. If the hand be put upon a piece of red-hot iron no one would say, "I believe it is hot;" he would know it, alas! too well. In your hand is a bank-bill; you believe it to be genuine, but you really do not know that it is until it is proven to be so by a proper test.

A proposition is made involving certain principles to be examined; a close train of reasoning follows, and a conclusion is arrived at; that conclusion is a belief. Belief is something of the mind; and it is as natural for us to believe or disbelieve as it is to eat or sleep. We find ourselves assenting to things every day—if we are thoughtful—which are new to us. There is a sense, then, in which belief is faith, and we cannot live without believing or exercising faith; it enters into life and helps to make it. It is a first mission of the human mind to seek out the truth and to discover and expose error. It was when angels forsook the truth and embraced error that they were dwarfed into devils; and by forsaking error and cleaving to the truth sinful men have arisen to the dignity of saints and the companionship of angels. Belief is the key of the world's progress. We believe in banks, and place in them our money. We believe in the coming around of the seasons, and adjust ourselves to these conditions. We believe in the purity and honor of our friends, and trust them with our holiest secrets. How much there is that we believe and act upon in the various relations of life of which we have no personal knowledge! We accept the statements of historians, ancient and modern, without a question. If any one should now rise up and proclaim that there never was such an event as the siege of Troy or the preaching of Peter the Hermit or the overthrow of Jerusalem by Titus, what would his standing be among intelligent people? There is a scientific instrument known as the spectroscope, of which very few persons have any practical knowledge; it is used mostly by astronomers, chemists, and teachers of science in our colleges. By its use the savants have ascertained many things far beyond ordinary comprehension—for instance, that there is hydrogen in the envelope that surrounds the sun; that copper or zinc or iron or some other metals, or all of them, abound in the substance of a star so distant from us that we cannot conceive of it. We may not know this ourselves, for we are not spectroscopists, and yet we accept the statement as true; that which is announced by so many eminent men as fully established by the investigations of science carries upon its face a claim which cannot consistently be ignored.

Sometimes men of science are mistaken, and things are declared to be true on insufficient grounds, but new revelations are made and opinions are changed. But even then this does not annul the statement that we believe things which we do not ourselves from our own personal experience know to be true. Science foretells an eclipse of the sun or moon, fixing definitely the day, the hour, and the minute; no one doubts it. Is it asked why? Because of the confidence people have in the statements of honest scientists. If some explorer should now return from the arctic regions and inform us that an open polar sea had been discovered, and that his ship had sailed its waters, the world, without seeing it, would believe in it. The adventures of Livingstone and Stanley in the heart of the Dark Continent are eagerly read; and though none of us have been there, and possibly we do not know any thing of the country, who would for one moment think of professing his unbelief in their statements? And if any one should be so incredulous as to declare his disbelief he would be laughed at and be looked upon as mentally defective.

The chemist has published to the world the fact that strychnine is a deadly poison. Suppose, now, not having any personal knowledge of this virulent narcotic, I should disregard the teachings of men and books and give this to my friend and thereby cause his death. The law would arrest me and try me, and, though I might plead ignorance and want of experience in the use of the deadly drug, it would justly punish me for murder or manslaughter, or send me to the asylum as an insane and dangerous person. It is my duty to know of its destructive qualities, or to believe what others have written and said of it. In this case I certainly would be responsible for my belief. In our courts of justice ignorance of the common law is never appealed to as an extenuation of criminal acts. If they were, what greater lawlessness there would be! No one can go before a judge and jury and say, "I did not know that I was committing a crime," with much expectation on that ground. Why do so many persons base their opinions and their actions in secular affairs on the personal testimony of others, without any knowledge of their own, and not unfrequently at the risk of health, property, and life, and then when they come to the Bible and the Christian doctrine begin to object and tell us that the evidence is not sufficient? To all such there is one text of Scripture which is most applicable— that last appeal where the great Teacher said, "If any man will do his will, he shall know of the doctrine, whether it be of God, or whether I speak of myself."

CHAPTER XXIV.

THE LOGIC OF EXPERIENCE.

THE birth of Christ was an event which may well be described as "the miracle of miracles." Births, like deaths, are of every moment occurrence, but the number of the former far exceeds that of the latter. The birth of Christ includes every essential feature of a human birth; but it was far more than that—it was the enswathement in human flesh of the supreme Divinity; a personal manifestation of the Infinite in the sphere of the finite. That one event alone in our earth history is of all the most marvelous and mysterious; and is, indeed, the sum of all Bible teachings.

It is one of the greatest facts recorded in Holy Writ that God was "manifest in the flesh." Jesus was not merely a man divinely commissioned to do a particular work, but he was Divinity himself.

That he was rejected by the very people from whom he sprang, and to whom he came first—"his own"—is another great fact in the religious history of the world. There was no fiction here; Jesus was not a myth, but a man. There was something in his magnetic nature or in his demeanor or his words that drew men about him; "great multitudes followed him." A long line of distinguished prophets had in various forms of speech, in prose and in poetry, in metaphor and vision, proclaimed his advent; and not only Jews, but Gentiles, looked anxiously for the coming of a Teacher of men. The old prophets had pointed out with somewhat of particularity the place where he should be born, and had described his person and character with marvelous exactness. The child Jesus, who was born in "Bethlehem of Judea," answered to these pen-pictures of the ancient seers so minutely that it is difficult to see how any one after examining them can possibly be a disbeliever in the Messiahship of Jesus of Nazareth. The birth, the life, the death of Jesus Christ have passed into history, and are among its leading and most sublime and substantial facts. Men of modern times have discovered nothing new in relation to the Nazarene. In his own day some of his neighbors said, "He is a good man;" others said, "He deceiveth the people;" then, as now, he was not esteemed alike by all. The fact that there are many who turn away from him and look upon his followers as the victims of delusions is no argument against the religion of Jesus. Christianity is fast becoming the religion of the whole world. The objections are not arrayed against the moral system which he inaugurated, but against his claim to be the Teacher and Saviour of all men, as well as against the miraculous birth, his resurrection from the dead, and his "wonderful works." When these are under review we hear the exclamation even yet, "How can these things be?"

The human heart does not always and naturally turn to the good and the pure; mankind do not always follow the path which leads to their highest and best interest. Why? It must be because the eye is blinded and the nature vitiated. But what has done this? Sin.

Sin is, then, the most startling and awful fact in the world's history. But when this is charged upon men we must not lose sight of another fact, namely, that there are some people who, though not followers of Christ in a purely spiritual sense, who are not Christians, yet are kind and loving fathers, tender mothers, dutiful children, honest, patriotic, and noble-souled. Furthermore, sin has degrees; it ranges from that of the least deflection from a life of personal purity to the utmost depravity of the heart. What is this condition but spiritual negativeness—an absence of the divine life in the soul with the natural traits of human character—the instincts and impulses left intact? Sin, therefore, in the human heart is reconcilable with intelligence, affection for friends, and integrity of character. To say that man is a sinner may mean that he is vicious in character, a very fiend in the malignity of his purposes, or it may mean that he is a pauper on the spiritual side, an *atheos*— one "without God." For the purpose of illustration on this point, suppose we should take an elegantly wrought vase, and, dashing it upon the pavement, shatter it into a hundred pieces, each fragment of that vase would preserve the delicate workmanship of the whole. Man is that broken vase. There are traces of wonderful workmanship in his make even as he is to-day—even in his moral depression is he God-like. But there is something wrong in his nature when he refuses the good and the pure and deliberately elects the base—the vile. Look at the depth of his sympathy, the grasp of his intellect, the power of his will; each one of these traits, like a fragment of the broken vase, tells of the original and wonderful being as he came from the hand of his God. Is it not true that among the philosophers, statesmen, scientists, poets, and teachers there are to be found persons of the greatest culture who spiritually are cast down and broken? The sublime unity is absent, and the harmony which results from a holy heart is wanting. There can be no genuine religion without some culture of the mind. Christianity is a system of instruction; the world must be taught before it can fully believe; but education is not piety. A beautiful work of art would not be appreciated by rude barbarians. Cultivation makes art effective. The developed soul and the art production are related to each other as the eye and the light; one is the complement of the other. The world needs to be taught in order that it may appreciate the beautiful. Therefore, to instruct mankind is a first mission of the Church. Jesus Christ said, "Go teach all nations"—in other words, make *scholars* of them. All the efforts which the Christian Church is putting forth to elevate the human race, intellectually as well as morally, are a part of her divine mission.

The world must be saved intellectually as well as spiritually and morally. It must be regenerated; but regeneration is something which we cannot explain, for it involves mystery. The laws which regulate the spiritual life of the world are incomprehensible by all who are not able to discern things from their spiritual side. Faith is a mystery in its religious aspects; so is electricity in its scientific aspects. But we accept all that is taught in reference to electrical science, and send our messages without a quibble or a murmuring doubt. We lose sight of the mystery in the recognized benefit received. Prayer is a mystery, so is the action of the will and the beating of the heart, but we all believe in will-power and heart-throbs. If the new birth in man is a mystery of the Christian belief, surely no less so is the new birth and growth of a plant in the spring-time; yet men are ever asking of the one, "How can these things be?" while the other does not raise even a question. It is characteristic of the Scriptures that they require our assent to statements of belief which seem to thwart the pathway of reason. We talk about the Trinity; ask the mathematician if he can explain how three can be one, and he will tell you that it involves a contradiction in the law of numbers, and so it does. The word trinity is not in the Bible, and yet that the trinality of the Godhead is taught there, even in the face of a mathematical incongruity, is evident.

The resurrection of the dead is another mystery. We ask the scientist to explain it to us, but it is impossible for him to do so from his stand-point; he can give us no scientific answer. He has many wonderful and delicate instruments, but none by which he can collect the dust of the long-entombed dead. Man's science is wonderful, but God's science is more so—it is infinite. In man's hand the crude carbon is only carbon; but in God's hand it is transformed into the flashing diamond, queen of the jewels. Science cannot explain how the diamond is formed nor how the dead are raised up; but God has created the diamond, and he can raise the dead. The doctrine of the resurrection lies out beyond all science; it belongs in the region of the unexplainable. The Bible does not tell us how; it simply declares it—"Thy dead shall live again." All the questions which mankind have ever asked concerning it must remain unanswered until the resurrection shall explain its own mode. Let us wait and hope for the time when

> "They now rising from the dead
> In luster brighter far shall shine,
> Revive with ever-during hope,
> Safe from diseases and decline."

And so it is. Every one who has reached accountable years, doubtless, has often thought of the mysterious things which surround us on every side, in human life as well as in the providence that is over the world. Life is a mystery in its origin and in its perpetuation. Death is all around us on every hand, and yet no one knows just what death is, for none have come back from the "undiscovered country" to inform us. We love our friends, but how constantly they are going away from us to return no more! Human nature is gifted with mental faculties which are content only with knowing, and yet the great universe is largely hidden away in impenetrable depths. We are invited by our instincts to enter God's great temple, but when we courageously approach the threshold we are ushered only within the vestibule. The angel which stands guard at the doorway says, "Thus far shalt thou go, but no farther." The venerable man with whitened locks and wrinkled brow stands peering into the great deep sea very much as he stood and gazed when, as a mere child, he wandered along its pebbly beach, only perhaps that he stands a little nearer, even where the sea-foam may moisten his garments. But the scores of years which have transformed the child into the man and given courage in place of timidity have not made the sea any more shallow; there are the same hidden depths beneath the wild and tumultuous billows, the same unveiled mystery of God's great deep.

In nature every-where there are voices calling to us and saying, "Come and see," and then at every step an impassable barrier confronts us, or an oppressive darkness enshrouds us. Perhaps this is the plan of the Father by which to lure us on toward our destiny. The most bewitching point in space is where the vision is bounded—the hazy rim where the visible merges into the invisible. God intends that we shall think of the beyond—the world where our faith shall be lost in sight. He intends us to learn of the future as well as the present, the invisible as well as the visible. The pathway meanders up the mountain-side; the eye follows it until it is lost in the shadows of the darkened forest, but then we know it leads on, even though its course eludes our vision. So in the deep spiritual things of this life, what clouds of thick darkness surround us and hang in the sky over us! How often do they gather alike over the mind and over the heart! But God in any thing is its solution. Without his presence all is darkness and mystery every-where; with it all is brightness and beauty.

> "If all our hopes and all our fears
>   Were prisoned in life's narrow bound;
> If, travelers through this vale of tears,
>   We saw no better world beyond,
> O, what could check the rising sigh?
>   What earthly thing could pleasure give?
> O, who could venture then to die?
>   O, who could then endure to live?"

The Scriptures enjoin upon us the performance of duties that are impossible to our unaided selves. We are required to "love our enemies," and our nature cries out, "Impossible!" It is in human nature to crush out our enemies and destroy them. We are also commanded to love the Lord our God with all the heart, soul, mind, and strength. How can we do this? How can we love a Being which "no man hath seen at any time?" Where is he? What is he?

Let me illustrate: once there stood in the presence of Jesus a man with a withered arm; it hung palsied by his side, a constant reminder of the death of the body. He had, doubtless, heard of this wonderful Healer, and came to him for help. The poor man's condition excited the sympathy of the Lord, who knew and felt it all, and so he said to him, "Reach hither thy hand." But how can this withered arm respond to such a demand? Jesus might as well have required him to roll back the tides or to create a world as to comply with such a condition. It was impossible for him to obey. How often he had tried to lift it up, and how often had he failed! But just then, possibly, there flashed upon him a new thought, that of endeavor simply, "I will try." No sooner is the volition put forth than the arm which had so long failed to meet the demands of the will now is vested with new strength and is made whole as the other. Impossibilities always vanish when God helps, whether it be in matters of belief or of practice. "I can do all things through Christ which strengtheneth me." So, too, we can believe "all things through Christ which strengtheneth" us.

There is a sense in which it may be said that every

healthy mind is naturally skeptical. We use the word in a good sense—that is, it is always seeking knowledge, and it desires to be convinced of the truthfulness of a statement before perfectly accepting it. A child believes whatever it is told; but as it grows in years and knowledge it begins to question itself and others, and so may develop into skepticism. We all know that society in its infancy is credulous and superstitious. Christianity among the ignorant is largely an emotion; among the more highly cultivated it is, alas! too apt to be a mere intellection. The true type lies between these extremes, *in media res.*

We have the charity to believe that a good many people drift off into spiritual destitution, not really from choice, not because they prefer doubt to faith, but who indeed may even desire to understand Christianity. The difficulty is they test it by the wrong methods. It is subjected to the alembic of the brain to the exclusion of the heart. And of all the unfair tests which have been employed in investigating Christianity that of cold and exacting science is most unfair. Science, in her own dominions, is fair and reasonable, but her province does not include the purely spiritual.

Science has achieved much, and when used by Christian men is the handmaid of religion. Questions of science must be settled by scientific methods; philosophy, which enters into the region of pure thought, must be examined in the light of intuitions and primitive judgments; history must make its appeal, not to imagination or dramatic fiction, but to facts. Every thing in this world has its own logic; every truth with which the mind deals has its own methods of proof; and hence the measurements are diverse. If we would know how much gold there is in a given ingot, it must be weighed by a particular scale; if we wish to ascertain how much iron there is in a car-load, it must be weighed in another sort of scale. If we wish to ascertain how many acres of land there are in a certain area, it must be tested by the compass and chain of the surveyor. If it be necessary to know the exact number of men in a congregation, they must be counted. Wheat is not measured with a tape-line, nor lumber sold by the ton. The eye passes judgment on distance; the ear determines the quality of sound, while temperature is ascertained by the finger-tips or the thermometer. Some objects which engross the human heart and affect the human life have their ultimate determination by the intellect; this is their final test. In ascertaining the difference between two circles or squares, or between a cone and a pyramid, the intelligence, not the conscience, must come into play. The business interests of life—the ledger accounts, which show the debtor and credit sides—do not involve the emotions and the affections, but lie in the region of our powers of calculation. There are other subjects which relate to our moral nature. Our friendships in life are not determined by pure reason; we do not graduate our love for our families by a mathematical scale; we do not regulate the intensity of our affections for friends by the height and weight of their bodies; were we to do so some would get more than their share; alas for others! Love is not a conclusion merely to be arrived at by mathematical equations or searched out by chemical re-agents.

Our Lord said to his disciples, on one occasion, what was very full of import: "Unto you it is given to know the mysteries of the kingdom of heaven, but unto them it is not given." In another place he says: "I thank thee, O Father, Lord of heaven and earth, because thou hast hid these things from the wise and prudent, and hast revealed them unto babes."

Too many apply the intellect where the heart only should be the standard. "Unto you it is given to know the mysteries of the kingdom," said Jesus. Why? Because you have yielded to it your hearts. Spiritual things are judged of by spiritual tests. The heart is the center and seat of our sympathies; spiritual life does not come by the eye or the ear, or by logic, or rhetoric, or music. "Eye hath not seen, nor ear heard, neither have entered into the heart of man, the things which God hath prepared for them that love him. But God hath revealed them unto us by his Spirit."

This brings us to the great question, Has the truth of the Christian religion been demonstrated? The ethics of Christianity have been established beyond a doubt; the world accepts the moral code fully and freely. A revolution in that code would destroy the social fabric; it would be in the moral world like the blotting out of the sun in the natural world.

Some men talk glibly about the division of the Church into sects, and sneer at what they call the *odium theologicum;* but what about the *odium medicum?* See how the learned doctors are divided into "schools," and, though learned and honest, how essentially different; but who thinks of repudiating medicine because of these divisions? There is nothing more certain in this world of religious thought than the possibility of reaching a plane where the human heart is quickened and comforted by the touch of Infinite love. "But now, in Christ Jesus, ye who sometime were afar off are made nigh by the blood of Christ." Is it true that we may be saved from our sins? If so, it is a more wonderful truth than any which science has ever published to the world. They tell us that the Buddhists in their temples often place broad-leaved lilies directly in front of their altars as sacred symbols setting forth a great moral truth; that as the pure white flower may spring out of the mire and the filth and bloom in loveliness, so may the heart of man rise above the wicked and corrupt world into a state of moral purity.

Christianity has its own arguments, its own logic, its own modes, and they are convincing to the Christian. How faithful and clear is the word! "As many as are led by the Spirit of God, they are the sons of God." How, then, are we to know that we are saved? By science? No. By art? No. By culture of the mind? Nay, verily. By philosophy? by the logical faculties? by natural intuitions? By none of these. They are all serviceable, all play their part in life; "But because ye are sons of God, he hath sent forth his Spirit into your hearts, crying, Abba, Father." "He that believeth hath the witness in himself." "If any man will do his will he shall know of the doctrine." "I know in whom I have believed, and am persuaded that he is able to keep that which I have committed unto him until that day."

If what we have said be true, then it follows that the main pillar in this temple is *experience*. Here is true

Christian logic, the rock on which we build, "Christ in you formed the hope of glory." "The natural man receiveth not the things of the Spirit of God: for they are foolishness unto him: neither can he know them, because they are spiritually discerned. But he that is spiritual judgeth all things, yet he himself is judged of no man."* Weighed in the balance of the heart, in the emotional soul-life, the religion of Jesus will never be found wanting. This is our vantage-ground; here are arguments which only they who have followed the leadings of the Spirit can employ. Scoffers may denounce, men of the world may ridicule, but none of these can argue successfully against the Christian's faith. The case of the man who was born blind is in point; when inquired of concerning the wonderful cure effected by the Saviour he answered, "Whether he be a sinner or no, I know not: one thing I know, that whereas I was blind, now I see."

There is no answer to the jeers and scoffs of disbelievers so effective as the testimony of a good heart and a pure life. One may know nothing of science, nothing of general literature, be quite ignorant of philosophy, and yet be filled with joy, peace, and light. "This is the victory that overcometh the world, even our faith." Christianity can never be destroyed by its enemies; for the final test being a spiritual one, how can men witness against what, by their own confession, they have never experienced in their hearts? A blind man when asked to give his idea of scarlet said it was like the sound of a bugle. So a blind man cannot discuss color very successfully with one who can see; a

---

* 1 Cor. ii, 14, 15.

deaf man would be a poor critic of music; a dumb man would hardly be thought of as a teacher of elocution. He who supposes that Christianity is a hard experience, is a delusion, a fiction, or superstition, is as much disqualified for his self-assumed position of critic as the blind man who claims to be able to give direction in the choice of colors for a lady's dress. The unbeliever is a negative witness. A witness who on the stand knows nothing about the case on trial will not be allowed to consume the time of the court. The positive witness is important; all true believers, in all ages and lands, bear witness to Christ's power to save from sin and to give comfort; and on their word and testimony rests this grand and beautiful structure, THE CHURCH OF THE LIVING GOD.

CHAPTER XXV.

THE GOAL.

To understand the real meaning of the word *life*, as it relates to us in this world, would make a great change in the manner in which many of us spend our years. Most of us think too much and too solemnly about heaven—about "the life that is to come," about where and what we shall be a thousand or ten thousand years hence; we are far too anxious to reach a heaven of some kind with its promised and expected joys, as if the main object in this life were to get well out of it and enter some other and unknown state and be "happy." That is, in a sense, all well enough, but let us remember that the joys of that life will not atone for duties left undone in this. If we think right, grow right, live right here and now, the future will be blissful enough. It is therefore with the world as it is, with its struggles, trials, temptations, labors, joys, mysteries, poverty, riches, sickness, and all that makes it, we have to do. The Bible was written to guide us in our life journey; it has no other meaning or purpose. The greatest thing in the universe is life, and of all the living beings on this earth man is the noblest, grandest.

To live is something more than simply to exist. An object which is purely inanimate, without thought or consciousness, exists; but the difference between that which lives and that which exists merely is almost the difference between the finite and the infinite. "Never shall I forget the phenomenon in myself," said Jean Paul Richter, "never till now recited, when I stood by the birth of my own self-consciousness, the place and time of which are distinct in my memory. It was on a certain forenoon that I stood, when a very young child, within the house-door, and was looking out toward the wood-pile, when in an instant the inner revelation, I AM I, like lightning from heaven, flashed and stood brightly before me; in that moment had I seen myself, as I, for the first time and forever."

A good many of us have had the same experience, if it did not dawn upon us quite so suddenly and so vividly. But who, after all, can define life in such terms as to tell us of its depth and meaning? The philosophies of a thousand years have not been able fully to explore the chambers and measure the powers of the human soul. Eternity will startle us with its revelations; then and then only will we understand fully the doings and beings of time.

We have endeavored in this book to present such thoughts and to inculcate such beliefs as would lead the reader to the study of the true life of man as held up and illustrated in the word of God. It has also been the constant effort to hold the mind close to the truths that are spiritual.

We have seen how universal life is; how it surrounds us every-where—on the one hand so minute as to be invisible to the keenest vision, and on the other in its larger and more tangible forms, not only in the animal, but in the vegetable world. When the grass is woven into velvet under our feet in spring-time we say it lives; the worm which crawls across our pathway is also endowed with life.

Life is every-where; earth, air, and sea are full of it. It ranges from the ephemera of an hour up to the angels in heaven, and to the Father of all, whose being was without beginning and is without end, for God lives. But it is with human life, as we see it and live it ourselves—this every-day life, full of cares and crosses, temptations and sorrows—this life of hope and joy—that we have to do.

We are taught that life is a probation, by which it is only meant that we are on a journey to somewhere and to something yet to be, yet to know, yet to experience; and all we see and know and do in this life shall in some way influence and make us in that. Every thing that has been written in this book, whether of the earth itself, the invisible animalculæ, the sea-monsters, the hordes of animals, wild or domestic, every thing, from worm to star, in some way affects the conditions of human life.

This state of being in which we now are placed is not always exactly to our liking. Our faces are turned sunward, but the way is often rough. There are many conditions, not of our choosing; left to our judgment, so poor and feeble, things would not be as they are always; but, alas! how human plans would have left the world in darkness and misery! Some one has said, "The web of life is of mingled yarn, good and ill together. Our virtues would be proud if it were not for our conscious faults, and our crimes would despair if they were not balanced by our virtues."

We have been writing about the Bible, and wherefore? Because all of its laws, morals, inspirations, examples, are directed to the human upbuilding. Man, intelligent, conscious, moral, is the objective point toward which all this points. If it does nothing in us, in our lives, then so far as we are concerned the book might as well not be. This life is not all; there is a beyond, a place, a condition to which this world-pilgrimage leads; and this Bible is our chart, our compass, our anchor.

Not unfrequently we find ourselves growing disheartened because of our weakness and our sinfulness, and we call this a hard and unfriendly world; we think of our pathway as a stony one. Many a heart has ached and many a soul has felt sad in this life journey. But if the pillow on which we lie is sometimes painful it is often our own wrong-doings that have made it so. And if the way of life is lonely and burdensome, yet we may have sweet sleep and glorious visions. It was when Jacob was lying on the rock-pillow of Bethel, in the darkness and alone, that the ladder was placed with its foot by his side while its top reached to heaven, and on which the angels of God ascended and descended. So is it with us, from our lowest estates of sorrow and humiliation God kindly permits us to look up into heaven.

If we would enjoy life we must take the world as it is. Of what is life composed? Right well do we know that a thousand spots of sunshine, a cloud here and there, the bright sky, a storm to-day, a calm to-morrow, the chill, piercing winds of winter and the bland, reviving air of summer—these make up the experiences of life. The secret of success in this world depends on that most precious of all possessions, power over self, power to endure trials, to suffer hardships, to meet dangers heroically, power to follow our convictions, no matter where they lead us, the ability to be calm in the hour of danger and to be courageous when it is darkest. In a physical sense it is through inward health that we enjoy all outward worldly things; in like manner from a spiritual stand-point the world is shaped and colored largely by our own mental and moral conditions.

This constant contact with the world was never intended to be always restful. The great Teacher said, "In the world ye shall have tribulation," or, literally, "In the world ye shall be beaten with a flail." It is quite easy when we mingle with the world around us to walk in its footsteps, imbibe its spirit, drift with its current. It is easy when we are alone to live as we wish. Society is a hard master and has many willing slaves. The great point to be gained is for us to carry into life, as we are jostled about in the crowd, the sweetness and independence of solitude. Jesus Christ summed it all up in that wonderful prayer, "I pray not that thou shouldest take them out of the world, but that thou shouldest keep them from the evil." Human trials vary with our years; and though we think, too often rightly, that sufferings and disappointments are but "barren trees, whereon grow neither flowers nor fruit," it is because we have not received them in the spirit in which they were intended. God means that all things shall work together for our good; and so tribulations should bear a rich harvest of experience. An uninspired poet wrote, "Sweet are the uses of adversity;" an inspired apostle said that chastisements "bear the peaceable fruits of righteousness."

How often we trouble ourselves more than is necessary by our anticipations of the future! The power to anticipate may be used to our advantage, to enlarge us, and to lure us on like imagination to a higher destiny. So far all is well; but the mistake is that we too often anticipate evils, dangers, and troubles that never come. Let us not forget that this life is one of perpetual contest, and if so how mad are they, and how unwise, who fail to arm themselves for the battle! We hear life spoken of as a voyage to some distant country, and the sea of life as often a stormy one. How mistaken is he who sleeps while his bark is being driven before fierce winds upon hidden rocks! If life be a pilgrimage, as it is often called, how unwise is the man who strays from the plain pathway of truth and right into the mazes of sin and does not even seek any return until the twilight shades of death gather about him! A voice speaks to us from out the dim and shadowy past, saying, "Man that is born of a woman is of few days, and full of trouble;" but the same voice cries, "Though he slay me, yet will I trust in him."

People who complain most of the evils of this world are generally those who are most unwilling to practice self-denial or to submit to such disciplines as are salutary and on which the highest happiness is founded. We are told by the natural historian that the frost which nips the foliage of the mulberry-trees does not kill the silk-worm cradled in its leaves. So calamities may overtake us and envelop us; but if we are right-minded our real life may not be touched. Some one has compared the human heart to a feather-bed, which needs to be roughly handled, well shaken, and exposed to a variety of turns to prevent it from becoming hard and knotty. The illustration is homely but true.

We murmur and complain a good deal at the hardships of life, but are generally unwilling to die and leave them. People who are always talking about their willingness to leave the world are generally the very ones to be most alarmed when death threatens. There is some real good in the actual evils of this life, for they deliver us, while they do last, from a thousand worse ones which the imagination may create. The difference between men is often like that between some species of serpents and honeybees: they extract the same juices from some plants, but the one converts them into poison, the other into honey. An ill, a great disappointment, will drive one man to Christ, another to Satan. While many of us fret and worry over the doubtful, the mysterious in life, all must submit to the inevitable. Some flowers need to be crushed that they may emit their imprisoned fragrance; so in human life, the crushing process is often the way to the highest moral development. The beautiful paper on which these words are impressed was made from old and possibly filthy rags; but the acids purified them and the iron-toothed machine tore them into fragments and ground them into pulp first. Out of great losses and tribulations are often developed the noblest characters, as the finest gold comes from the seven times heated furnace. Jesus of Nazareth told us that the way to save life is to lose it. Plunge into the battle of life and win, even though it be by dying.

This seems like a hard saying, for most of us prefer

to live rather than to die even in a good cause. But he who falls in the pathway of duty deserves a nobler name than the general who leads a victorious army over the ruins of a conquered kingdom. "Except a corn of wheat fall into the ground and die, it abideth alone; but if it die, it bringeth forth much fruit." Yes, life has its hardships, and should have, for in them the heart grows strong and the faith may become almost omnipotent. The difficulty is, we too often double the real evils that environ us by pondering over them too closely, until in our broodings a mere scratch becomes a wound, a slight an injury, a playful jest an insult, a small peril a great danger. Brooding apprehensions may convert health into sickness and darken a sky which God has made bright. You have felt many a pang and many a trouble, dear reader, possibly; but often those which have vexed you most have been such as you were merely expecting. That which we dread most is often passed by with ease.

Is it not well that God has made the plan of our lives, and not we ourselves? He has mingled sunshine and shadow, mountain and valley, rocky ledge and grassy slope, to make up the picture of life. Constant prosperity may harden the heart, as perpetual sunshine does the earth; but when the heart is softened by the tears of sorrow, and the earth by the refreshing showers, alike they yield the best of fruits. Goodness is twice blessed—in what it gives and what it receives. The peace and comfort we impart to others is restored to our own bosoms by the satisfaction of an approving conscience, as the vapors which ascend through the day fall back at night in rain-showers upon the land.

The danger is that the powers of our minds, when unbounded and expanded by too much worldly good, too much sunshine, may luxuriate into sin and folly rather than blossom into genuine goodness of heart. More human souls have grown great under the storms of adversity than from the sunshine of good fortune. The spirit which recognizes the good in the world is far wiser and better than that which is always on the search for evil. God's plan is to compel our thought and reflection, and thus increase wisdom and knowledge in us, which can never be acquired without both pains and application. These are alike troublesome and perplexing; but, like deep digging for pure water, when you reach the fountain the water is sure to rise up and meet you. That is the point of victory.

The problem of life is not solved by merely looking at the dark side. What does life become? What is its use? In other words, why do we live; who or what is ever benefited by the days we, as individuals, spend on earth? These are pertinent questions and are ever confronting us. Who has not looked upon some poor mortal greatly cast down in the circumstances of life, overthrown in worldly fortune, health gone, and friends few in number? But, turning from such human depressions, have we not seen something in the great world-book around us to shed light on the dark scene? We have seen how God can carpet the sterile rock with the velvet moss; how the ivy under the touch of his finger will cling to the moldering ruin; how the pine and cedar will remain fresh and fadeless amid the mutations of the dying year. Life comes from death every-where.

In the coldest and darkest hour of life God's smile puts a rainbow in the sky. Something green and beautiful, something grateful and refreshing to the soul, the Father has left untouched by death. It matters not what may be our life-lot, there are still spiritual vines to twine their tendrils around the altars and broken arches of the otherwise desolate temples of the human heart. They who have only the good of this life are poor indeed. The truest riches, like the purest joys, are spiritual. There is a difference between necessities and wants. The wants of life for the greater part are merely artificial. God has amply provided for life's necessities. We must seek our true joy and our highest good where they can only be found—in ourselves as gifts of God. Here we shall discover a greater resource than all outer objects are capable of affording. Alas for those who have no hope beyond the present! What is life to them but one long care for its mere temporal benefits, one perpetual struggle with moral evil?

Pleasure and pain alike tend to destroy our energies, and there is probably a period in almost every one's life when the soul as earnestly desires the repose of the grave as the body does the rest and quiet of the night. "Godliness with contentment is great gain;" and a man's life "consisteth not in the abundance of the things which he possesseth." Real happiness only begins where our wishes end; they who are ever pining after more really enjoy nothing.

If we are not content with such things as we have we might not be satisfied with the things we most desire were we to possess them; for it is not what we own and control so much as what we are in ourselves that forms the basis of our happiness and constitutes our true life.

If we allow ourselves to dwell with envy upon the riches, honors, or ease of those around us in society we irritate ourselves, so that a mere congestion becomes an inflammation, and that turns into gangrene and death; besides, we may be finding fault with Providence.

It is a common mistake with many to regard those things as necessary which are only ornamental, and to depend upon outward surroundings for inward happiness. The only true happiness which the world can ever know arises from virtue and communion with God. All this discipline of which we have been talking does something in us; we are either made better or worse by it. A man who passes through life meeting all its disappointments bravely, enduring all its trials heroically, and withal remaining sweet in temper may, indeed, be called a perfect man. "He is a weak man who cannot twist and weave the threads of his feelings, however fine, however tangled, however strained, or however strong, into the great cable of purpose by which he lies moored to his life of action."

Life is intended to develop in us what may be called true heroism—sturdiness of character. He who looks upon life as merely an extended play is like one who attempts to shield himself from the blasts of winter with garments of thread-lace, or who endeavors to satisfy his hunger with condiments and flavoring extracts. God tries men sometimes in the furnace to save them from themselves and from melancholy. More than half of the melancholy one meets in life is the result of indolence. There are thousands of rich and idle people in the world who imagine themselves ill, but who are only lazy. Were they to rush out into life seeking for channels of good work and scattering their money with a lavish hand upon the poor and needy they would have cheeks like roses and eyes of fire; they would reach a height of happiness which neither money nor ease can ever purchase. The burden of work is on the world. The Master has said: "Son, go work in my vineyard." The very best cure for low spirits is hard work.

To be deprived of much makes us love the little we have and think of the destitute. And what is true of life generally is particularly true of our spiritual lives. Success means surrender: "The meek shall inherit the earth." "Pleasure loves the garden and the flowers; labor loves the field and the plow; devotion loves the mountain, the skies, and God." The happiest people in the world are those who labor in some calling. God never gave organization to a body to be motionless and idle. Some of the greatest battles of history have been fought by a few troops, but they were turning-points in the world's history. So in human life, small things are great. It requires more courage often to cast aside a small sin than it does to risk ten thousand dollars in a doubtful speculation. Some sins have no hold upon us but in connection with some other sin. When a man forsakes a pet sin, one he has loved, he is like the woodsman who cuts down a tree—the branches fall with the trunk. In like manner virtue has its connections; we cannot be holy to-day and sinful to-morrow—holy in one thing and sinful in another. No; there is no heavenliness in sinful indulgences; there are pleasures, but such pleasures are for the most part short-lived, false, and deceitful, and, like drunkenness, they revenge the jolly madness of one hour with the sad repentance of many. A vicious habit, an indulged little sin, a neglected duty, can easily be taken care of to-day if we are so minded, but let alone may send one's soul into the shades of night.

A man's goodness should not be measured by his occasional exertion, but by his every-day life. No one ever thinks of buying a house from a specimen brick; nor should we judge of a man by his capabilities, but by what he actually does or tries to do for the world around him. Great talents render a man famous; great merit will command respect everywhere; extensive learning will gain esteem, but a good heart wins the world.

It requires a great deal of real heroism to confess one's ignorance at times, and yet that is what we all must do more or less if we would gain knowledge. The thoughtful life is made up largely of interrogation-points. The great Franklin said, "Ask questions about what you do not understand, ask modestly and seriously, then listen to the answers and think well of them. A man who knows nothing can give you no light on any subject; but almost any one can tell you something you don't know. I have gained some valuable information from the humble blacksmith who shoes my horse." There are two classes of persons who can afford to be modest—those who possess a large amount of knowledge and those who have but little. But it is one of the lessons we must learn, not to think of ourselves "more highly than we ought to think." When one's self-esteem is so great that he regards himself as wiser than his fellows, and when he supposes his faults to be better than other people's virtues, we may say truthfully that he has rather an exalted opinion of himself.

The world judges of us not by what we say, but by what we do and what we love. When a man manifests delight in low and sordid objects—the vulgar song, the ribald jest—or takes pleasure in the misfortunes of other men, or in cruelty, even though it be toward the meanest living thing, it somehow determines the complexion of character. On the other hand, they who love purity, modesty, truth, who pursue virtuous things in life, impress themselves upon us as righteous.

"Thoughts, melancholy and gay, careless and bitter, how like innumerable fairy fingers they are ever playing on that mysterious harp, the human soul! Who can trace them through their long continuous course or define their dim and shadowy relations with each other? Every human soul is a volume in itself, bound together by reason, though fancy may vary and gild the pages."

Life is far more than we know now or can know. Only eternity can reveal the value of time, and death alone can show us what life really is. The weakness and folly of childhood, the vanity and vices of youth, the bustle and care of mid-life, and the infirmities of old age, what do they give us? Experience. A short life indeed; yet man has a soul of vast desires and vast possibilities, and eternity is before him. He is capable of much and aims at more.; many things he cannot attain, and many are not worth the effort made to attain them. O, it is a pity that he should not know how always to choose the good and refuse the evil, as well as to know how to make the most and best of so short a life! The way of life divides at the grave; the soul goes upward or it goes downward, goes into darkness or into light. One thing we must remember—never to make the avoidance of punishment a reason for avoiding sin; in other words, never seek heaven simply to be happy, but because it is best and right.

The spiritual life—the "heaven-begun-below" life—is the only one which satisfies the soul. "Man shall not live by bread alone."

"The world can never give
The bliss for which we sigh."

The life fullest of God is the one fullest of joy. It was this which made one of old cry out, "My cup runneth over."

"True riches consist in that which sufficeth, and not in that which is superfluous." "Our brains are seventy-year clocks," wrote Oliver Wendell Holmes. "The angel of life winds them up once for all, then closes the case and gives the key into the hand of the angel of the resurrection." We live, we die, we are swallowed up in the great abyss; there is a ripple on the surface for a moment only, the earth closes over us, and the world goes on just as it did; only a few watchers at the tomb will hold us in remembrance. But this is not all; this is not the end: life stretches away into the future, far beyond the reach of the wildest imagination. Do we ask, What is life? It is a throb, an inspiration, a great duty, an expectancy, a hope, a thrill! All the waters of the globe have come out of the sea, and all are going back again into its bosom. We have all come into being by the power of God, and we are all turning back into infinity again. Therefore the life most true, most valuable to the world, and the one surest of bliss in the "undiscovered country" is the one with the most of God in it. As we study it here and now we are looking at it only partially. The spiritual lies very close to the natural: only a thin veil separates the two worlds. No one knows or can know where heaven is. The universe is God's house. This world is one of the rooms in that house. There are two possible heavens to every mortal—that above and out of sight, and that which is within us; it is possible to fail of both; but this we know—the heaven within is first and is essential to the heaven without.

We may travel the world over to find the beautiful; but if the sense of the beautiful is not in us we shall never see it. We may roam the universe through to find heaven, and yet we will never find it, if it be not in our own hearts. People have sometimes quarreled over their religious creeds; but they who are always disputing about their religion give proof to the world that they have not much to dispute about.

Some people are like the old Moravians, who, it is said, made gardens of their grave-yards, while others are like the Jews, who made grave-yards of their gardens. True religion is first pure, then peaceable, and puts beauty every-where. The restless spirit argues, the peaceful mind judges, the strong arm may load the scales, but only the quiet hand can hold the balance. How much peace has been banished from the world by heresy-hunters and by fierce theological combats over nothing! As two chords keyed alike in two instruments in a room will answer the one to the other, so is there a correspondence between this heaven and that. Death is but the door-way out of this world into that higher and better one, and so death to a Christian is a triumphal march witnessed by the innumerable company of "just men made perfect," and such a death is glorious. Glory is so enchanting that we love whatever we associate with it, even war or death." The apostle of old said, "For to me to live is Christ, and to die is gain." We care not how rich or great or learned, that life is a failure which is not lured forward by thoughts of heaven and immortality. We are going upward on our pathway of destiny. Every day stamps us with some mark or design or impression, and these we shall carry with us forever. We shall be there what this life makes us here; let us not forget that conduct is destiny! Our thoughts, our words, our affections, and as certainly our afflictions, all unite to make us one thing or the other. Again we ask, "What is your life?" Only God knows; only eternity can tell. "It doth not yet appear what we shall be." "Man is the hero of the eternal epic composed by the divine intelligence."

"Man's actions here," wrote Thomas Carlyle, "are of infinite moment to him, and never die or end at all. Man reaches upward high as heaven, downward low as hell, and in his threescore years of time holds an eternity fearfully and wonderfully hidden. The universe is the realized thought of God."

> "'Tis immortality deciphers man,
> And opens all the mystery of his make."

THE END.